Springer Textbooks in Law

Springer Textbooks in Law compiles high-quality educational content aimed at undergraduate and graduate students in all areas of law. All self-contained volumes are authored by accomplished academics and suitable for use in class as well as individual study. Many of them include chapter abstracts, definitions of technical terms, cases and self-assessment exercises, as well as recommended reading sections. This series is an invaluable resource for students and lecturers alike and spans the full range of topics in international and European law, including fundamentals of law and comparative law. Special attention is paid to current and emerging topics such as IT law, intellectual property, human rights as well as dispute resolution, mediation, arbitration – and many more.

Juan J Garcia Blesa
Editor

Contemporary Methods in International Legal Research

Between Legal Interpretivism and Empirical Inquiry

Springer

Editor
Juan J Garcia Blesa
FernUniversität in Hagen
Hagen/Westfalen, Germany

ISSN 2509-999X ISSN 2510-0009 (electronic)
Springer Textbooks in Law
ISBN 978-3-031-69521-6 ISBN 978-3-031-69522-3 (eBook)
https://doi.org/10.1007/978-3-031-69522-3

This Springer imprint is published by the registered company Springer Nature Switzerland AG
The registered company address is: Gewerbestrasse 11, 6330 Cham, Switzerland

Contents

Introduction

Juan J. Garcia Blesa

Contents

The contemporary theory and practice of legal research is fractured by deep disagreements about method.[1] The notion of method as a procedure for finding some certainty or ultimate social truth in the law has been swept away by the postmodern critique.[2] And yet, while some postmodern ways of thinking and doing legal research have become widely accepted by the mainstream academia, traditional styles of work and argumentation are still hegemonic in legal discourse and need to be acknowledged by any person (also postmodern thinkers) willing to engage other legal professionals in debates about alternative views on the law.

In this context, this book aims to help postgraduate students and early career researchers to get acquainted with the theory and practice of a selection of alternative modes of legal research widely used in international law today. The book also encourages a meaningful dialogue with traditional doctrinal styles of research. This aspiration to link with mainstream scholarship as the still dominant language of the global community of international lawyers, however, is not meant as an invitation to embrace any sort of cut-and-dried eclecticism. Though it does not repudiate eclectic approaches, the book tries to follow in the footsteps of different forms of critical legal thinking without diluting them. This is done in particular by warning early on against the problems and limitations of any pragmatic

[1] See generally Davies (1994), Buckel et al. (2009), Van Hoecke (2011), Cahillane and Schweppe (2016). See also Derrida (1989–1990).

[2] See e.g. Carty (1990), and Litowitz (1997).

J. J. Garcia Blesa (✉)
FernUniversität in Hagen, Hagen/Westfalen, Germany
e-mail: juan.garciablesa@fernuni-hagen.de

J. J. Garcia Blesa (ed.), *Contemporary Methods in International Legal Research*,
Springer Textbooks in Law, https://doi.org/10.1007/978-3-031-69522-3_1

reconciliations suggested in the book. But the critical orientation drives the book in more general aspects as well—from the selection of the approaches presented in the chapters to the methodological landscape that the first chapter describes to contextualise the book within broader methodological debates to the manner in which traditional legal research is featured in the chapter devoted to "Mainstream Approaches to International Law".

In this sense, it is important to note that the book repudiates the rigid disciplinary boundaries that separate international legal research from other areas of legal inquiry by reducing international law to the traditional commonplaces of a community of lawyers who serve (or imagine to serve) sovereign states and international institutional power. Without denying their importance, mainstream disciplinary boundaries today tend to function as devices that hinder the development of new insights about the intertwined and dynamic existence of global legal relations. Such relations hinge upon complex clusters of ideas and practices with deep socioeconomic, political and cultural roots that stem from and deploy their effects on all levels of international and domestic life. In other words, the book also aims to contribute to the 'disordering of international law' with a view to facilitating its critical reconstitution.[3] Thus, for instance, it highlights issues that traverse the international and domestic law divide, and features examples from national law that transcend disciplinary borders when illustrating some of the approaches presented, particularly in the chapters dealing with Feminist Approaches and Empirical Legal Research.

On the other hand, while it tries to offer a faithful account of the approaches it presents, the book also aims to be succinct. It is primarily intended as a concise practical guide to some of the most relevant forms of alternative thinking and doing international legal research today. Moreover, it takes an essentially practical approach as it aims to facilitate the applied learning of the modes of research presented. Thus, given its purpose, simplification is inevitable. For the sake of explanation, otherwise evolving constellations of singular and polyhydric approaches to legal research must be reduced to and encapsulated in a few pages. Here, detail and nuance inevitably become a secondary concern.

At the same time, the book tries to do justice to the approaches it presents, above all, by remaining self-aware of its weaknesses and warning the reader of its necessary limitations. In this regard, the book covers from the first to the last chapter a wide span of literature and makes the conscious decision to select certain references and discard others. Therefore, along with more recent literature, this work draws heavily on early sources in order to track central debates at their inception and benefit from the efforts that the pioneers of each approach made to explain their methodological endeavour in their own terms.

The book is arranged in six chapters. The opening chapter begins by situating the book within broader methodological debates and stressing the connections between contemporary legal inquiry and social thought. The chapter dealing with "Mainstream Approaches to International Law" aims to add some more texture to this

[3] Kelsall (2022).

background picture by providing further information about the traditional approaches to (international) law, that is, the methodological mindset against which the other approaches have evolved historically. The remaining four chapters present in detail four alternative modes of research that include Critical International Law, Feminist Approaches to International Law and Third World Approaches to International Law, completed with the study of empirical legal research methods in the last chapter.

These four chapters ("Critical International Law", "Feminist Approaches to International Law", "Third World Approaches to International Law (TWAIL)", and "Empirical Legal Research") have all the same structure. Each starts with an explanation of the approaches selected describing their main features and main applications in practical legal research. This opening part is supplemented by the list of references at the end of each chapter which contains literature that the authors recommend as further reading. In the second part of these four chapters, readers will find some examples of how each research approach presented can be applied in practice. Readers can examine these examples in order to get a clearer understanding of the practical application and challenges of each approach—and try to connect them to their own research.

Finally, the last part of these four chapters offers some exercises that invite readers to apply the research approaches discussed in a limited but meaningful manner through small practical tasks. The goal of these exercises is to facilitate some practical learning that readers can transfer later to their own research. As pointed out above, although this book is addressed particularly to the field of international legal research, the ever-growing entanglement between national and international law as well as the pervasive impact of international law on domestic legal affairs make the book and the alternative approaches it presents applicable to many domestic law debates, especially at the widening intersections between national and international law.

References

Buckel, S., Christensen, R., & Fischer-Lescano, A. (2009). *Neue Theorien des Rechts* (2nd ed.). Lucius & Lucius.

Cahillane, L., & Schweppe, J. (2016). *Legal research methods. Principles and practicalities*. Clarus Press.

Carty, A. (1990). *Post-modern Law: Enlightenment, revolution and the death of man*. Edinburgh University Press.

Davies, M. (1994). *Asking the law question*. The Law Book Company (Sweet & Maxwell).

Derrida J (1989–1990) Force de loi: le 'fondement mystique de l'autorité'. Cardozo Law Review 11:920-1045

Kelsall, M. S. (2022). Disordering international law. *European Journal of International Law, 33*(3), 729–759.

Litowitz, D. E. (1997). *Postmodern philosophy & law: Rorty, Nietzsche, Lyotard, Derrida, Foucault*. Kansas University Press.

Van Hoecke, M. (2011). *Methodologies of legal research. Which kind of method for what kind of discipline?* Hart Publishing.

Legal Method in the Context of Social Thought

Juan J. Garcia Blesa

Contents

This chapter aims to situate the book within the context of broader debates about method in law and the social sciences. It offers a theoretical ground plan to locate the legal approaches discussed in the rest of the book and encourages reflection on the connections between them. The chapter explores the relation between legal and social inquiry after the philosophical demise of legal and scientific positivism, understood as the origin of the different families of contemporary non-positivist/non-doctrinal legal research. It also delves into interpretivist legal research as the most relevant of these families in relation to the approaches presented in this book.

J. J. Garcia Blesa (✉)
FernUniversität in Hagen, Hagen/Westfalen, Germany
e-mail: juan.garciablesa@fernuni-hagen.de

J. J. Garcia Blesa (ed.), *Contemporary Methods in International Legal Research*, Springer Textbooks in Law, https://doi.org/10.1007/978-3-031-69522-3_2

1 From Legal Order to Methodological Disorder

The origin of the problem of method in contemporary legal studies can be traced to the philosophical decline of the *legal order* tradition dominant in Western legal thought.[1] Although connected to different philosophical strands of political liberalism (utilitarianism, contractarianism, etc.), the construction of legal order is the historical project of legal positivism and is predicated upon a number of common assumptions about language, law and society.[2] These assumptions include in particular the notion that language is a code of names that point at things—words usually having clear meanings—and that, therefore, legal materials contain a system of norms which, correctly applied through a special form of doctrinal reasoning, determines necessary answers to all possible questions of social life reflecting a coherent view of human relations that is generally applied in practice.[3]

One after another such premises have been debunked by different movements of social and legal thought during the twentieth century.[4] Primarily, the indeterminacy critique negates that legal materials can determine *per se* any necessary solutions supposedly contained in statutes, case-law, etc.; and the critique of formalism rejects the existence of any special form of reasoning that would grant the legal researcher or the legal profession at large any special capacity to discover such answers in legal materials.[5] The critique of legal order has also rejected the idea that the law can reflect a coherent view of social order and pointed out that law may have in fact only a marginal impact on social behaviour.[6] As a result of the critique, the assumptions of the legal order tradition have been progressively abandoned by leading legal scholarship since the 1970s; although the tradition still is broadly accepted among judges and practicing lawyers –as well as in the mainstream of legal academia.[7]

---

[1]Trubek (1984), p. 577.

[2]Dyzenhaus (2004), pp. 42–43. The term 'positive law', however, originates within the natural law tradition to define as law that which has been 'posited' not only by the sovereign, but also by other 'social-fact sources', especially courts, and oppose this to the laws of reason as a guide and a critical standpoint. Positivism, in contrast, strives to reduce the 'posited' law to that simply willed by the sovereign or, in the liberal tradition, by legislative power, Finnis (2000), pp. 1601–1602, and Unger (1984), pp. 70–72.

[3]Unger (1977), pp. 52–57, 176–181, and Unger (1984), pp. 88–98. Other features of the positivist project of legal order are the idea that the construction of validity from one single social-fact source—the modern state—is a political moral good in itself; the continuous effort to improve the clarity and determinacy of the will manifested by the sovereign/legislature as the only source of law; the sharp distinction law-making/law-application and the struggle to deny judicial law-making, Dyzenhaus (2004), pp. 41–45. See also chapters on "Mainstream Approaches to International Law" and "Critical International Law" below.

[4]Trubek (1984), pp. 577–578. See chapters on "Mainstream Approaches to International Law" and "Critical International Law" below.

[5]See also chapters on "Mainstream Approaches to International Law" and "Critical International Law" below.

[6]Unger (1984), pp. 97–98; Trubek (1984), p. 578; Gessner and Winter (2011), pp. 170–177.

[7]Posner (2002), p. 1326; Bianchi (2016), pp. 21–27.

On the other hand, given that not every point of this critique is generally upheld or understood in the same manner by every critical lawyer, the critics of the mainstream legal order tradition and doctrinal approaches have produced in turn no homogenous movement capable of asserting itself as a new dominant tradition.[8] Instead, the critique of the traditional foundations of legal thinking has opened up the field of legal studies—perhaps more intensely in the area of international law than in any other discipline—to a quickly evolving range of new research approaches, tools and practices that try to understand law's complex existence beyond doctrinal routines. This diversity of non-doctrinal ways of analysing and narrating the law crucially improves legal studies by asking new questions, reformulating old problems and identifying new ones that are out of the reach of traditional doctrinal inquiries.

Such abundance, however, may also be confusing and cumbersome for legal researchers to navigate and integrate into their work. Thus, in order to situate the approaches presented in the chapters below within larger families of non-doctrinal thought, it is useful to describe some of the main methodological streams existing today in line with Max Weber's ideal or pure type constructions. As heuristic instruments, pure types function as relatively clear benchmarks against which we can describe and grasp particular events—always in merely approximate terms.[9] That is, as ideal or pure types, the methodological labels used in this chapter are not meant to reproduce in detail all the elements and practices of each stream. Rather, they consist of sharp distinctions that help draw a map of the field wherein the approaches selected in the other chapters can be better grasped.[10]

To this end, the following begins by looking at the aspect that most non-doctrinal approaches have in common: the main question they ask. Whereas doctrinal or mainstream research is exclusively interested in what the law 'is' or 'ought to be'—i.e. the solution that legal materials supposedly prescribe or should prescribe for a particular case (the so-called 'black-letter law' or 'law in the books' approach);[11] non-doctrinal approaches enquire about what law 'does' in society (e.g. the 'law in action' perspective).[12] Surely, this common question is tackled from different perspectives and answered in very different ways by each non-doctrinal approach, but these approaches are generally characterized by a preoccupation for the study of law in a social context, which situates the alternative modes of research within the common coordinates of modern social thought and its constitutive problems—particularly, the problem of method.

---

[8] See generally, Kennedy (2006), pp. 72–73.

[9] Weber (1922), p. 10.

[10] Ibid, pp. 1, 4, 10, 13.

[11] See e.g. Hutchinson (1999).

[12] Trubek (1984), pp. 586–587.

2 The Question of Legal Method as a Problem of Social Thought

The social study of law in its different manifestations makes non-doctrinal researchers wonder about the role of law in society and brings them into direct contact with modern social theory's main unresolved questions about method, social order and modernity itself.[13] Moreover, like in the social sciences, when we ask what the law 'does' in society (instead of what the law 'is' according to legal materials) several background philosophical questions crop up (epistemological, metaphysical, ethical) which drive the most crucial methodological debates.[14] Some of these debates appear to have subsided today or, perhaps, they have always been too specialized to reach broader academic audiences. Be that as it may, the controversies that animate them are still strongly felt in every form of socially oriented non-doctrinal legal inquiry.

In the main, all questions of method can be traced to epistemological disputes, that is, differences about the definition and justification of knowledge.[15] From this viewpoint, the central methodological divide splits modern social thought into two types of research: naturalist and interpretivist.[16] Naturalist approaches to social study are defined by the fundamental belief that, pertaining to the natural world, individuals and societies must be explained from a perspective that is external to them and according to the same method and standards as the natural sciences, i.e., by the empirical verification of causal relations that allow us to know the laws of nature and make predictions about events in order to control our environment.[17] Typically defined as logical empiricism or scientific positivism, however, the most extreme versions of this vision of knowledge and the methods necessary to acquire such knowledge ceased to dominate the natural and the social sciences in the 1970s; since then, the social sciences are not openly positivistic, although the naturalistic approaches that have replaced scientific positivism retain weakened versions of positivism's defining traits.[18]

Interpretivist approaches, in contrast, consider that the attempt to explain human action and social life through the lens of natural sciences—in particular, through the

[13] Unger (1977), p. 44.

[14] Rosenberg (2018), pp. 3–9.

[15] Ibid, p. 11. Surely, the most fundamental epistemological dispute is that between empiricism (knowledge comes from experience and is only certified by observable predictions) and rationalism (knowledge is derived from *a priori* ideas independent from experience), ibid, p. 30.

[16] Ibid, pp. 11–33, and Hollis (2002), pp. 8–11, 16.

[17] Rosenberg (2018), pp. 12–15.

[18] Ibid, pp. 14, 31. In the natural sciences, this has been described as the paradigm change from Newtonian to quantum mechanics, Kuhn (1996), p. 48. In the social sciences, on the other hand, it is generally accepted since the 'Positivismusstreit" of the 1960s that 'social reality does not exist objectively, but emerges intersubjectively. Science also shapes social reality. For sociology there is nothing which can be simply counted and measured. But counting and measuring continued...", Gessner and Winter (2011), p. 159. On the 'Positivismusstreit", see Adorno et al. (1969, 1972).

old positivist paradigm—ignores the most characteristic elements of human life—i.e. intentionality and meaning. These elements are, from the interpretivist viewpoint, the main source of social knowledge and that which social studies should strive to understand and explain.[19] Therefore, from this viewpoint, the aim of social inquiry is not to produce causal explanations and predictions to control human behaviour, but to comprehend action, to render it intelligible by studying its purpose and meaning. Accordingly, human action must be approached with a method that is specific to the social sciences and does not aim to causally explain and predict, but to understand and, perhaps, move social life towards emancipation by looking at it from within.[20] Disagreement among interpretivists, however, arises on whether the comprehension of human action is to be defined exclusively by reference to the (subjective) meaning social agents give to their own actions or according to some other (objective) external perspective.[21]

This is connected to another important methodological divide that traverses the main naturalistic/interpretivist dichotomy. Depending on social researchers' beliefs about the source of social order and change, some researchers concentrate on the study of structural relations, whereas others are mainly concerned with individuals.[22] The first type of research, also called holistic, takes the view that social order is produced by systems or hidden structures of meaning that hold individuals together, induce their actions in a *top-down* relation and are, thus, the essential stuff of social knowledge.[23] Conversely, the second type of research, also called individualistic, holds that individuals are the elements that make up society in a *bottom-up* direction, and, thus, their desires, decisions and actions are the only source of social knowledge and the main object of social study.[24]

Certainly, many eclectic approaches traverse these lines of methodological division striving to escape the problems and limitations of the extreme poles described; and, surely, much of contemporary social research is situated in intermediate positions—no matter how internally contradictory or incoherent such positions might be.[25] The crude sketch in this section, however, serves two of the main purposes of this chapter. First, it provides legal researchers with a rough map to navigate the multiplicity of social research perspectives that inspire non-doctrinal legal research, especially those presented in this book. And second, it suggests that

[19] Phenomenology, structuralism, semiotics, hermeneutics, postmodernism or deconstruction are different developments of the interpretivist type of social research, Rosenberg (2018), p. 31. See also Rorty (1982), pp. 195–198.

[20] Rosenberg (2018), pp. 25–27.

[21] Fay (1996), p. 113.

[22] Hollis (2002), pp. 5–12.

[23] Ibid, pp. 6–7, 17–18, and Fay (1996), pp. 50–52.

[24] Hollis (2002), pp. 10–11, 19, and Fay (1996), pp. 31–32.

[25] Rosenberg (2018), p. 29.

legal researchers, just as social researchers, have to make methodological and, thus, philosophical choices—whether they like it or not.[26]

This is a liberating insight in many ways. Because all possible methodological perspectives existing along or across these lines—especially eclectic positions—are vulnerable, researchers should not feel afraid of choosing the 'wrong' option. It is an invitation to work within and experiment beyond well-known limitations. On the other hand, it places on researchers a stronger requirement of intellectual honesty and academic ethics. Whatever their motivations (political, professional or else), their methodological and philosophical choices should be conscious and explicit for other researchers and for the society at large to grasp and challenge.

In this vein, this book also makes a choice and concentrates on approaches inspired by interpretivist thinking. Yet, as pointed out above, the focus on meaning rather than causal explanation that derives from this choice does not preclude this work from pointing at eclectic or pragmatic avenues, in particular those derived from the use of some empirical tools of research included in the last chapter. Therefore, while the next section examines some of the basic elements and limitations of interpretivism succinctly, the rest of this chapter discusses how general methodological debates shape interpretivist legal research (especially its critical or emancipatory strands) and its possible combination with the type of empirical legal research suggested in this book.

3 Meaning as Method: Interpretivism and the Basic Scheme of Explanation in Social Sciences

Naturalism and interpretivism in social research express different responses to the common methodological problem of the 'severely limited fund of basic schemes of explanation available to modern Western thought'.[27] Following Rosenberg, this is first related to the conceptual apparatus that social sciences generally rely upon. While the natural sciences reject 'folk' descriptive categories for the explanation of natural phenomena and replace them with new concepts considered more adequate for the search of natural laws; social research retains the conceptual repertoire that 'folk psychology' uses to explain individual actions in terms of their intentionality, that is, as behaviour guided by desire and belief.[28] Such categories reflect the common-sense idea that people do things for some purpose. The resulting conceptual apparatus, thus, functions 'by identifying our desires about how we want to rearrange our circumstances, and our beliefs about how our circumstances can be shaped to satisfy our desires, to narrow down the range of actions that will attain the desires in light of the beliefs.'[29]

---

[26] Ibid, pp. 28–30.

[27] Unger (1977), p. 9.

[28] Rosenberg (2018), pp. 20–21.

[29] Ibid, p. 25–26.

This common-sense explanatory strategy can be expressed as an 'if…then…' proposition: if a person desires something and believes that a certain action is a means to fulfil their desires; then that person will perform that action.[30] But why and how exactly does action result from desire and belief? What kind of connection does link them together? The interpretivist response grows out of opposition to naturalism. Naturalist social researchers construe this link as a cause-effect relation, where desire and belief *determine* action, and from which generalizations and laws can be discovered and verified through empirical observation and experimentation to predict human behaviour.[31] It is in that sense, e.g., that social research connected to neuroscience tries to describe beliefs and desires as physical (brain) states that determine behaviour and from which the neurophysiological laws governing individual and collective action can be identified.[32]

However, there seem to be too many unresolved questions about the possibility of establishing any causal relation between belief, desire and action. In particular, the impracticability of capturing the exact beliefs and desires causing action—as any desire and belief makes only sense by reference to larger systems of other beliefs and desires—; or our inability to understand just how beliefs and desires are actually 'contained' in and retrieved by our braincells (the so-called mind-body problem). These and other problems would account for the failure of naturalist social research to develop any sound laws of human behaviour on that basis.[33]

Rejecting deterministic naturalism, interpretivists hold that beliefs and desires cannot be comprehended as causes that determine action, but as 'reasons' that render action intelligible by highlighting how actors justify it, i.e. by showing its meaning.[34] From this viewpoint, the connection between action and reasons for action is semantic. In other words, the basic categories of social research operate by making actors' beliefs and desires explicit and linking them to action in a sort of redefinition. This redefinition transforms the description of *behaviour* from mere bodily movement into *action* which is then comprehended as the *relative coherence* between behaviour and intentional states or psychological attitudes towards the propositional content of certain statements (beliefs and desires).[35]

But how does interpretivism extend the conceptual apparatus of folk psychology from the interpretation of individual interactions to interactions between institutions, social groups or cultures? Instead of seeking linear causal connections between social phenomena, interpretivist research acknowledges the reciprocal interrelatedness of social events and tries to explain how and why they interlock without any of

[30] Ibid, p. 39. Needless to say, there are other schemes of explanation of human action in the social sciences, although this is the most widespread one, ibid, p. 40.

[31] Correlation and probability being the weaker or more 'modest' versions of the deterministic form of connection under the current naturalistic paradigm, Hollis (2002), pp. 47–50.

[32] Rosenberg (2018), pp. 44, 61.

[33] Ibid, pp. 41–50, 55–71.

[34] Ibid, pp. 43, 56.

[35] Ibid, pp. 57–60, 64.

them determining the rest.[36] Conceived as the *relative correspondence* between belief and action, the notion of meaning is applied to explain such interrelation.[37] Actions, beliefs and desires constitute inseparable units of meaning that gather into larger semantic clusters based on collective systems of meaning. Thus, the semantic unity of a social situation is connected to the visions of life shared by its participants; a totality of meaning that derives from its constituent parts and, at the same time, gives meaning to them in a dynamic and changing relation (e.g. specific legal doctrines can be connected to certain forms of legal consciousness and visions of life).[38]

Insofar as causation and determinism are abandoned,[39] the problems with the use of the traditional categories of social sciences can be regarded not as unsurmountable obstacles to fruitful research, but as the inherent limits of any study of society. Thus, rather than further aping the natural sciences, acceptance of these limits requires researchers to become critically self-aware regarding methodological issues. Given that specific beliefs and desires may be a function of all or most of our other beliefs and desires—possibly a state of our whole brain or consciousness—; given that beliefs and desires also have a collective dimension; and given that the identification of such psychological states usually takes place indirectly through speech (a form of action); social inquiry in these terms is always sketchy and largely based on guesswork.[40] Therefore, for interpretivists, prediction and the ability to control human behaviour cannot be the benchmark for measuring the success of social studies. Rather, the goal of this type of research is the interpretation of action in order to understand it, i.e. to establish some coherence between reasons and actions, and possibly transform action by transforming or affecting the reasons that motivate it.

Similarly, interpretivist research cannot solve once and for all the dilemmas of individual/structural sources of meaning and social order mentioned above or the problem of combining people's (subjective) self-understanding with the observer's or system's (objective) perspective.[41] Neither can interpretivism more generally escape the recurring dilemma between abstract vagueness and meaningless precision in scientific explanation that plagues every research approach: i.e. the more explanatory simplicity research offers, the less descriptive fidelity it can provide; and, vice-versa, the more descriptive accuracy, the less explanatory power.[42] In practice, thus, interpretivism, as any other form of research, is always compelled to seek some sort

[36] Unger (1977), p. 14.

[37] Ibid, p. 246.

[38] Ibid, p. 249.

[39] Determinism understood as the belief in and search for the laws of the social world that would determine human action beyond human will, Trubek (1984), p. 580.

[40] Rosenberg (2018), pp. 64–65, 69.

[41] Unger (1977), pp. 15–17.

[42] Ibid, pp. 20–22.

of reconciliation between concrete perception and abstract knowledge.[43] The need to balance all these extremes results in a variety of strands, eclectic strategies and idiosyncratic modes of interpretivist research which, despite their differences, seek to overcome similar limitations and constraints.

Despite the weaknesses of the interpretivist approach and its conceptual apparatus, interpretivism's optimistic view on the potential of anti-naturalist approaches to the study of human behaviour seems to offer the only way out of the pessimism (and cynicism) to which the naturalist approach has led social research throughout the twentieth century.[44] As a result, interpretivist thought has driven the most characteristic and fruitful debates in the social sciences—and in non-doctrinal legal research—for decades. The following, therefore, deals with the interpretivist type of legal research focusing on some of its critical strands—i.e. Critical, Feminist and Third World approaches supplemented by some of the empirical (qualitative) modes of inquiry that are best suited to the interpretivist endeavour.

4 Legal Interpretivism: Systems of Legal Belief and Ideology Critique

Legal interpretivism is based on the notion that human action and social order are embedded in legal belief with which they form an inseparable unit of meaning. From this viewpoint, individual beliefs generally depend upon complex systems of ideas, i.e., wide compounds of interrelated beliefs that cluster together into meaningful wholes. Legal ideas, thus, constitute systems of belief that are not isolated from other systems of meaning; they are interwoven with other cultural systems, and are a piece of larger semantic wholes and visions of life.[45] Interpretivist studies in law focus on how legal beliefs and practices are organised according to certain principles of meaning and how these principles form variable structures interwoven with nonlegal cultural systems so as to explain human action and social order.[46]

By redefining social interactions and institutions in terms of legal belief, that is, by making explicit the meaning they have for different groups of social actors, legal interpretivism stresses the unity of human action and belief. In other words, it shows that legal beliefs not only have a bearing upon action; legal beliefs do constitute social action and institutions in a real sense. Even when they diverge for some reason (e.g. due to conflicting subsystems of meaning, social actors' mistake or inattention to the consequences of action, etc.), there is no strong distinction between belief and action, consciousness and order, ideas and practice.[47] As a result, for interpretivists, if we change dominant legal beliefs and consciousness, we are not only changing

[43] Ibid, p. 15, and Hollis (2002), pp. 180–182 and ch. 9.

[44] Rosenberg (2018), p. 70.

[45] Unger (1977), pp. 250–252.

[46] Trubek (1984), p. 604.

[47] Ibid, pp. 589–592.

legal ideas, we are also at the same time changing the social order in a meaningful way.

These insights, however, prompt radically contrasting attitudes among interpretivist researchers and give rise to different types of interpretivist legal scholarship. By tracking their research agendas, two main types can be distinguished. First, there is a type of interpretivist scholarship that seeks to adapt and rehabilitate the traditional legal order ideas and practices as represented by political liberalism and its institutional decision-making processes.[48] In opposition to this, there is a critical type of legal interpretivism that seeks to overcome different aspects of (neo)liberal legalism understood as a belief system that justifies unnecessary domination or illegitimate power asymmetries, and usher some kind of emancipatory social change.[49]

This second broad type of interpretivist scholarship, which covers the family of approaches this book focuses on, seeks to reveal to social actors the deep, unrealized meanings of their actions and the social institutions they participate in. The notion of a deeper meaning that is unknown to or neglected by social actors implies the identification of some beliefs and desires as unfounded visions contrary to the actors' interests, i.e. as some sort of ideological delusion, which, once exposed, the actors will reject or abandon if the social conditions allow for a process of free self-reflection and debate that would lead to more free beliefs instead of new ideological impositions.[50] Other versions of this approach seek to identify and denounce unjustified power asymmetries that are ideologically justified by law without necessarily alluding to hidden structures.[51] Nevertheless, the search for the unrealized, ideological meanings of legal beliefs and practices is often conducted by reference to a variety of deep patterns or structures of meaning—like the (neo)liberal, patriarchal, (neo)colonial or imperialist—that work as provisional maps of meaning and tools of critical analysis.[52]

In any case, however essential to critical interpretivist legal research, the element of evaluative critique may lead to confusion about its relation to the style and methodological assumptions of the mainstream approaches within the legal order

---

[48] See Stavropoulos (2021), and Altman (1986, 1990).

[49] See chapters on "Critical International Law", "Feminist Approaches to International Law", and "Third World Approaches to International Law (TWAIL)" below.

[50] This critical strand of interpretivism emerges in European Continental philosophy (from Marx to the Frankfurt School to Habermas, Foucault or Bourdieu), Rosenberg (2018), pp. 150–170, and Geuss (1981), pp. 4–44). However, its application to law is strongly linked to the Anglo-American critical legal movement, where Feminist, anticolonial or Third World approaches to legal research are also rooted, see e.g. Hunt (1985), pp. 19–31, Hunt (1986), pp. 12–13, Balkin (1987), pp. 422–431, Munger and Seron (1984), pp. 279–284, Coombe (1989), pp. 105–111, and Kennedy (1998) 147–179. On ideology critique and its limitations, see generally Desautels-Stein and Rasulov (2021), and chapter on "Critical International Law" below.

[51] Marks (2001, 2009).

[52] See e.g. Brown and Halley (2002), and Anghie (2007).

tradition.[53] Yet, critical interpretivism differs significantly from the latter. First, by adhering to the distinction descriptive/normative (is/ought) about law, traditional approaches (both in the natural law and the legal positivist versions) as well as their contemporary derivates, reproduce the assumptions of naturalist social thought—especially, its vision of language, the sharp distinction between fact and value, or the search for a social-fact source as the best way to acquire relevant legal knowledge.[54]

Furthermore, given that traditional is/ought debates also deal with political morality and sometimes borrow from the same categories of 'folk psychology' as legal interpretivism,[55] there is an apparent overlap and the temptation to assess (critical) interpretivist legal research against naturalist/positivist standards and expectations. In particular, legal interpretivist work might be expected to produce causal, linear explanations about *why* a particular social situation is the one-directional effect of a set of legal ideas or a form of legal consciousness.[56] This objection, however, confuses the link between belief and action with a surrogate form of causation. That is, it fundamentally misunderstands the repudiation of causation as a scheme of explanation by interpretivist analysis which, instead of causal relations, explores the connections between action and belief, social order and legal consciousness through the complex 'logic of situations'—i.e. 'the sense an act

[53] See e.g. Corten (2009), pp. 45–68.

[54] According to its self-image, legal positivism emerges as a reaction against the natural law tradition and bestows upon modern legal scholarship the character of a 'science' comparable to the natural sciences by identifying the predictable and stable source of the legal order in the consensual basis of liberal political theory, see Mensch (1998), pp. 25–26. However, the main difference between natural law and legal positivism is not the acceptance or rejection of the distinction is/ought (fact/value), as the positivist critics of natural law would have it, but the way both traditions define the social-fact source from which law emanates ('is'). Particularly, whether this should include alternative forms of law-making as a way to channel morality into the posited law, Finnis (2000), pp. 1604–1605. By accepting this inclusion, part of contemporary legal positivism (the so-called 'inclusive' positivism) seems to have collapsed into natural law, Goldsworthy (1990), pp. 485–486.

Ironically, since the early twentieth century, the denial of traditional legal positivism's scientific character by naturalist non-doctrinal legal research is coupled with the latter's attempt to retain for law the scientific authority of the natural sciences through the discovery of extra-legal sources of legal order, Munger and Seron (1984), pp. 287–288, at n 10. Legal behaviourism, for instance, is a naturalistic-deterministic non-doctrinal approach that aims to establish causal explanations about the externally observable behaviour of people when their conduct is affected by legal rules and predict how law, as an external constraint, can help produce (determine) desired behaviour in certain circumstances, Trubek (1984), pp. 602–603.

[55] See e.g. H.L.A. Hart's positivist method of conceptual analysis as a 'descriptive sociology' that analyses 'the uses to which the concept is actually put in real social practices' or Hart's description of legal rules as an inquiry into how people feel they have an obligation of obedience as opposed to feeling merely obliged by the threat of sanctions, Coleman and Leiter (2010), pp. 229, 232. Kelsen's normativist positivism does also claim to be based not only on 'scientific' descriptions of actual legal systems, but also on the meanings people give to them, Davies (1994), p. 107.

[56] Hunt (1986), pp. 11–17.

makes against the background of a social code of rules, practices and beliefs', using the 'language of purpose'.[57]

Therefore, the interpretivist critique about the politics of law, judicial law-making, etc. takes place in a completely different methodological framework and is motivated by radically divergent professional goals and expectations. Whether inspired by natural law or legal positivism, mainstream or doctrinal legal work is in general methodologically geared to the revamp and continuation of the legal order tradition and institutions. In contrast, the interpretivist critique aims to understand and influence the legal consciousness of society or specific groups (e.g. courts) with a view to reducing domination and perhaps transforming law and legal institutions into forums of social deliberation or tools of emancipation.[58] On the other hand, while it cannot be assessed from the legal order framework or the empiricist-deterministic premises of social naturalism, interpretivist legal research is not disconnected from empirical inquiry.

5 The Limits of Meaning: Critical Empirical Work and the Persistence of Scientistic Modes of Representation

Despite its anti-positivist inspiration, legal interpretivism is, in a broad sense, 'empirical' as it seeks to comprehend what law 'does' in social life.[59] In fact, interpretivist thinking makes, at its roots, no claim that absolutely everything is consciousness, that 'there's nothing out there outside our minds' which researchers need to take into consideration.[60] On the contrary, early studies on the application of interpretivist insights to legal research give fair warning about the limits of the 'method of common meaning' and the risk that exclusive focus on belief and consciousness may slide back into an arcane sort of idealism.[61]

The study of legal belief, thus, does not excuse the empirical study of social action and its relation to consciousness. Rather, it requires certain forms of empirical research, especially because, for the most part, psychological states (beliefs, desires, consciousness) must be identified indirectly through speech (above all, spoken or written language).[62] Moreover, it is crucial for critical interpretivist work to improve our understanding of the relationship between legal belief systems and social action

[57] Unger (1977), p. 254. 'The "logic of the situation" may make some acts in any given circumstance more probable than others, not because they result from specific causes, but because of the tendency of social phenomena to join into meaningful wholes', ibid, p. 255.

[58] Kennedy (1998), p. 70.

[59] Trubek (1984), p. 600.

[60] Gessner and Winter (2011), pp. 159–160.

[61] Unger (1977), p. 256.

[62] Rosenberg (2018), p. 48. On the study of case-law as empirical work in the rhetorical analysis of law, see e.g. Sobota (1992), pp. 232–233.

as well as the impact of legal consciousness on social organization and institutions.[63] In particular, interpretivist legal research cannot neglect the study of how action recreates systems and subsystems of legal meaning every day.[64]

In this sense, critical empirical work tries to address these issues by practising different forms of factual inquiry detached from positivistic-deterministic premises.[65] Linked to philosophical pragmatism, critical empirical research not only repudiates the positivist value-fact dichotomy and the deterministic idea of discovering the laws that drive human action; it also rejects the notion that the purpose of knowledge be the representation of 'reality'.[66] From this perspective, thanks to empirical legal research we can know more about the semantic relations of mutual reinforcement and/or conflict between legal belief and social action; while we also learn something valuable about the conditions and consequences of different policy choices.[67]

Moreover, to some extent the use of empirical legal work can also help interpretivist researchers to reconcile their critical aspirations with the limitations that any alternative to positivist determinism must face as long as we remain within the confines of the Western *scientistic* culture.[68] For all the contemporary epistemic struggles, we still live in a *scientistic age* where our ways of thinking, speaking and writing are dominated by 'discourses of the real' that aim to 'produce necessities through realities and facts'.[69] Although the scientistic foundations of law have been removed by the critique of legal order, legal discourse in general is still characterized by the primacy of references to 'the real', even when expressing counter-scientistic positions.[70] Thus, the references to 'empirical reality' are an 'inescapable genre'.[71] And as such, certain forms of empirical inquiry can be strategically mobilized by researchers for critical purposes without necessarily seeking a reactionary rehabilitation of positivistic-deterministic discourses.

On the other hand, this must begin by acknowledging the need for a type of empirical research that is self-aware of its own risks and limitations.[72] Several issues,

---

[63] Trubek (1984), p. 615.

[64] Unger (1977), p. 252.

[65] Trubek (1984), pp. 581–582.

[66] Whitford (2011), pp. 182–183, and Rorty (1982), pp. 160–166.

[67] E.g. Van den Meerssche (2022), Corkery and Khalil (2018), and Alston (2016).

[68] The term scientistic (*szientistisch*) was originally coined by Karl Popper to define only the most orthodox forms of scientific positivism, Adorno (1969, 1972), p. 9.

[69] D'Aspremont (2022), pp. 680–681, 684.

[70] Ibid, pp. 687ff.

[71] Ibid, p. 690.

[72] On the problems of conceptualism (facts do not exist independently of concepts, i.e. language—which is inherently indeterminate) and agency (the definition and interpretation of the facts observed depend on the observer's values, preferences, etc.) in empirical research, see Whitford (2011), pp. 179–180. See also the problem of 'empirical' legal positivists' rhetorical appeals to (naturalistic) sociological inquiry based on no serious sociology—e.g. H.L.A. Hart's positivist 'method' was purportedly empirical, although he did no substantial empirical work, which led him

like the possible difference between stated and actual beliefs, actors' mistake about the effects of their actions, internal value conflicts, the existence of conflicting subsystems of meaning and the excessive focus on dominant cultures, call for precaution. Similarly, the idea that empirical legal research could act as critical guidance for legal doctrine (e.g. courts) or policy-making (ministries, parliaments, agencies, etc.) by processing empirical results theoretically and then evaluating and directing policy reform has often proved to be less than effective and capable of leading to counterproductive results.[73] Although it can potentially help legal research to achieve an emancipatory impact on the legal beliefs of society,[74] this sort of legal pragmatism in general can paradoxically transform critical research into an indirect source of support for traditional legal thought,[75] or become a cynical routine with potentially repressive effects on legal thinking and imagination.[76]

Being aware of these risks and given the strategic importance of empirical legal research for the use of the other approaches presented in this book, the last chapter presents some qualitative methods of empirical research in law as a means to complete and supplement the other chapters. Their use in combination with Critical, Feminist or Third World approaches is neither necessary nor is it always advisable. This will depend on the variable goals and circumstances of each researcher and their projects. And yet, making these tools available to critical researchers today seems more indispensable than ever before to improve the quality and impact of legal research conducted on a critical interpretivist basis.

References

Adorno, T.W., Dahrendorf, R., Pilot, H., Albert, H., Habermas, J., & Popper, K.R. (1969, 1970). *Der Positivismusstreit in der deutschen Soziologie*. Hermann Luchterhand,

Alston, P. (2016). *Report of the special rapporteur on extreme poverty and human rights to the thirty second sessions of the human rights council* (UN Doc. A/HRC/32/31).

Altman, A. (1986). Legal realism, critical legal studies, and Dworkin. *Philosophy & Public Affairs, 15*(3), 205–235.

Altman, A. (1990). *Critical legal studies. A liberal critique*. Princeton University Press.

Anghie, A. (2007). *Imperialism, sovereignty and the making of international law*. Cambridge University Press.

Balkin, J. M. (1987). Taking ideology seriously: Ronald Dworkin and the CLS critique. *UMKC Law Review, 55*, 392–433.

to massive speculation about legal systems other than the English (those he termed 'primitive' legal systems incidentally), Davies (1994), pp. 106–107.

[73] Cf. e.g. Krever (2013). As the fate of empirical legal sociology after the 1960s shows, due to deep-rooted professional power struggles and the still hegemonic role of doctrinal thinking, empirical information tends to be selected by legal doctrine and policy-makers and cleansed from any theoretical insight to support preestablished goals—also discouraging in turn critical theoretical study in empirical research, Gessner and Winter (2011), pp. 162–168.

[74] Ibid, pp. 177–178.

[75] Desautels-Stein (2018), pp. 268–272.

[76] D'Aspremont (2022), pp. 691–693.

Bianchi, A. (2016). *International law theories. An inquiry into different ways of thinking*. Oxford University Press.
Brown, W., & Halley, J. (Eds.). (2002). *Left legalism/left critique*. Duke University Press.
Coleman, J. L., & Leiter, B. (2010). Legal positivism. In D. Patterson (Ed.), *A companion to philosophy of law and legal theory* (2nd ed., pp. 228–248). Wiley-Blackwell.
Coombe, R. J. (1989). Room for manoeuver: Toward a theory of practice in critical legal studies. *Law & Social Inquiry, 14*, 69–121.
Corkery, A., & Khalil, H. (2018). Do metric matter? Accountability for economic and social rights in post-revolution Egypt. In G. MacNaughton & D. F. Frey (Eds.), *Economic and social rights in a neoliberal world* (pp. 150–172). Cambridge University Press.
Corten, O. (2009). *Méthodologie du droit international public*. Editions de l'Université de Bruxelles.
D'Aspremont, J. (2022). International law and the rage against scientism. *European Journal of International Law, 33*(2), 679–694.
Davies, M. (1994). *Asking the law question*. The Law Book Company (Sweet & Maxwell).
Desautels-Stein, J. (2018). *The jurisprudence of style: A structuralist history of American pragmatism and liberal legal thought*. Cambridge University Press.
Desautels-Stein, J., & Rasulov, A. (2021). Deep cuts: Four critiques of legal ideology. *Journal of Law & the Humanities, 31*(2), 435–519.
Dyzenhaus, D. (2004). The genealogy of legal positivism. *Oxford Journal of Legal Studies, 24*(1), 39–67.
Fay, B. (1996). *Contemporary philosophy of social science: A multicultural approach*. Blackwell.
Finnis, J. M. (2000). On the incoherence of legal positivism. *Notre Dame Law Review, 75*(5), 1597–1611.
Gessner, V., & Winter, G. (2011). Empiricism and legal practice. *German Law Journal, 12*(1), 159–178.
Geuss, R. (1981). *The idea of a critical theory. Habermas and the Frankfurt School*. Cambridge University Press.
Goldsworthy, J. D. (1990). The self-destruction of legal positivism. *Oxford Journal of Legal Studies, 10*(4), 449–486.
Hollis, M. (2002). *The philosophy of social science. An Introduction (revised and updated)*. Cambridge University Press.
Hunt, A. (1985). The ideology of law: Advances and problems in recent applications of the concept of ideology to the analysis of law. *Law & Society Review, 19*(1), 11–37.
Hunt, A. (1986). The theory of critical legal studies. *Oxford Journal of Legal Studies, 6*(1), 1–45.
Hutchinson, A. C. (1999). Beyond black-letterism: Ethics in law and legal education. *The Law Teacher, 33*(3), 301–309.
Kennedy, D. (1998). *A critique of adjudication: Fin de siècle*. Harvard University Press.
Kennedy, D. (2006). Three globalizations of law and legal thought: 1850–2000. In D. M. Trubek & A. Santos (Eds.), *The new law and economic development. A critical appraisal* (pp. 19–73). Cambridge University Press.
Krever, T. (2013). Quantifying law: Legal indicator projects and the reproduction of Neoliberal common sense. *Third World Quarterly, 34*(1), 131–150.
Kuhn, T. S. (1996). *The structure of scientific revolutions* (3rd ed.). University of Chicago Press.
Marks, S. (2001). Big brother is bleeping us: With the message that ideology doesn't matter. *European Journal of International Law, 12*(1), 109–123.
Marks, S. (2009). False contingency. *Current Legal Problems, 62*(1), 1–21.
Mensch, E. (1998). The history of mainstream legal thought. In D. Kairys (Ed.), *The politics of law: A progressive critique* (3rd ed., pp. 23–53). Basic Books.
Munger, F., & Seron, C. (1984). Critical legal studies versus critical legal theory: A comment on method. *Law Policy, 6*(3), 257–297.
Posner, R. A. (2002). Legal scholarship today. *Harvard Law Review, 115*, 1314–1326.

Rorty, R. (1982). *Consequences of pragmatism (Essays: 1972-1980)*. University of Minnesota Press.
Rosenberg, A. (2018). *Philosophy of social sciences* (5th ed.). Routledge.
Sobota, K. (1992). Rhetorisches Seismogramm — eine neue Methode in der Rechtswissenschaft. *JuristenZeitung, 5*, 231–237.
Stavropoulos, N. (2021). Legal Interpretivism. In: Edward N. Zalta (ed) *The Stanford Encyclopedia of Philosophy*. URL: https://plato.stanford.edu/archives/spr2021/entries/law-interpretivist/
Trubek, D. M. (1984). Where the action is: Critical legal studies and empiricism. *Stanford Law Review, 36*(1/2), 575–622.
Unger, R. M. (1977). *Law in modern society. Toward a criticism of social theory*. The Free Press.
Unger, R. M. (1984). *Knowledge and politics*. The Free Press.
van den Meerssche, D. (2022). *The World Bank's lawyers: The life of international law as institutional practice*. Oxford University Press.
Weber, M. (1922). *Wirtschaft und Gesellschaft. Grundriss der Sozialökonomik 3. Abteilung*. J.C.B. Mohr (Paul Siebeck).
Whitford, W. C. (2011). Critical empiricism: a comment on David M. Trubek & John Esser, Gerd Winter & Volkmar Gessner. *German Law Journal, 12*(1), 179–185.

Mainstream Approaches to International Law

Juan J. Garcia Blesa

Contents

1 Introduction

Given that the approaches studied in the following chapters grow out of the critique against traditional legal methods, this chapter outlines some of the most typical features of mainstream approaches to legal work.[1] That is, in order to contextualise the critical and empirical approaches explained in the rest of the book, the following pages offer a brief account of the key ideas and practices that distinguish mainstream

[1] As explained below, the broad label 'mainstream' is meant to describe the customary form of international legal scholarship which, despite its internal incoherencies and well-known deficiencies, is the most widespread and familiar type of legal approach in international law. In this sense, the word mainstream is similar to and used here interchangeably with other terms employed in the literature on international legal methods such as orthodox, doctrinal, archetypal, traditional, default or practitioners' legal approach. See Sect. 2 of this chapter.

J. J. Garcia Blesa (✉)
FernUniversität in Hagen, Hagen/Westfalen, Germany
e-mail: juan.garciablesa@fernuni-hagen.de

J. J. Garcia Blesa (ed.), *Contemporary Methods in International Legal Research*, Springer Textbooks in Law, https://doi.org/10.1007/978-3-031-69522-3_3

approaches to international law (MAIL) in connection to some aspects that are characteristic of a broader underlying type of mainstream legal scholarship (MLS).[2]

The selectivity implied is justified by the plurality and heterogeneity of the beliefs and routines embraced by MLS/MAIL. Instead of aiming at an exhaustive account of these approaches, the chapter focuses on the familiar dominant style which, inspired by traditional legal positivism, unmistakably marks the bulk of legal scholarship and defines institutional work as well as the identity and consciousness of the legal profession—both in international and domestic law.[3]

More specifically, the kind of legal positivism that inspires MLS/MAIL is based on no coherent set of postulates and practices and can be better defined as a cultural tradition,[4] or as 'a process of socialisation and adaption' whose methods and practices constitute 'a culture more than an approach'.[5] Yet, the inconsistencies of the mainstream idea and practice of legal positivism are not related only to the inattention of mainstream practitioners and researchers to the profound theoretical problems of their work—as some philosophical positivists would seem to suggest.[6]

Since the early twentieth century, unresolved fundamental questions plague philosophical positivism which is defined today by theoretical controversy and a wide variety of internal positions that continuously expose and emphasize each other's weaknesses.[7] Typically, reconstruction attempts concede a measure of law-making power in law-application while they try to retain, at least partially, some traditional positivist ideas—in particular, the notion that there is a distinct legal method for the solution of legal questions connected to some kind of weakened formalism.[8] Yet, the general failure of MLS/MAIL to live up to the original legal positivist aspirations and the subsequent inability to transcend the self-imposed limits of traditional frameworks has led to an internally eclectic—fundamentally incoherent—mainstream jurisprudence that keeps MLS/MAIL trapped in the 'tourment intime né de l'insatisfaction provoquée par les solutions tour à tour adoptées'.[9]

---

[2] The picture provided here is supplemented by the discussion of other aspects of MLS/MAIL in the chapters below.

[3] Davies (1994), p. 76, Bianchi (2016), p. 21, and Kammerhofer (2021), p. 95.

[4] Observing the relative uniformity of mainstream approaches, Bianchi describes them as a tradition or a conservative cultural process where certain beliefs are formulated as truth claims and preserved and administered by groups of '"licensed" speakers', Bianchi (2016), p. 22.

[5] Kammerhofer calls it a *culture of orthodoxy*, a pragmatic tendency to respect authority and accommodate perceived political trends, Kammerhofer (2021), pp. 98–100.

[6] For Kammerhofer, for instance, this '"default positivism" is semi-conscious and half-reflected, more part of one's legal socialisation and culture than of a conscious choice and reflection', Kammerhofer (2021), p. 97.

[7] Forgó and Somek (2009), pp. 256–257. See e.g. Kammerhofer and d'Aspremont (2014).

[8] Kennedy (1973), p. 392. See also Rosenberg (1990), and Singh (2015).

[9] Ago (1956), p. 900. About the post-modern critique of philosophical legal positivism, see also this chapter.

In order to unpack these problems, Sect. 2 sketches some general, common markers of mainstream legal approaches pointing at instances of their eclectic reliance on different strands of legal thought from conceptualist and empirical positivism to natural law. Section 3 outlines how mainstream approaches to international legal research translate these basic traits into a disciplinary language of its own.

2 Separability, Formalism and Systematicity: The Eclectic Foundations of Mainstream Legal Work

As mentioned above, at the heart of mainstream legal research lies the positivist project of a legal science which is based on two fundamental premises: first, law is not dictated by God nor derived from any natural order or immanent rationality, but created and expressed ('posited') by people through empirically recognisable procedures (the social thesis); and second, law is essentially independent from morality, politics, culture, etc. (the separability thesis).[10] While the former premise is central to the historical construction of legal positivism in opposition to the natural law tradition; it is the latter that typically characterizes contemporary legal positivism—and its critique.[11]

According to the separability thesis, law is separate or at least separable from other dimensions of social life; that is, it exists as an entity that can be isolated and described objectively.[12] And just as scientific naturalism claims to be based on the objective and neutral observation of facts, MLS claims to be able to produce an objective description of law-making processes and of the existing (valid) laws thereby created—the 'law as it is'.[13] Although legality may overlap with morality, culture, etc., for traditional legal positivism/MLS, these are radically different and separate entities.

The notion of separability lies at the heart of the mainstream legal methodological claims to 'scientificity'.[14] Only insofar as legal research can provide a value-free account of law (free from the subjectivity of morality, politics, etc.) can it claim to be neutral and objective; and only insofar as it is neutral and objective can it claim to be 'scientific'.[15] MLS, thus, devotes much of its energies to the creation and protection of (intra- and extra-) disciplinary boundaries because only by banishing from legal

---

[10] Coleman and Leiter (2010), p. 228, and Ago (1956), pp. 873, 902.

[11] Hall (2001), p. 272, and Cryer et al. (2011), pp. 37–38. In fact, for strict legal positivists, who uphold the strong separability of law and morality, any challenge to this extreme position is understood as a way of advancing natural law in disguise, see Goldsworthy (1990).

[12] Forgó and Somek (2009), p. 258.

[13] Davies (1994), pp. 87–88.

[14] Ibid, p. 108, and Corten (2009), pp. 30–44.

[15] Davies (1994), pp. 115–117.

debate those aspects of social life deemed to be subjective can legal positivistic work appear neutral and objective.[16] Furthermore, at a more practical level, MLS's insistence on delimiting acceptable legal knowledge also simplifies the lawyer's work, it provides a professional identity vis-à-vis the rest of society, and secures the disciplinary and institutional power (real or aspirational) of those who join MLS's positivistic 'intellectual border patrol'.[17]

This quest for the negative demarcation of law also defines the traditional methods of legal analysis. Mainstream legal research claims to move from an aseptic description of the procedures that warrant the 'correct' creation of (valid) rules in a society to the determination of specific valid rules and finally to their application to particular cases.[18] Once the criteria for the determination of law's validity are identified, they are deployed as formal sources of law which enable the verification of the 'pedigree' of a norm (i.e., whether it has been correctly produced through the socially accepted means of normative production) and, thus, help draw a clear separation between valid rules and extra-legal considerations—the ultimate distinction between law and non-law.[19]

Confined in practice to the operation of a received set of formal sources of law, the archetypal MLS strongly depends on legal formalism. Of course, just as there are different views on how the scientific foundation and operation of the legal system should proceed within legal positivism;[20] there are different versions of legal formalism.[21] The archetypal MLS version of formalism propounds that the language of legal rules determines the outcomes of law-application thanks to a special legal technique that would secure the textually constrained interpretation and mechanical application of legal rules to objective facts.[22] Based on these assumptions, formalism pledges the exclusion of subjective values in law-application and the production of purely formal solutions that would reflect only the law as a pure or autonomous entity, transferring legitimacy from the legislator to the law-applier.[23]

In the face of the legal indeterminacy critique and its anti-formalist consequences, however, strong claims about the determination power of language, systems and

---

[16] Is/ought, *lex lata/lege ferenda*, description/evaluation, hard/soft, rule-based/extra-legal considerations are but a few of the usual disciplinary lines of exclusion whose transgression makes the legal researcher liable to charges of insufficient rigour, Bianchi (2016), pp. 24–29.

[17] Forgó and Somek (2009), p. 255. See also Bianchi (2016), pp. 22–24.

[18] Davies (1994), pp. 76–77, and Gardner (2001), p. 201.

[19] The idea of 'pedigree' to describe this way of thinking is Dowrkin's, see Dworkin (2013), pp. 32–33. See also Dyzenhaus (2004), p. 45, and Finnis (2000), pp. 1598–1601. In international law, see Ago (1956), pp. 874, 886, and Simma and Paulus (1999), pp. 305, 308.

[20] The classic account ranges from the more inductive common law tradition with the American case-method to the more deductive civil law tradition, Davies (1994), pp. 104–114.

[21] Schauer (1988), pp. 509–510, and Davies (1994), p. 115.

[22] Kennedy (1973), pp. 358–359, Dyzenhaus (2004), p. 45, and Rosenberg (1990), p. 1233.

[23] Kennedy (1973), p. 353, and Davies (1994), pp. 116–117.

processes of law are often replaced by arguments about the coherence and intelligibility of law as a professional practice of justification.[24] As the coherence and intelligibility standards of a professional community are intrinsically relative and not inevitably connected to one necessary interpretation of democratic legislative will, the legitimacy problems that this shift raises are whisked away by paradoxical arguments about the (false) contingency of legal decision-making (i.e. its being distinct from law-making).[25] In other words, revised versions of formalism have been forced by the post-modern critique to take up more modest positions and reach out to eclectic notions like 'the distinctive morality that marks coherent legal relationships'[26]—though this may also be occasionally displaced by sheer faith in the purity of one's liberal convictions.[27]

Be this as it may, within the MLS framework formally validated rules compose a normative mass which, in order to work as an autonomous system of law, must also be organized in accordance with the scientific values of logic, clarity, rationality, etc.[28] Mainstream legal work, thus, emerges as the effort to build a coherent structure, a rationally ordered and gapless system that determines normative creation, interpretation and legal problem-solving, keeping extra-legal considerations at bay.[29] In the final analysis, it is this closed, rational, and logical systematicity that is expected to preserve law's objectivity and independence from subjective values (non-law), and secure legal work's scientific character and identity.[30]

The connection between logic, scientificity and law can be traced at least back to the seventeenth century's scientific revolution and the attempt to derive all human knowledge from universal reason (natural law).[31] Nineteenth century legal positivism continues to treat logical reasoning as a central component of the legal method and the construction of a legal system by simply eliminating previous references to natural law, but not necessarily natural law's embedded role and aspirations.[32] Indeed, today the pursuit of systematicity and coherence as the markers of (international) law still reveals MLS/MAIL's search for a connection with a superior rationality, a sort of natural law in disguise that is at odds with the 'social thesis' of more philosophically consistent versions of legal positivism and, thus, a most genuine expression of the eclecticism and internal contradictions that lie at the positivistic heart of mainstream legal work.[33]

---

[24] E.g. Weinrib (2010), pp. 327, 336–337. See also Rosenberg (1990). About the indeterminacy critique, see this chapter.

[25] E.g. MacCormick (2005), p. 170; and Peat (2018), p. 671. For a compelling critique of the false contingency of legal decision-making, see Marks (2009).

[26] Weinrib (2010), p. 337.

[27] Van der Walt (2020), pp. 4–5.

[28] Schauer (1988), p. 536, at n.81, Ago (1956), pp. 919–920, and Visscher (1973), pp. 78–79.

[29] Rosenberg (1990), pp. 1233–1234, and Forgó and Somek (2009), pp. 255–256.

[30] Ago (1956), pp. 897–898.

[31] Hoeflich (1986), pp. 96–97.

[32] Ibid, pp. 102–112.

[33] Kammerhofer (2021), p. 103.

Furthermore, in practical terms, systematicity and coherence are not an objective fact nor the product of mere description; they require the creative effort of legal scholars and implies the realization of certain tasks with the mobilization of an argumentative style that characterizes mainstream legal research. The enterprise of building and preserving a legal order inspired by the premises of traditional legal positivism places upon legal researchers following MLS/MAIL the endless task of representing law as a unitary and coherent system that contains, at least potentially, all necessary answers to social problems and can constrain legal interpreters in a predictable manner.[34]

In this endeavour, the style of mainstream legal research is defined by rhetorical references to the logical syllogism,[35] a permanent quest for the improvement of the textual clarity of rules,[36] the prevention of fragmentation and the eradication of contradictions,[37] as well as the selection and rationalization of a mass of legal materials (legislation, decisions, etc.) in order to transform them into abstract, ordered principles that would allow the whole system and its parts to produce rational, coherent and, ultimately, intelligible justifications.[38]

While all these features occur across the international/domestic law divide, the efforts to develop an autonomous scientific discipline of international law have translated into a particular disciplinary language with specific methodological problems. The next section discusses some of the key traits of mainstream international legal work.

3 Mainstream Approaches to International Law (MAIL): Between Objectivism and Elite Management

In the province of international law, even though classical legal positivism and its extreme state voluntarism sunk officially in disgrace after World War I, the contemporary construction of the discipline is still rooted in many of the ideas that were developed to secure the recognition of international law as proper law according to

[34] Kilcommins (2016), pp. 9–12; Singh (2015), pp. 313–321.

[35] About the structure of legal reasoning as enthymeme or rhetorical syllogism, see e.g. Sobota (1991). For an MLS account of the use and limitations of logical syllogisms in legal reasoning, see Aldisert et al. (2007).

[36] Raz (1979), pp. 214–216.

[37] The above-mentioned construction of inter- and intra-disciplinary boundaries is, among other things, meant to reduce the number of rules potentially applicable to a particular case diminishing the potentiality of conflict between different rules and principles and, thus, constraining the choices available to rule-appliers. But this effort simultaneously reduces coherence between different, ever more dislocated normative areas. In other words, efforts to achieve determinacy lead to the reduction of coherence and *vice versa*, Edmundson (1996), pp. 6–7, 10–11, 20. See also Fragmentation of International Law: Difficulties Arising from the Diversification and Expansion of International Law, Report of the Study Group of the International Law Commission, A/CN.4/L.682, 13 April 2006, paras. 22, 33–35, 487.

[38] Davies (1994), pp. 93, 107–110, and Bianchi (2016), pp. 33–34.

classical positivist standards.[39] Above all, as mainstream international jurisprudence tries to move beyond classical positivism during the twentieth century, it advocates for a more 'scientific' study of law, but it also retains much of the classical positivistic style and aspirations—especially in its narrative about method.[40]

Thus, while MAIL strives to incorporate sociological and systemic considerations into its eclectical method, it cannot do away completely with the centrality of state will in its search for validly posited rules.[41] This continuity is expressed in the epistemic choices that still define the discipline's traditional methods—i.e., (a) the sovereign state is the most central element of international relations and international law; (b) politics plays a limited and constrained role in international law; and (c) language, which is mostly determinate and stable, can transport the exact meanings intended by law-makers, ensuring the separation of law-making and legal interpretation.[42]

From such a heterogenous methodological framework results a set of approaches that has also been described broadly as *objectivism*, in opposition to classical positivistic voluntarism or state subjectivism.[43] According to this, while voluntarism describes a doctrinal approach that only accepts as valid international law those rules strictly derived from state consent; objectivism encompasses doctrinal approaches that, relativizing state will, also link law's validity to ideas of necessary social solidarity, systemic constraints, etc.[44] In other words, the notion of objectivism defines MAIL's attempts to reinterpret and temper the inevitable reference to state consent with broader ideas about systemic logic, social reality, and so forth.[45]

Although arguments in favour of a more voluntarist approach to international law and warnings about the imperialist dangers of the ensuing relativization of sovereign equality and freedom are still part of disciplinary debates;[46] classical positivist voluntarism has been swept away by the objectivist eclectic style that, conscious

---

[39] Collins (2014), p. 25, and Hall (2001), pp. 279–301. However, as Koskenniemi notes, classical legal positivism was a deviation that did not reflect the historical and organic jurisprudence shared by most nineteenth century international law scholars. Yet, classical positivism has come to define the discipline's image of the international legal scholarship of that period, Koskenniemi (2001), p. 48. Furthermore, the basic notions of the international legal belief system originated earlier from pre-classical international law, Anghie (1996).

[40] See e.g. Ago (1956), pp. 915–918, Visscher (1973), p. 75, and Simma and Paulus (1999), pp. 304–305. Attempts to return to natural law foundations have also been part of this shifting away from classical positivism, see e.g. Verdross (1926).

[41] Ago (1956), pp. 931–932, and Simma and Paulus (1999), pp. 304, 306–308.

[42] Venzke (2014), pp. 182–189. For a recent call to transcend the received framework and re-imagine international law beyond the coordinates of the traditional liberal international legal order, see Kelsall (2022).

[43] Corten (2009), p. 46.

[44] Ibid, pp. 46–50.

[45] See e.g. Simma and Paulus (1999), pp. 304, 307, Visscher (1973), pp. 76, 79, Ago (1956), pp. 928–935, and Castberg (1933), pp. 342–351.

[46] Weil (1983).

or unconsciously, characterizes and dominates international doctrinal work today.[47] Methodological eclecticism, thus, defines MAIL and permeates the discipline's traditional tasks and routines.

3.1 The Tasks of MAIL

Generally speaking, the major task that MAIL takes upon itself is that of demonstrating that legal norms exist and function as such within the international legal system—that is, the verification of the 'law as it is'.[48]

MAIL, however, breaks this down into different more specific tasks which consist essentially of: (1) the theoretical description of the international legal system; (2) the determination of the validity of specific international legal rules; and (3) the interpretation of those valid rules so as to ascertain their content—which is also separated from the application of rules to the specific facts of a case.[49] In principle, this distinction aims both to assign different working methods to seemingly different tasks and to fence off professional work that is conducted within the limits of the legal order tradition (*internal* work; law) expelling other forms of research and knowledge from the realm of proper legal work (*external* work; non-law).[50] Yet, given the general features of MAIL, the exclusion/inclusion dynamic does not take place along stable, well-defined methodological lines.

Regarding the first task (1), as the purpose of international legal theory is the analytical explanation of the social foundations and structure of the international law system, MAIL's theoretical work rests on variable combinations of empirical observation of international relations (allegedly free of 'preconceived dogmatic notions'), logical deductions, inductions and so on.[51] For instance, despite his critique of (classical) legal positivism's focus on state will-based formal sources, Ago concedes that the strictly scientific study of law must persist in the analysis of norms that have been posited 'by someone' through some intentional external procedure, but it should also broaden its focus to cognize by induction any norms that 'exist' empirically in the world, norms that emerge by 'spontaneous formation'.[52] As a consequence of MAIL's internal diversity in this respect, social events may or may not be construed by international law scholars as legal sources depending on their (political, ethical, cultural) focus and the methodological blend applied.[53]

---

[47] Alvarez (2020), Tasioulas (2020), and Fastenrath (1993).

[48] Ago (1956), pp. 919–920.

[49] Corten (2009), pp. 34–35, Dominicé (1997), para 2 and 13c), and Azaria (2020), pp. 176–177.

[50] Corten (2009), pp. 30–33, and Bianchi (2016), p. 24.

[51] Dominicé (1997), para 10d), Visscher (1973), pp. 75–76, and Ago (1956), p. 903.

[52] Ago (1956), pp. 876–882, 931–932.

[53] See e.g. the ongoing debates about the need to expand the traditional sources of customary law beyond state practice and *opinio juris* to include that of international organisations and criminal

As to the second task (2), the determination of existing (valid) legal rules in accordance with the sources of international law draws on formal techniques that aim to establish the proof of a rule's existence independently of its content—that is, independently from subjective political or value programmes.[54] Here again, several methodological problems arise out of MAIL's general features. For instance, in customary rule ascertainment the increasing use of arguments about *soft law* or social and systemic needs to construe *opinio juris* or the relativization of the inductive study of state practice creates obvious tensions that tend to be solved through *authoritative assertion* as the main method.[55] The result is an array of flexible approaches through which formal (or informal) sources are variably mobilized to different effects depending on extra-legal factors—exposing MAIL's claims as to its ability to separate law from subjective value judgments.[56]

When it comes to the third task (3), the MAIL narrative about interpretative methods emphasizes a formalist 'technique juridique' that focuses on the plain meaning of language in the operation of primary sources.[57] The traditional methods of legal interpretation (textual, subjective/intentional, teleological), epitomized by the rules on treaty interpretation enshrined in Articles 31–33 of the 1969 Vienna Convention on the Law of the Treaties, assume the existence of a 'correct', pre-existent meaning embedded in the legal text that can be extracted and clarified in good faith from the ordinary meaning of words, the intention of the parties or the object and purpose of the relevant instrument (all of which refers back to the 'true' intent or state will contained in the text).[58]

The most serious challenge to the core assumption about pre-existent meanings and 'correct' interpretations comes from the problem of legal indeterminacy, which is discussed elsewhere in this volume.[59] Remaining now within MAIL's own framework, the convoluted resort to textualism, intentionalism and purposivism in interpretative practice as well as its widespread use of dynamic and contextual forms of interpretation increase the interpreter's freedom to a degree that undermines MAIL's ability to extract the meaning of a rule and determine its content and scope in a technically constrained manner, raising questions about the political and law-making nature of legal interpretation.[60]

---

tribunals, Baker (2010), pp. 176–184. See also e.g. the idea of 'potential sources' in Hernández (2022), p. 33.

[54] Dominicé (1997), para 11a).

[55] Talmon (2015), pp. 429–440, and Corten (2009), pp. 149–178.

[56] See e.g. the 'pragmatic' use of judicial precedent as the main source in international investment arbitration, Ureña (2014). See also Alvarez (2020), pp. 80–81.

[57] Hernández (2014), pp. 319, 330–331. See also Waibel (2011). Indeed, any attempts to abandon the semantic thesis of positivism seem incompatible with the social thesis apparently upheld by MAIL, Goldsworthy (1990), p. 474.

[58] Crawford (2013), paras 189–190, d'Aspremont (2021), pp. 1–13. See also Hernández (2014), pp. 326–329.

[59] About the indeterminacy critique, see next chapter.

[60] Linderfalk (2015), pp. 188–189, Hernández (2014), pp. 335–339, and Koskenniemi (2005), pp. 333–345.

In fact, as they collapse into each other in practice, the very distinction between these three tasks is highly problematic. For instance, MAIL's theoretical work strives to delimit the sources of international law as the defining criteria on which the subsequent determination of a rule's validity depends. Yet, even slight differences in the construction of sources (e.g., due to varying degrees of importance attributed to state will or different views on systemic and social constraints) will determine the possibilities and limits of rule determination which, in turn, also overlaps with rule interpretation (especially in customary law).[61] Ultimately, the effort to keep these tasks separated aims to both sustain an illusion of coherence and transfer polemical aspects of legal work to the theoretical realm, preserving to some extent the supposedly more neutrally technical tasks of rule determination and interpretation from controversy.[62] This discursive strategy allows MAIL to project onto theoretical work an image of openness, while shielding the determination and interpretation tasks, even when the distinction between them and their technical neutrality remains elusive in practice.

3.2 MAIL and the 'Collegiality of Elites from Different Countries'

Borrowing from Koskenniemi's analysis of the structure of international legal argumentation, MAIL's eclectic objectivism described above reflects the discipline's general effort to mediate the *ascending* and *descending* patterns of international legal argument (ascending arguments relying on state consent and descending arguments expressing systemic, sociological or justice claims)—an effort that is characterized by deep structural problems.[63] In particular, Koskenniemi describes how ascending and descending arguments are both mutually exclusive and simultaneously dependent upon each other. That is, they are mutually exclusive because they provide utterly contradictory and irreconcilable modes of justification for international law; and yet, they are mutually dependent because, if taken individually to their ultimate consequences, they are self-defeating (state will arguments alone lead to the dissolution of international law's bindingness, and systemic/sociological/justice arguments alone dissolve the principle of sovereignty and self-determination—and thus, international law as such).[64] As a result, neither type of argument can be preferred nor fully discarded; both must be incorporated into international legal work and reconciled through a variety of discursive strategies that inevitably

[61] Azaria (2020), p. 177; Corten (2009), p. 213.

[62] Which also explains MAIL's relative disdain for theoretical debate, Koskenniemi (1991), p. 3; and Verhoeven (2000), p. 892.

[63] Koskenniemi (2005), pp. 58–69.

[64] Koskenniemi also explains these patterns and their mutual relation through international law's need to be simultaneously concrete and normative, i.e. while ascending arguments aim to be *concrete* (verifiable by reference to concrete state behaviour); descending arguments aim to be *normative* (prescriptive, judging state behaviour independently of its mere existence). Thus, the two ways of justifying international law are contradictory, yet simultaneously necessary, ibid, p. 58–60.

produce a systemically incoherent type of argumentation that can only be persuasive through the mobilization of legal rhetoric.[65]

Of course, when practitioners and scholars use MAIL, they might believe in the objectivity of what they do and feel that their work is neutrally determined by legal rules or the system as a whole.[66] Moreover, there might well be important social virtues in the formalism defended by MAIL that even critics should not ignore.[67] Yet, MAIL's eclectic combination and re-combination of different methodological choices comes down in practice to strategic rhetorical moves primarily intended to convince a professional audience of the 'correctness' of the arguments and the solutions that a lawyer defends.[68]

In other words, MAIL does not manage the inbuilt tensions of traditional legal work with logical deductions, inductions and syllogisms, but with rhetorical tools.[69] The familiar style cultivated by traditional international legal research strives to maintain a tone of objectivity based on truisms, rhetorical use of the language of logic, the depersonalization of legal decisions and other typical rhetorical figures.[70] But more importantly, as the twentieth century critique of legal positivism compellingly shows, the experience of rationality, coherence, intelligibility and linguistic determinacy that these rhetorical strategies produce in certain audiences is generated by reference to moral, cultural and political frames shared by relatively homogenous interpretive communities—the 'international collegiality of elites from different countries'.[71]

In this context, international legal research should pay much more attention to this 'invisible college of international lawyers'.[72] MAIL, however, ignores or dismisses reflection upon such interpretive communities and their 'reason-construing frames' as a lack of professional rigour or as something external to law, thus, keeping the power, interests and value-preferences of these disciplinary 'licensed speakers' systematically in the blind spot of mainstream research.[73] In the face of critique about the constitutive importance of the group interests and ideological make-up of these interpretive communities, MAIL has traditionally turned to crude assumptions about the special moral qualities of the profession.[74]

---

[65] Ibid, pp. 62–64. Tacit consent being the usual reconciliation strategy, ibid, pp. 64, 325–333.

[66] d'Aspremont (2014), p. 126.

[67] Davies (1994), p. 118, and Koskenniemi (2001), pp. 494–509. See also Blum (1990), pp. 69–70.

[68] Koskenniemi (2005), p. 36, and Corten (2009), pp. 82–83.

[69] Bianchi (2016), pp. 36–39.

[70] The list of the usual rhetorical figures upon which the discipline's image of coherence and order rests is long and complex for the scope of this chapter. For a deeper study of the rhetorical style and strategies of international legal positivism, see Kennedy (1987), and Salmon (2014).

[71] Vagts (1993), p. 480. See also this chapter.

[72] See e.g. Soares Pereira and Ridi (2021).

[73] Bianchi (2016), pp. 22, 32.

[74] E.g. Higgins (2010), pp. 287–288.

This methodological blindness characterizes the discipline since its nineteenth century's re-foundation around a group of (white, upper-class, Western, mostly Protestant) men and their ideas about the moral and juridical conscience of the civilized world, which they claimed to represent.[75] And it continues today in the traditional appeals to axiological neutrality in legal research, the vindication of a clear separation between the researcher and the law as a relation between observer and object of study or the admonition to keep the researcher's emotions and values out of their work (or at least not to express them, for instance, by suppressing the use of adjectives).[76]

Even as recent (neo)positivist scholarship calls for more methodological self-awareness and the acknowledgement of the influence of politics and ideology in legal work,[77] mainstream methodological choices continue to sustain structural blind spots and hidden value preferences.[78] To the limited extent that the problem has been dealt with by MAIL, mainstream scholarship trusts in the technical quality and legitimacy of its outputs on the grounds that they are measured and controlled by reference to the consensus of professional interpretive communities ('Konsens der Rechtsgemeinschaft') that provide stability through their communitarian semantics.[79] That is, revised versions of MAIL share some of post-modern critique's insights about the inevitability of decisionism and elite management; however, they do so in a general attitude of self-assertiveness (whether optimistic, cynical or tragic)[80] and trust in authorized experts (either individually or as a community).[81]

An especially deep scrutiny and critical attitude vis-à-vis international law-appliers and the politics they advance or hinder is justified by the power they

[75] Koskenniemi (2001), pp. 52–54. Although the make-up of interpretive communities of international law-appliers is today more diverse in terms of geographical origin, their socio-economic (class) and ideological (educational, political, etc.) homogeneity is still remarkable, Brekoulakis (2013), Eberhardt and Olivet (2012), Puchkov (2018), and Faure and Ma (2020).

[76] See e.g. Corten (2009), pp. 119–120, 124–125.

[77] Simma and Paulus (1999), pp. 307–308, and Kammerhofer and d'Aspremont (2014), pp. 6–7.

[78] Needless to say, value preferences and blind spots are behind every methodological choice, Ratner and Slaughter (1999), p. 292. One of MAIL's typical blind spots, for instance, results from the re-elaboration of international law as an order or system of principles and rules primarily created by sovereign states. As the minimum political conditions are not met for the fulfilment of the state-based legal method's promises of security and well-being, this methodological choice merely simplifies the management of complexity by excluding important political, economic, cultural and historical aspects of social relations, Carty (1986), p. 5. The ensuing expulsion of complexity leads to the discipline's structural disregard for crucial aspects of social life—for example, the way the world underclasses tend to experience (or suffer) the global system of law as a unitary system where no difference between international and domestic, public and private law exists, while MAIL sustains a realm above domestic politics that protects and favours the interests of state and global elites and advances a variety of (neo)liberal and (neo)imperial agendas across the world, see Cooper (2012), p. 488, and Kennedy (2004), pp. 3–35.

[79] Beckett (2012), pp. 152–153, and Forgó und Somek (2009), p. 258.

[80] See e.g. D'Aspremont (2021b).

[81] See e.g. Simma and Paulus (1999), p. 303; Hernandez (2012), pp. 206–207, and D'Aspremont (2021a) pp. 58–59.

wield. Yet, the critique of the mainstream's confidence in the interpretive communities of international law-appliers should also serve as a caveat for critical scholars. In the absence of a healthy dose of honesty, self-reflection and scepticism about the very positions we take, the approaches featured in the following chapters of this book might lead to just the same kind of unreflective practice produced by MAIL leaving the door open to similar problems of groupthink and attitudes of self-righteousness.[82]

3.3 A Meeting Point for Mainstream and Critique?

In *The Gentle Civilizer of Nations*, Martti Koskenniemi concludes with a reflection on formalism as a professional culture and its meaning for the legal profession's *raison d'être*.[83] This culture, argues Koskenniemi, exists today in the uneasy space between the impossibility of undoing the critique or returning to a naïve and arrogant formalism, on one hand; and, on the other, the problems of anti-formalism and the managerial language of deformalized reasoning which, deployed on the basis of moral truths, can be as dogmatic and politically dangerous as traditional formalism.[84]

In contrast to these two extreme positions, the *culture of formalism* that Koskenniemi evokes allows for the articulation of our particularist claims and provides a common ground for the (potential) comprehension of those of others by reference to the universal/common formal language furnished by international law. While this formal language remains open-ended and cannot be the ultimate basis for any substantive claims, it is precisely its openness towards other particularisms (due to its lack of any definitive substantive meaning) that turns it into a possible basis for a non-imperialist universality.[85]

Yet, the possibility of such an approach to MAIL's formalism requires, first, a critical comprehension and repudiation of MAIL's flawed assumptions. That is, Koskenniemi's call for preserving a culture of formalism cannot be understood as an appeal to preserve the traditional identity and consciousness of the legal profession untouched. If the lawyer retains their traditional professional identity wholesale, why would they even think of transcending the traditional formalism that provides their very identity (and social power) in the first place?[86]

Moreover, it is a particular culture (and ethics) of formalism that Koskenniemi advocates. The moral thrust behind it stems from a concern for the radical scepticism about universality and truth that threatens to render the critique of ideology meaningless making the claims of the oppressor indistinguishable from those of the

[82] Günther (2020).

[83] Koskenniemi (2001), pp. 494–509.

[84] Ibid, pp. 495–503.

[85] Ibid, p. 506.

[86] Though see D'Aspremont (2021b).

oppressed.[87] Rising against the paralysis of democratic politics caused by social antagonism, Koskenniemi's culture of formalism would allow not only for changes in the ownership of power, but also a change in 'the form of that power itself'.[88] Yet, such culture of formalism seems of little help in the face of an opponent's strategic behaviour. In other words, it requires a particular ethics from all the participants in the legal debate that we would be too naïve to expect from all jurists.

Notwithstanding these issues, and insofar as the question about the valid law remains the main question for lawyers, the idea of a culture of formalism suggests interesting ways of transporting critical legal thinking into the legal work that, for strategic reasons or due to institutional and professional constraints, critical researchers must conduct within the framework and in the language of MAIL. More specifically, Koskenniemi's culture of formalism seems to imply or, at any rate, fit into a rhetorical understanding of law which traverses the critical legal approaches discussed in the following chapters. Provided that any alternative to the strategic use of rhetoric is available, a (critical) culture of formalism understood in those terms may actually help transform legal routines and institutions into spaces of 'ideological dialogue and evolution'.[89]

References

Ago, R. (1956). Science juridique et droit international. *Recueil des Cours de l'Académie de Droit International, 90*, 859–958.

Aldisert, R. J., Clowney, S., & Paterson, J. D. (2007). Logic for law students: How to think like a lawyer. *University of Pittsburgh Law Review, 69*(1), 1–22.

Alvarez, J. E. (2020). The relativity apocalypse is nigh. *AJIL Unbound, 114*, 77–81.

Anghie, A. (1996). Francisco de Vitoria and the colonial origins of international law. *Social & Legal Studies, 5*(3), 321–336.

Azaria, D. (2020). 'Codification by Interpretation': The international law commission as an interpreter of international law. *European Journal of International Law, 31*(1), 171–200.

Baker, R. B. (2010). Customary international law in the 21st century: Old challenges and new debates. *European Journal of International Law, 21*(1), 173–204.

Beckett, J. A. (2012). Faith and resignation. A journey through international law. In M. Stone, I. R. Wall, & C. Douzinas (Eds.), *New critical legal thinking. law and the political* (pp. 145–166). Routledge.

Bianchi, A. (2016). *International law theories. An inquiry into different ways of thinking*. Oxford University Press.

Blum, J. M. (1990). Critical legal studies and the rule of law. *Buffalo Law Review, 38*, 59–155.

Brekoulakis, S. (2013). Systemic bias and the institution of international arbitration: A new approach to arbitral decision making. *Journal of International Dispute Settlement, 4*(3), 553–585.

Carty, A. (1986). *The decay of international law? A reappraisal of the limits of legal imagination in international affairs*. Manchester University Press.

[87] Ibid, p. 505.

[88] Ibid.

[89] Kennedy (1998), p. 70.

Castberg, F. (1933). La méthodologie du droit international public. *Recueil des Cours de l'Académie de Droit International, 43*, 313–383.

Coleman, J. L., & Leiter, B. (2010). Legal positivism. In D. Patterson (Ed.), *A companion to philosophy of law and legal theory* (2nd ed., pp. 228–248). Wiley-Blackwell.

Collins, R. (2014). Classical legal positivism in international law revisited. In J. Kammerhofer & J. d'Aspremont (Eds.), *International legal positivism in a post-modern world* (pp. 23–49). Cambridge University Press.

Cooper, F. (2012). Social rights and human rights in the time of decolonization. *Humanity, 3*, 473–492.

Corten, O. (2009). *Méthodologie du droit international public*. Editions de l'Université de Bruxelles.

Crawford, J. R. (2013). Chance, order, change: The course of international law. *Recueil des Cours de l'Académie de Droit International, 365*(2013), 9–390.

Cryer, R., Hervey, T., & Sokhi-Bulley, B. (2011). *Research methodologies in EU and international law*. Hart Publishing.

D'Aspremont, J. (2014). The idea of 'Rules' in the sources of international law. *British Yearbook of International Law, 84*(1), 103–130.

D'Aspremont, J. (2021a). *After meaning*. Edward Elgar.

D'Aspremont, J. (2021b). International legal methods: Working for a tragic and cynical routine. In R. Deplano & N. Tsagourias (Eds.), *Research methods in international law. A handbook* (pp. 42–59). Edward Elgar.

Davies, M. (1994). *Asking the law question*. The Law Book Company (Sweet & Maxwell).

Dominicé, C. (1997). Methodology of international law. In *L'ordre juridique international entre tradition et innovation* (pp. 3–12. Available online: http://books.openedition.org/iheid/1334). Graduate Institute Publications. https://doi.org/10.4000/books.iheid.1334

Dworkin, R. (2013). *Taking rights seriously*. Bloomsbury.

Dyzenhaus, D. (2004). The genealogy of legal positivism. *Oxford Journal of Legal Studies, 24*(1), 39–67.

Eberhardt, P., & Olivet, C. (2012). *Profiting from injustice: How law firms, arbitrators and financiers are fuelling an investment arbitration boom*. Corporate Europe Observatory and Transnational Institute.

Edmundson, W. A. (1996). The antinomy of coherence and determinacy. *Iowa Law Review, 82*(1), 1–20.

Fastenrath, U. (1993). Relative normativity in international law. *European Journal of International Law, 4*, 305–340.

Faure, M., & Ma, W. (2020). Investor-state arbitration: Economic and empirical perspectives. *Michigan Journal of International Law, 41*(1), 1–61.

Finnis, J. M. (2000). On the incoherence of legal positivism. *Notre Dame Law Review, 75*(5), 1597–1611.

Forgó, N., & Somek, A. (2009). Nachpositivistisches Rechtsdenken. In S. Buckel, R. Christensen, & A. Fischer-Lescano (Eds.), *Neue Theorien des Rechts* (2nd ed., pp. 253–269). Lucius & Lucius.

Gardner, J. (2001). Legal positivism: 5 ½ myths. *American Journal of Jurisprudence, 46*(1), 199–227.

Goldsworthy, J. D. (1990). The self-destruction of legal positivism. *Oxford Journal of Legal Studies, 10*(4), 449–486.

Günther, P. (2020). Groupthink bias in international adjudication. *Journal of International Dispute Settlement, 11*(1), 91–126.

Hall, S. (2001). The persistent spectre: Natural law, international order and the limits of legal positivism. *European Journal of International Law, 12*(2), 269–307.

Hernandez, G. I. (2012). Impartiality, bias, and the International Court of Justice. *Cambridge Journal of International and Comparative Law, 1*(3), 183–207.

Hernández, G. I. (2014). Interpretation. In J. Kammerhofer & J. d'Aspremont (Eds.), *International legal positivism in a post-modern world* (pp. 317–348). Cambridge University Press.
Hernández, G. I. (2022). *International law*. Oxford University Press.
Higgins, R. (2010). Ethics and international law. *Leiden Journal of International Law, 23*, 277–289.
Hoeflich, M. M. (1986). Law and geometry: Legal science from Leibniz to Langdell. *American Journal of Legal History, 30*(2), 95–121.
Kammerhofer, J. (2021). International legal positivist research methods. In R. Deplano & N. Tsagourias (Eds.), *Research methods in international law. A handbook* (pp. 95–110). Edward Elgar.
Kammerhofer, J., & d'Aspremont, J. (2014). Introduction. In J. Kammerhofer & J. d'Aspremont (Eds.), *International legal positivism in a post-modern world* (pp. 1–19). Cambridge University Press.
Kelsall, M. S. (2022). Disordering international law. *European Journal of International Law, 33*(3), 729–759.
Kennedy, D. (1973). Legal formality. *Journal of Legal Studies, 2*, 351–398.
Kennedy, D. (1987). *International legal structures*. Nomos.
Kennedy, D. (1998). *A critique of adjudication: fin de siècle*. Harvard University Press.
Kennedy, D. (2004). *The Dark Sides of Virtue: Reassessing International Humanitarianism*. Princeton University Press.
Kilcommins, S. (2016). Doctrinal legal method (Black-Letterism): Assumptions, commitments and shortcomings. In L. Cahillane & J. Schweppe (Eds.), *Legal research methods. Principles and practicalities* (pp. 7–19). Clarus Press.
Koskenniemi, M. (1991). Theory: Implications for practitioners. In P. Allot, A. Carty, M. Koskenniemi, & C. Warbrick (Eds.), *Theory and international law: An introduction* (pp. 3–45). British Institute of International and Comparative Law.
Koskenniemi, M. (2001). *The gentle civilizer of nations. The rise and fall of international law 1870–1960*. Cambridge University Press.
Koskenniemi, M. (2005). *From apology to Utopia. The structure of international legal argument*. Cambridge University Press.
Linderfalk, U. (2015). Is treaty interpretation an art or a science? International law and rational decision making. *European Journal of International Law, 26*(1), 169–189.
MacCormick, N. (2005). *Rhetoric and the rule of law. A theory of legal reasoning*. Oxford University Press.
Marks, S. (2009). False contingency. *Current Legal Problems, 62*(1), 22–70.
Peat, D. (2018). International investment law and the public law analogy: The fallacies of the general principles method. *Journal of International Dispute Settlement, 9*, 654–678.
Puchkov, S. (2018). Subconscious bias as a factor influencing arbitral decision-making. *International Journal of Arbitration, Mediation and Dispute Management, 84*(1), 52–76.
Ratner, S. R., & Slaughter, A. M. (1999). Appraising the methods of international law: A prospectus for readers. *The American Journal of International Law, 93*, 291–302.
Raz, J. (1979). *The authority of law: Essays on law and morality*. Clarendon Press.
Rosenberg, M. (1990). Deconstruction and legal interpretation: Conflict, indeterminacy and the temptations of the new legal formalism. *Cardozo Law Review, 11*, 1211–1267.
Salmon, J. (2014). *Droit International et Argumentation*. Bruylant.
Schauer, F. (1988). Formalism. *Yale Law Journal, 97*(4), 509–548.
Simma, B., & Paulus, A. L. (1999). The responsibility of individuals for human rights abuses in internal conflicts: A positivist view. *The American Journal of International Law, 93*, 302–316.
Singh, S. (2015). Narrative and theory: Formalism's recurrent return. *British Yearbook of International Law, 84*(1), 304–343.
Soares Pereira, L. L., & Ridi, N. (2021). Mapping the 'invisible college of international lawyers' through obituaries. *Leiden Journal of International Law, 34*(1), 67–91.
Sobota, K. (1991). System and flexibility in law. *Argumentation, 5*, 275–282.

Talmon, S. (2015). Determining customary international law: The ICJ's methodology between induction, deduction and assertion. *European Journal of International Law, 26*(2), 417–443.
Tasioulas, J. (2020). Prosper Weil and the Mask of Classicism. *AJIL Unbound, 114*, 92–96.
Ureña, R. (2014). Of precedents and ideology. Law making by investment arbitration tribunals. In P. Singh & B. Mayer (Eds.), *Critical international law: Postrealism, postcolonialism, and transnationalism* (pp. 276–303). Oxford University Press.
Vagts, D. F. (1993). Treaty interpretation and the New American ways of law reading. *European Journal of International Law, 4*, 472–505.
Van der Walt, J. (2020). *The concept of liberal democratic law*. Glasshouse (Routledge).
Venzke, I. (2014). Post-modern perspectives on orthodox positivism. In J. Kammerhofer & J. d'Aspremont (Eds.), *International legal positivism in a post-modern world* (pp. 182–210). Cambridge University Press.
Verdross, A. (1926). *Die Verfassung der Völkerrechtsgemeinschaft*. Springer.
Verhoeven, J. (2000). Charles de Visscher: Living and thinking international law. *European Journal of International Law, 11*, 887–904.
Visscher Ch de. (1973). Méthode et système en droit international. *Recueil des Cours de l'Académie de Droit International, 138*, 75–79.
Waibel, M. (2011). Demystifying the art of interpretation. *European Journal of International Law, 22*(2), 571–588.
Weil, P. (1983). Towards relative normativity in international law? *American Journal of International Law, 77*(3), 413–442.
Weinrib, E. J. (2010). Legal formalism. In D. Patterson (Ed.), *A companion to philosophy of law and legal theory* (2nd ed., pp. 327–338). Wiley-Blackwell.

Critical International Law

Juan J. Garcia Blesa

Contents

1 Introduction

This chapter introduces the reader to critical international law, an internally diverse and heterogeneous movement in international legal academia. Due to the heterogeneity of critical legal scholarship in international law, this is only a summary of some of its main traits. The central aim of the chapter is to guide the reader into the realm

Acknowledgements: Parts of this chapter were developed with the support of the Erasmus+ Programme for Strategic Partnerships (2015-1-DE01-KA203-002169).

J. J. Garcia Blesa (✉)
FernUniversität in Hagen, Hagen/Westfalen, Germany
e-mail: juan.garciablesa@fernuni-hagen.de

J. J. Garcia Blesa (ed.), *Contemporary Methods in International Legal Research*,
Springer Textbooks in Law, https://doi.org/10.1007/978-3-031-69522-3_4

of practice by offering a concise appraisal of the most common working methods in critical international law.

For this purpose, Sect. 2 offers an account of the main features of critical international legal thinking and some of its working methods: the deconstructive and rhetorical analyses of international legal discourse. Section 3 delves into these modes of critical international legal work through examples from practice. And Sect. 4 ends with a few exercises that invite the reader to transfer the ideas learned in this chapter into their own research work. The chapter does not delve into the historical development and transformations of critical international legal scholarship. The reader can find such information in the list of literature at the end of the chapter.

2 What is Critical International Law?[1]

Critical International Law (CIL) can be understood in general as the application of post-modern critical legal thinking –especially the insights of the *Critical Legal Studies* (CLS) movement—to the discipline of international law.[2] Being critical legal thinking a rather diverse set of theories and approaches to legal scholarship, critical international law also presents itself as a heterogeneous set of ideas and perspectives on international legal scholarship irreducible to a unified theory.

Notwithstanding, it is possible to identify a number of common features and themes that give CIL a common identity in spite of its diversity and lack of theoretical uniformity. These common themes are to an important extent a continuation of some of the common themes of critical legal thinking in general and of CLS in particular. These themes include the critique of liberal legalism, modern legal consciousness, law as ideology and a project of emancipation and empowerment for

[1] Parts of this section draw on Garcia Blesa (2022), and Garcia Blesa (2024).

[2] Whereas critical legal scholarship has changed over the years and split into different strands that focus on a diversity of issues and geographical contexts, there is no denying that many of their basic themes, tools and styles have remained more or less stable since the 1970s and 1980s. Given that the purpose of this chapter is to offer a practical portray of some of these more stable features, it will rely on those authors and strands that have devoted more significant efforts to explain critical legal work as a specific way of thinking and doing research. Admittedly, this selectivity may imply a certain Western male bias, especially in its North-American form, due to the strong reliance of this chapter on the self-reflective work of CLS scholars. This, however, is particularly useful in explaining the basic methodological aspects of legal critique. Therefore, it is important to stress the heterogeneity of CIL and highlight the work of many other authors who have made valuable contributions to critical international legal scholarship, e.g. Anne Orford, Luis Eslava, Sundhya Pahuja and many others. Although Western male biases are held in check by two other chapters of this book (see the chapters on "Feminist Approaches to International Law" and "Third World Approaches to International Law (TWAIL)" below), part of this chapter also adds to this effort by offering some examples of how the critical deconstructive approach has been used by non-Western CIL scholars, and looking into Susan Marks's and Wendy Brown's important contributions to the critique of ideology in international law and neoliberal rationality respectively.

[3] Carty (1991), p. 1.

the weakest members of society. As Anthony Carty, one of the leading CIL scholars, put it:

> 'Critical' international legal studies constitute a so-called post-modern approach to international law. This is to assert that the discipline is governed by a particular, historically conditioned discourse which is, *in fact*, quite simply, the translation onto the international domain of some basic tenets of liberal political theory. It opposes itself to positivist international law, as representative of an actual consensus among states. The crucial question is simply whether a positive system of universal international law actually exists, or whether particular states and their representative legal scholars merely appeal to such positivist discourse so as to impose a particularist language upon others *as if it were a universally accepted legal discourse*. So post-modernism is concerned to unearth difference, heterogeneity and conflict as *reality* in place of *fictional* representations of universality and consensus.[3]

The rest of this section explores some of the themes that provide CIL with a basic common identity.

2.1 Legal Indeterminacy and the Critique of (International) Liberal Legalism

Much of CIL work is connected to the CLS critique about the pervasive impact of liberal political theory (and its shortcomings) on contemporary legal thinking. CLS insights serve as an analytical framework to understand how mainstream international legal discourses represent the world system to us. The critique posits that, through the lens of mainstream liberal legalism, the world is portrayed as an atomized society of free, territorially defined state-individuals in search of a common legal order the legitimacy of which is simultaneously based on their axiomatic freedom and their regulatory limitation. According to this image, that system is expressed in legal materials which contain determinate (or at least determinable) and neutral solutions that can be bureaucratically extracted from such materials by trained legal operators. This, for instance, is the view encapsulated in the UN Declaration on Principles of International Law concerning Friendly Relations and Co-operation among States, the *magna carta* of international legal liberalism.[4]

Critical lawyers strongly object to this image and the claims to neutrality and objectivity it implies. They do not see law as an abstracted, objectified and

---

[4]UN General Assembly Resolution 2625 (XXV), of 24 October 1970.

[5]Contemporary linguistic philosophy propounds that language is not a simple list or code of words describing the exact meaning we can extract from them because that could not explain the room for play and innovation existing in language, see Wittgenstein (2009), para. 151, 185, 201, and Derrida (2001), pp. 351–370. Legal semiotic critique also targets the linguistic concept of *code* in mainstream legal scholarship, see Goodrich (1981), pp. 65–70. Yet, contemporary critical legal research goes beyond mere linguistic indeterminacy and posits a stronger claim to value and systemic indeterminacy, Kelman (1987), pp. 12–13. See also Balkin (1986), pp. 67–74.; Coombe (1989), pp. 100ff; Kennedy (1973), pp. 394ff; Kennedy (1998), pp. 157ff, 308ff; Schlag (1988), p. 957.

conceptualized set of rules that can be bureaucratically interpreted in some 'correct' manner so as to obtain a neutral answer embedded in materials that are the expression of the will and social needs of sovereign states. In this regard, CIL draws on CLS's indeterminacy critique.

Since the 1970s and linked to twentieth century linguistic philosophy, CLS has pointed at how legal materials cannot determine *per se* legal decision-making.[5] But CLS's claim about the fundamental indeterminacy of legal materials goes beyond the old (realist) critique of linguistic indeterminacy and delves into the fundamental structure of liberal legal discourse which is based on radically contradictory values. One of the founders of the CLS movement, Mark Kelman, put it this way:

> . . .the legal system is invariably simultaneously *philosophically committed* to mirror-image contradictory norms, each of which dictates the opposite result in any case (no matter how 'easy' the case first appears). While settled practice is not unattainable, the CLS claim is that settled justificatory schemes are in fact unattainable. Efforts at norm legitimation are radically indeterminate not because the source of authority cannot speak clearly (though, rather incidentally, she often cannot) but because if pressed, she would not want to.[6]

Fundamental oppositions such as individualism/communalism, freedom/order, self-reliance/altruism, free will/determinism and many others are pervasive throughout liberal legal thought and make a permanent choice between any of the terms of these oppositions unworkable.[7] Therefore, in a liberal legal system law-makers do inevitably uphold opposite values simultaneously. They cannot escape these dichotomies which inevitably appear in the legal materials they produce justifying potentially incoherent legal solutions.[8] As a result, it is beyond the interpreter's means to exclude the possibility of contradictory interpretations derived from the same legal materials. In the final analysis, law cannot offer universal, determinative

[6] Kelman (1987), p. 13.

[7] Kennedy (1979), pp. 211–221. In fact, a choice between any of the two dichotomous terms is self-defeating to the extent that each term eventually collapses into its opposite. For instance, in the dichotomy self/others, pure individualism and freedom collapse into chaos and the impossibility of freedom due to all-out conflict or the dictatorship of the strongest, while pure communalism and order eliminate freedom and the basis of its own legitimacy becoming tyrannical or oligarchic rule (the absolute freedom of a few).

[8] This is also related to the difficulty of translating the interests of a plurality of individuals into one clear legal command, see Levine (1981), pp. 49–62.

[9] Also drawing on contemporary linguistic philosophy, the ability of language users to produce common meaning out of words depends on their sharing common interests, understandings or a 'form of life', Wittgenstein (2009), para. 241–242. Critical legal scholarship translates these insights into the field of law, see e.g. Schlag (1988), p. 938, Cotterrell (1996), pp. 104ff, 230ff, and Kennedy (1998), pp. 228ff.

[10] Marks (2009), pp. 1–21, and Kennedy (1998), pp. 288–289, 293–294.

[11] Kennedy (1987), pp. 293–294.

prescriptions based on mechanical relations between law and society; and the distinction between law-making and law-application vanishes.

Moreover, if legal texts do not determine legal decisions, the relative predictability of legal decision-making and its stable meanings can only stem from the collective values of specific communities of law-appliers.[9] Thus, against traditional positivism, critical legal thinking rejects not only the necessity of legal reasoning, but also the contingency of that reasoning, whose outcomes are seen as the stable products of the beliefs and value-preferences shared by the communities that generate them.[10]

Mainstream international legal scholarship is exposed by CIL as a relentless, yet hopeless activity devoted to hiding these antinomies or fundamental oppositions in order to create an illusion of determinacy that can never be fulfilled.[11] In sum, as an antinomy-ridden system, contemporary international law is incapable of producing *per se* necessary legal solutions. Critical scholars do not deny the relative predictability of legal outcomes in particular institutional or social contexts; rather, they indicate that these outcomes are dependent upon the value-preferences shared by groups of law-appliers and the institutional context within which they work. Therefore, legal solutions are not the result of law's compelling textual objectivity or systematicity, but the product of a rhetorical activity that can only 'make sense' and be persuasive within a specific interpretive community.

2.2 Law as Rhetoric and the Shift to the Margins of Society

CIL scholarship perceives international lawyering as a type of rhetorical activity rather than as an objective science or a neutral technique.[12] As Koskenniemi puts it:

> *International law* is an argumentative practice. It is about persuading target audiences such as courts, colleagues, politicians, and readers of legal texts about the legal correctness — lawfulness, *legitimacy*, justice, permissibility, validity, etc—of the position one defends. What passes for method, in other words, has to do with what counts as persuasive arguments in international law. Key to persuasiveness is that the argument is recognizable as a good *legal* argument and not, for example, a strong *moral* point, a plausible *political* position, or a convincing *sociological* description of something.[13]

It is all about persuasion, and persuasion as well as the way in which it can be produced in international law are defined by reference to what a specific professional community or audience thinks is arguable and convincing:

> . . . it is the consensus in the profession—the *invisible college* of international lawyers—that determines, at any moment, whether a particular argument is or is not persuasive. . . The methodology of international law is best seen as being about criteria that legal arguments

[12] Ibid, p. 7, Koskenniemi (2005), pp. 58-69, and Carty (1986), pp. 1ff, 128ff.

[13] Koskenniemi (2007), p.1.

[14] Ibid.

ought typically to fulfil in different contexts—including the academic context—in order to seem plausible.[14]

CIL exposes mainstream approaches to international law as a set of rhetorical techniques of persuasion that can be put to the service of different interests in different contexts. That is, mainstream approaches operate by reference to what the professional target audience understands to be acceptable and persuasive.

Yet, such emphasis on *relative persuasiveness* may project too much of a *nihilistic/sophistic* image about CIL that would be misleading. In the text cited above, Koskenniemi only points at how mainstream international lawyering works in practice from a CIL perspective, i.e. as a technique and a language deployed to convince a specific type of audience about the preferred solution to a particular issue. But CIL does not mean to mobilize this knowledge for the sake of just any outcome. On the contrary, CIL combines its insights about the rhetorical nature of mainstream international lawyering with the study of its practical context and outcomes (cultural, social, economic, political, moral, etc.), which connects critical scholarship in international law with James B. White's more general ideas about constitutive rhetoric and rhetorical criticism.

According to White, Modernity separates law from rhetoric presenting the law as a set of rules institutionally managed in order to fit with the bureaucratic idea of politics as ends-means rationality.[15] In this manner, law is misrepresented as a set of objectified choices made by institutions through abstract, mechanic calculations separated from human experience about life. Such notion of law, however, is generally unaware of the social outcomes it produces.[16] In contrast, the rhetorical approach sees law as a language that lawyers use to talk about issues related to justice and injustice, community and freedom, etc.; a language that is spoken in a specific community with a particular culture within which it makes sense.[17]

Spoken to this particular audience, legal language can be persuasive and produce somewhat stable results; but even if its resources and materials appear sometimes clear, there is always an imperfect agreement about their scope, force and value, because the meaning and authority of legal materials are always arguable. Speaking the language of the law, thus, is a creative process of argumentative play that recreates meaning and authority. To some degree, legal language itself is always modified by the utterances of each legal speaker.[18] Law becomes that which is said by lawyers within the margins of that which the professional community considers possible or arguable, even if these margins are inherently fluid.

[15] White (1985), p. 685.

[16] Ibid, p. 686.

[17] Ibid, p. 689.

[18] Ibid, p. 690.

[19] Ibid, pp. 691-692.

[20] Ibid, p. 692.

[21] Ibid, pp. 692-693.

For White, law is a cultural discourse that configures the identity of the members of the community that speaks the legal language. At the same time, it is a fluid process in which the speakers, their choices and their identities are permanently changing.[19] Moreover, law is seen as a way of talking about something speakers think is 'out there', 'real' events, and about their meaning. Accordingly, lawyering is also a way of telling a story, a narrative activity.[20] Law becomes a type of constitutive rhetoric because it construes a story, it translates something into legal language and gives it new meanings, roles and expectations, creating and recreating a social universe of relations and shared meanings.[21]

In this vein, the rhetorical approach to law propounded by White carries a great critical potential as '[t]his way of conceiving of law invites us to include in our zone of attention and field of discourse what others, operating under present suppositions, cut out, including both the radical uncertainty of most forms of knowledge and the fact that we, and our resources, are constantly remade by our own collective activities'.[22] This critical perspective stands in sharp contrast to other rhetorical approaches to law whose reference to 'the social' is only vague and distant. Instead, critical rhetorical approaches to law treat 'the rhetoric of law as a primary datum to be evaluated... against the background of the institutional power and social relations of inequality, of superordination and subordination, that underpin that rhetoric and determine its semantic content...'.[23]

This way of looking at lawyering is also part of CIL. Critical international lawyers tend to see international law as a rhetorical activity that translates a certain view of something called 'international relations' into a legal language that allows the community of international lawyers (academics and practitioners) to articulate and recreate that object for different purposes. Through its patterned argumentative strategies, however, this language produces a specific and stable narrative.[24] In contemporary international law, the dominant argumentative practice generates a narrative that perpetuates the liberal illusion that the law is based on consent, which can produce a determinate and objectively operated legal order. CIL tries to expose this narrative by applying deconstructive and rhetorical criticisms of international law which allow critical lawyers to claim the inclusion in the legal debate of things that are excluded by the mainstream legal discourse.

Beyond the rejection of the mystifying and bureaucratic theory and practice of international law, the critical international lawyer enquires about international law's collective meanings asking questions such as: are international legal materials internally and externally coherent? How do they represent society? What kind of world and community is their narrative advocating for? Who or what is left out,

---

[22] Ibid, p. 698. As White points out, the rhetorical perspective allows for a rhetorical criticism of the law that is more open to non-lawyers and outsiders because it goes beyond the mechanistic idea of the law and the bureaucratic ends-means notion of politics, ibid. 697-698.

[23] Goodrich (1987), pp. 123-124.

[24] See Kennedy (1981).

[25] Kennedy (1988), p. 48.

excluded from the mainstream narrative? What kind of power asymmetries does it support? In the words of another leading CIL scholar:

> Seeing institutions and legal materials in this way – as unified languages – highlights the exclusionary practices of these disciplines in a more comprehensive fashion. [. . .]
>
> If we changed our optic to see the entire struggle for inclusion as simply part of the rhetorical fabric [. . .] we might be able to imagine a more thorough turn to the margins. [. . .] Thinking about international law and institutions as a common language suggests a more expansive approach to the politics of inclusion and privilege, one which challenges the common lexicon of law and state rather than relying upon the struggle between law and state.[25]

As discussed below, legal deconstruction and the rhetorical analysis of law are the most powerful tools of critical legal thought in the struggle to turn the focus of legal theory and practice to the margins of society. However, in and of themselves these tools do not serve any definite critical purpose beyond the theoretical (and somewhat elitist) challenge to liberal legal thought. In fact, part of the foundational deconstructive work of CIL has been accused of being too detached from the political, economic and social realities that the discipline deals with.[26] Therefore, what defines the identity of CIL is not only its analytical style, but also the deliberate addition of a normative dimension to the task of deconstruction, i.e. the turn to the margins of society already noted above. Legal deconstruction alone could not deliver this result.

In practice, although focused on the destabilization of traditional legal discourse (whether combined or not with empirical legal research),[27] the critical shift to the margins implies a turn outwards towards the weakest members of society, the excluded by the dominant discourses and institutions, drawing attention to a large variety of issues including, for instance, economic exploitation, neo-colonial domination, social inequality, racism, gender discrimination or the environment. Only the pursuit of this ultimate goal gives meaning to CIL and its most characteristic tools, the deconstructive and rhetorical analysis of law.

---

[26] This is the case of David Kennedy's *International Legal Structures* which has been criticized for targeting only theoretical, doctrinal and institutional materials excluding external or sociological factors in the elaboration of their meaning, see Carty (1991), pp. 6-7. For David Kennedy, on the other hand, international history, theory and institutions must be analyzed as rhetorical devices. This *internal* analysis of international legal materials is performed from the point of view of rhetoric regardless of sociological contexts in the hope of destabilizing the very internal images of international legal history, theory, doctrine and institutions, Kennedy (1988), p. 11.

[27] For more information about the use of empirical methods in legal research, see chapter "Third World Approaches to International Law (TWAIL)".

[28] Kelman (1987), pp. 3-4.

[29] Ibid, p.3.

2.3 Legal Deconstructive Analysis

There is not only one way of understanding and doing legal deconstruction. There probably are as many styles of legal deconstruction as there are legal deconstructionists so that an exhaustive account of this approach is problematic, to say the least. The goal of this section, therefore, is to present the reader with a basic account of legal deconstruction as often understood in critical legal scholarship itself, and explain how it has been generally translated into the disciplinary coordinates of public international law.

A useful description of the process of legal deconstruction is presented by Mark Kelman in his *Guide to Critical Legal Studies*.[28] For Kelman, the 'standard four-part critical method' helps to unveil mainstream liberal legalism as a system of thought simultaneously beset by contradiction (irreducible conflict) and the repression of these contradictions (mediation strategies).[29] In Kelman's account, when using the method of legal deconstruction critics do the following:

Standard Four-Part Critical Method of Legal Deconstruction

(1) IDENTIFY A CONTRADICTION IN LIBERAL LEGAL THOUGHT. These appear as paired rhetorical arguments that:

a. Resolve cases in incompatible ways; and
b. Correspond to different and opposing visions of human nature and fulfillment

In Kelman's view, there are three central contradictions in liberal legal thought:[30]

1. Commitment to mechanically applicable rules to resolve disputes **vs.** commitment to situation-sensitive, *ad hoc* standards;
2. Commitment to the notion of subjectivity of values and objectivity of facts (or reason) **vs.** commitment to the belief in the possibility of 'knowing' social and ethical truths objectively or that one can transcend the distinction between subjectivity and objectivity in seeking moral truth;
3. Commitment to intentionalistic discourse (i.e. human action is the product of self-determining human will) **vs.** commitment to deterministic discourse (i.e. human action merits neither respect nor reproach for it is only the outcome of structural forces).

(2) DEMONSTRATE THE PERVASIVE DESTABILIZING POWER OF THESE CONTRADICTIONS in all legal controversies.

(continued)

[30] Other authors concentrate on other contradictions, see section on legal indeterminacy above.

a. The repressed contradictory impulse is always present even in apparently settled practice. One need only push that practice to reveal its grounds;
b. There are no easy cases, even if some are predictable.

(3) EXPOSE HOW ONE TERM OF EACH CONTRADICTORY PAIR OF VALUES IS *PRIVILEGED* IN MAINSTREAM LIBERAL LEGAL THOUGHT. These terms are privileged in 3 ways:

a. The privileged term is presented as normative for the resolution of the dispute;
b. The privileged term is assumed to govern the bulk of conflict situations;
c. Departures from the privileged term are considered exceptions and need justification.

In general, liberal legal discourse is committed to privilege individualism, the notion of subjective value, intentionalism and an uncritical respect for the announced choices of individuals (dismissing without further scrutiny the possibility that these choices might be inconsistent with other choices of the individual, relatively unfree choices or just bad choices).

(4) RESUSCITATE THE UNPRIVILEGED POSITIONS which might be better grounded in the cultural tradition of liberalism itself. The privileged choices are remarkably aligned with a right-wing, quasi-libertarian program.

Based on Kelman (1987), pp. 3-4

CIL displays a deconstructive style similar to this CLS benchmark.[31] The method consists in searching rhetorical patterns of opposition (and mediation) across international law—what Koskenniemi calls 'controlling contradictions'.[32] State consent vs systemic constraints, public vs private, the domestic realm vs the international realm, sovereign autonomy vs sovereign cooperation, substance vs process, objective fact vs subjective value, political force vs neutral form; these are only a few of

[31] Kennedy (1988), p. 7; Koskenniemi (2005), pp. 11f, 533ff.

[32] Koskenniemi (2005), p. 63.

[33] See generally Kennedy (1987) and the commentary on his work below.

[34] Despite the 21st century's economic and political globalization, contemporary international law finds it impossible to exist in the absence of state sovereignty. In fact, its regulation is totally parasitic of the problems of nation-state, its validity and interests being still based on the typical categories of property, sovereignty, the clash of sovereign vs sovereign or sovereign vs community, Kennedy (1987), pp. 229-233.

[35] Kennedy (1988), p. 7.

the infinite and fluid combinations of opposing terms that structure the discipline and that deconstruction seeks to expose and destabilize.[33]

The deconstructive analysis is the basis for a critique of international law that takes apart the doctrines and arguments that flesh out the discipline in order to expose and reassess the ideas and assumptions which constitute the mainstream's ideological framework. For David Kennedy, for instance, critical international law puts the finger on two of the most pervasive ideas that underlie public international law and constitute its identity. The first is the state-centered social paradigm embedded in international law that reproduces in legal discourse the image of a society that is primarily articulated by sovereign states.[34]

The second idea is the discipline's particular understanding of the relation between law and the society of states. According to the mainstream view, public international law needs to be descriptive and express state will and behavior as the only relevant source of power; yet, at the same time, it needs to be normative and remain distanced from the state in order to control its behavior. In other words, the mainstream idea of the relation between law and the state society requires the development of a discipline that is simultaneously political and non-political.[35]

This notion is also linked to two collective fantasies in the mind of mainstream international lawyers: (1) serving the state in a similarly contradictory role of simultaneously critical distance from and apologetic service to the state; and (2) a naïve view of politics and sovereign statehood where the state is the only arena for all conscious, open, public and visible struggle of interests perfectly articulated through rights, leaving little or no room for unconscious or hidden politics.[36]

Legal deconstruction, instead, approaches law and its relation to politics as a type of rhetoric, an argument about something we call 'law' and 'society'. This argument is created by a particular language which projects through its rhetorical structures a stable relation between the spheres it constructs (e.g. public vs private).[37] Mainstream historical, theoretical and doctrinal justifications are, thus, critically reinterpreted as discourses of mediation, argumentative constructions whose deployment and effectiveness (persuasiveness) within the interpretive communities that

[36] Ibid, pp. 8-9. For Kennedy, as a result of these features, the discipline is trapped in eclectic insecurity, a move towards institutionalization and the analogy to domestic law.

[37] Ibid, p. 8.

[38] This approach can also be applied to institutional reforms that are seen as the enactment of the rhetorical moves of mainstream legal doctrine, ibid, p. 10.

[39] This section and the practical example of critical rhetorical analysis below elaborate on Garcia Blesa (2023); and Garcia Blesa (2024).

[40] Balkin (1996), pp. 214, 220. About the technical modes of persuasion (ethos, logos, pathos) and their role in legal discourse, see generally Aristotle (1991), pp. 74-75, Chapter 1.2, para 1356a, and Sobota (1994), pp. 155-171.

[41] Sobota (1994), pp. 157-159. See e.g. Paso (2012), Ervo (2016), Pinho (2018).

[42] Sobota (1994), p. 157. Logos, understood as argumentation in the narrow sense, includes implicit references that make their identification hard –that is, rather than a mechanical technique, its analysis 'is primarily a matter of intuition', ibid.

produce, use and diffuse them can also be explained (and countered) as rhetorical moves.[38]

2.4 The Rhetorical Analysis of Law[39]

As an extension or special case of the deconstructive work described above, the rhetorical analysis of law approaches the deconstruction of mainstream legal discourse through the lens of the classical Aristotelian modes of persuasion, i.e., *logos* (appeals to reason), *ethos* (authority) and *pathos* (emotion).[40] In this type of analysis, the basic concepts of liberal legalism are classified following the three classical rhetorical categories and then applied to the analysis of specific legal discourses.[41]

Accordingly, *logos* is expressed in propositions that 'hint to a reason', for instance, arguments that resort to deductive or inductive language, codification, principles or common sense.[42] *Ethos* consists of references to authority, professional or institutional traditions and cultures, for example, the scientific authority of the interpreter, the authority of text or other sources, etc.[43] *Pathos* appears through emotional topics (*topoi*) like dignity, freedom, fairness, etc. or certain rhetorical figures that can move the audience to feelings of sympathy, pity, trust, scepticism, fear and so on.[44]

In practice, *ethos* and *pathos* appear intertwined in a chain of argumentation (*logos*) which they support and substitute at points where *logos* alone is less persuasive.[45] The chain of argument normally starts with some general *topoi*—that

[43] Ibid, p. 158.

[44] Ibid, pp. 158-159. These figures are numerous and typically include metaphor, association, dissociation, concession (*apologismus*), intensifiers, etc. Sobota's catalogue e.g. includes 37 figures, ibid.

[45] Paso (2012), p. 20. Courts, for instance, mix *logos*, *ethos* and *pathos* when they stress workers' ethical and personal qualities or emphasize their own *ethos* as protectors of workers' rights, Sobota (1994), pp. 168-169.

[46] Against traditional positivist accounts, judicial reasoning does not proceed through logical syllogistic deductions that move from general normative premises to specific facts and finally normative conclusions. Instead, it is normally arranged as an enthymeme or rhetorical syllogism that begins with the formulation of a problem and develops as a heuristic discussion about possible solutions based on commonplace ideas or *topoi*, Sobota (1991), pp. 276-279; Aristotle (1991), para1395b-1397a.

[47] Germany v United States of America, Judgment of 27 June 2001; and Mexico v United States of America, Judgment of 31 March 2004.

[48] Pinho (2018), pp. 147-152. About the 'tree of arguments', see von Schlieffen (2005), p. 422.

[49] Paso (2012), p. 18, and Goodrich (1987), p. 168.

[50] The dominant rationalistic strand of legal rhetorical analysis insists that only *logos* and *ethos* are relevant among legal audiences, who are imagined as especially rational groups, see e.g. MacCormick (2005), pp. 2, 14f, 237f, 255, 261, 280, and Alexy (1989), Part C. See also the 'New Rhetoric' and its dialectic aspirations in Perelman et al. (1971), pp. 26, 30. A similar stance was characteristic among some members of the 'School of Mainz' at its origins, see Sobota (1991), p. 276.

is, inconclusive, open-ended ideas or social pre-formulations—that function as a common ground for the speaker and their audience from which the argumentation unfolds. This can be applied to different forms of legal argumentation, in particular, to judicial discourses.[46] Based on the work of Sobota/von Schlieffen, for instance, Pinho analyses the Vienna Convention on Consular Relations Cases (*LaGrand* and *Avena and Other Mexican Nationals*)[47] and shows the 'tree of supporting arguments' (including *ethos* and *pathos*) that the International Court of Justice develops around one central common place, the *topos* of human dignity.[48]

Once the structure of *topoi* and their supporting patterns of *pathos* and *ethos* are revealed, the rhetorical analysis of law can identify the emotional attitudes, value preferences and background beliefs that animate a particular piece of legal discourse—and the interpretive community that produced it.[49] Against the dominant argumentation theory that ignores or downplays the emotional aspect of legal language,[50] this critical step links with the turn to ideology critique in twentieth century rhetorical studies which tries to overcome 'neo-Aristotelian' scholarship's failure to apply the study of linguistic structures to improve our understanding of how these structures are appropriated and mobilised for the development of a legitimation framework with political purposes.[51]

In this sense, critical rhetorical analysis highlights that legal discourse is influenced by a language (emotive topics, images, metaphors) that escapes rational argument and creates the emotional setting upon which the persuasiveness of *logos* (reason) depends.[52] Yet, this influence is not a one-directional, transparent relation. First, because the language that conveys *pathos* is not necessarily articulated through *logos*, and the background values and mindsets it expresses are not easy to reduce to an exact set of principles.[53] Moreover, in order to maintain a closed control of legal meaning in the hands of the legal profession, legal discourse explicitly strives to suppress emotional language and deny the influence of extra-legal discourses.[54] And finally, as the non-legal discourses in which legal discourse is embedded are fluid and changing, their mutual relation is difficult to pinpoint.[55]As a result, no neat and

[51] Wang (2020), pp. 10, 15-17.

[52] Farber and Sherry (1996), pp. 41, 52. Research in the field of moral psychology today seems to confirm the thesis that language operates primarily on an unconscious, non-rational level, see Haidt (2013), Parts I and III, and Baumeister and Vohs (2007), pp. 588–89.

[53] Farber and Sherry (1996), p. 49. These unconscious or 'tacit understandings' are mostly communicated through 'images, stories and other symbols' embedded in discourse, ibid.

[54] Goodrich (1987), p. 187.

[55] Cotterrell (1996), pp. 8-9, 249-273.

[56] In other words, '[l]egal language . . . is not purely and simply the malleable or transparent instrument of ideological purposes', Goodrich (1987), p. 169.

[57] Ibid, pp. 111-112. For instance, it is 'incontestable that aspects of the content of law are only explicable in terms of their expression of economic relations', in particular 'the conflicting interests of labour and capital', Goodrich (1987), pp. 185-186. See also Dardot and Laval (2017), pp. 8-9, 12.

clean 'causal' connection to non-legal discourses and value-programmes is likely to appear in legal discourse.[56]

And yet, the *ethos* and *pathos* that support legal discourse tend to form patterns that cluster around certain principles revealing the 'politics of legal language'.[57] That is, their arrangement is not totally random or coincidental; they are dynamically organised according to certain value-preferences and principles of meaning which stem from different normative frameworks. The critical rhetorical analysis of law highlights these discursive elements and patterns to show how they help reproduce and re-elaborate certain political themes reflecting unstated world views which can be read in the context of the political struggles of our time.

By pointing at 'underlying shared assumptions', biases and 'blind spots', this type of legal work exposes unexamined political positions, shows a lack of neutral, technical determination in legal work and, more importantly, opens up new rhetorical avenues to challenge such assumptions. In sum, whatever form of critical deconstructive work we carry out, the examination of the structural or ideological background against which the patterns and preferences expressed in mainstream legal discourse 'make sense' is a transversal aspect of critical legal research that needs to be explained in some detail.

2.5 The Critique of Ideology[58]

In critical legal scholarship, the analysis of legal discourse's background factors is often articulated around the notion of *ideology*.[59] The critique of ideology seeks to expose different legal discourses, institutions and practices as a set of legitimizing strategies for a particular (contingent) *status quo*.[60] As critical scholars acknowledge, however, there are certain problems and limitations to the use of this term as an analytical tool. Above all, there are difficulties with the definition of the concept of ideology and its relations to social action.[61] And yet, the notion of ideology still is a valuable element of legal critique. As Hunt put it:

> Ideology is and will remain a difficult, slippery, and ambiguous concept, and there is little to be gained by searching for a 'better' definition. Problems cannot be avoided, for ideology involves issues that go to the heart of the puzzling interrelationship between human

[58] This section elaborates on Garcia Blesa (2022), Garcia Blesa (2023), and Garcia Blesa (2024).

[59] For an overview of the different traditions of identifying the politics of international (legal) expertise, see Kennedy (2005), pp. 21-28.

[60] Kennedy (1998), pp. 288-289, 293-294.

[61] Ibid, pp. 286-287, 294, and Hunt (1986), pp. 11-17.

[62] Hunt (1985), p. 31.

[63] See e.g. Desautels-Stein and Rasulov (2021), and Marks (2001).

[64] Kairys (1998), p. 14, and Kennedy (1998), p. 287.

[65] The problem about demonstrating the relations between ideology and social action seems to stem partly from the mistaken expectation that 'ideology critique' must live up to a strict naturalist/

> subjectivity and social action. Yet, handled with care, the concept 'ideology' provides an indispensable and irreplaceable tool of analysis.[62]

Thus, while recent critical legal scholarship also criticizes previous work on the notion; instead of abandoning the critique of ideology it calls for an update that can suit the circumstances of the twenty-first century.[63]

Indeed, this sense of calculated risk has always characterized the use of the term in legal critique. Critical legal scholars have traditionally warned that, as legal '[d] ecisions are predicated upon a complex mixture of social, political, institutional, experiential, and personal factors . . .', they cannot be reduced to sweeping claims about the uniformity and causality of any deep structure such as 'capitalism' for the left –or 'efficiency theory' for the right.[64] Therefore, the notion of ideology is not used in a strong systematizing sense by most critical scholars. Rather, it is often conceived of as a flexible analytical framework applied to understand and explain legal ideas and practices in connection to broad systems of extra-legal beliefs and their consequences in broader socio-political contexts.[65]

In this vein, Susan Marks reconstructs the critique of ideology in international legal scholarship by defining it as the 'analysis of the involvement of systems of meaning with relations of power'.[66] For Marks, ideology critique cannot be grasped as a neutral categorization of different political traditions or as the mere uncovering of the mistaken epistemological status of certain beliefs.[67] Rather, Marks's ideology critique focuses on the way legal discourses are deployed, not simply because they are erroneous, but more importantly because of their function and ethical/political effects, namely the legitimation of power asymmetries that are 'instrumental to injustice'.[68]

Ideology is not conceived of by Marks as a monolith to be studied with the arrogance of an external observer. On the contrary, in her view, ideology exists as a feedback loop between epistemological mistakes and the practices in which we all participate, not really due to unawareness of the mistaken assumptions that ground our social and professional practices, but owing to inattention to the way our 'acting *as if*' reproduces social problems.[69] Consequently, the mainstream 'problem-

positivist standard of causality, which ignores its being rooted in social interpretivism, see e.g. Hunt (1986), pp. 12-16.

[66] Marks (2001), p. 117. See also Marks (2009).

[67] As is the case to some extent in the traditional critique of ideology, see Geuss (1981), pp. 13-19.

[68] Marks (2001), pp. 111-112, 115.

[69] E.g. 'acting *as if* labour relations were based on free exchange among equals', ibid, p. 113.

[70] Ibid, pp. 118-119.

[71] See e.g. MacNaughton and Frey (2018), Golder and McLoughlin (2018), Brabazon (2017), Trubek and Santos (2006). Although defined in different ways, neoliberalism is often understood as a fluid set of political-economic projects and discourses epitomized by the financialization and marketization of global relations and their consequences –e.g. the substantive shifts of power occurred across the world affecting social, economic and political structures, Harvey (2005). See also Dardot and Laval (2017), and Keter (2012).

solving' type of legal work that 'seeks to isolate problems and propose remedial action on the footing of a framework of ideas and practices which is not itself in question' is seen as another ideological strategy which (intended or unintendedly) 'helps to obscure and legitimate relations of domination'.[70]

Similarly, another interesting reconstruction of ideology critique is the study of different types of normative *rationality* in mainstream legal discourse—often connected to the critique of neoliberalism and neoliberal legalism.[71] In this sense, rationality does not mean logical consistency or the absolute exclusion of other normative preferences in legal discourse. Rather, it implies a degree of relative normative coherence, a matter of 'making sense' when legal discourse is taken together in a specific social or institutional context. In line with the Foucauldian insight that '[p]ower itself does not exist either as raw domination or in a material substratum of existence independent of thought and language', the term 'neoliberal rationality' advances the idea that neoliberal ideology can be grasped as a '*normative reason* from which governing is forged' and which constitutes 'the condition of possibility and legitimacy' of power.[72]

But the analysis of legal discourse in relation to a broader type of normative reason looks into policies, practices and actors that are in permanent transformation and, thus, require continued revision. Moreover, any dominant form of normative rationality does always coexist, struggle or draw upon other marginal discourses and value-programmes.[73] Thus, such analytical strategy must avoid closed conceptual definitions by approaching global and local manifestations of neoliberal rationality as a continuing process of socio-regulatory adaption;[74] and admit the imbrication of and reciprocal influence between legal discourses and the neoliberal governmental normative rationality (neoliberal rationality limits legal discourses and legal discourses re-create neoliberal rationality).[75]

In any case, whether expressed in terms of governmental rationality, political bias, ideological mindsets or else, many CIL scholars have turned to the analysis of how international law is mobilized as an instrument of neoliberalism.[76] The field of international economic law is particularly fruitful for this type of inquiry. Research in the area of international investment arbitration is a good illustration thereof. Critical scholarship in this area, for instance, aims to identify patterns and tendencies in the decisions issued by international mechanisms of dispute settlement and see

[72]Brown (2015), pp. 115–25 (emphasis added). See also Dardot and Laval (2017), pp. 4–6, 180–191.

[73]Peck (2010), pp. 24-25, 31–34.

[74]Ibid, pp. 33-34.

[75]This links with Weberian, Foucauldian and the Frankfurt School's insights about techno-bureaucratic rationality in modern societies, Brown (2015), pp. 116ff, and Kennedy (2001), pp. 1161-1163.

[76]Butler and Crawley (2018).

[77]Ureña (2014), p. 300.

[78]Behn (2015), p. 411, and Faure and Ma (2020), p. 59.

how and to what degree they help underpin the *status quo* of neoliberal globalization.

Pointing at the indeterminacy of international investment legal materials and the apparent incoherence of investment arbitration's outcomes, international legal critique in this field endeavors to show how investment arbitration awards are not just a collection of discrete, contingent decisions disconnected from each other. Rather, they actually follow certain ideological (neoliberal, neo-colonial) patterns. This implies unearthing professional conventions that generate stable practices and patterns of meaning within investment arbitration. One such pattern is the 'failed law premise', described by Ureña, whereby investment arbitration usually follows a narrative that 'features domestic law as *failed* (or about to be), and therefore in need of correction or complement by the investment tribunal.'[77]

This general pattern hinges on an entrenched disregard for domestic law and is closely linked to a well-documented tendency of investment tribunals to find developing states in breach of their investment protection obligations significantly more often than developed states.[78] In the analysis of this tendency, Odumosu identifies three technologies or strategies frequently deployed by investment tribunals. These encompass the exclusion of any genuine participation of grassroots movements from host societies that is not mediated by NGO workers 'socialized' in investment law; the systematic treatment of public interests as a private property issue; and, finally, the purported separation of investment law from its serious socio-economic, political and cultural ramifications under the slogan of 'depoliticization'.[79]

These and other patterns in investment decision-making are indicative of a political orientation intended or unintendedly aligned with neoliberal postulates.[80] Legal discourses that deal with economic matters of the highest social and political importance through the narrow lens of private property and construe the rights of private capital as fundamental rights (while weakening public protection of the environment and the rights of local populations in the name of global free movement of capital) give expression to a political economy that promotes the marketization of all human transactions on a global scale and the privatization of governance across borders through a 'polycentric web' of international rules and non-state institutions that displaces and alters traditional state goals and structures.[81]

These features expose two central aspects of international investment arbitration. First, in view of the fact that such patterns do not stem from the indeterminate investment law materials themselves, their source must be located within the 'background assumptions' and shared interests and understandings that define the

[79] Odumosu (2007), pp. 260-265. See also Shalakany (2000).

[80] Prieto-Rios (2015).

[81] Shalakany (2000), pp. 452ff, Nicol (2011), p. 243, Cooper (2012), p. 488, Slobodian (2018), pp. 271-218. For a more detailed analysis of how neoliberal ideology is reproduced in dispute resolution mechanisms outside the state, masking power asymmetries and advancing the criterion of 'utility maximization', see Cohen (2009), pp. 63–69.

[82] Norton (2018), p. 300, and Roberts (2010), pp. 179-178, 188ff.

community of investment law language users, i.e. the interpretive community of investment lawyers and arbitrators itself. While this may offer a modicum of predictability or stability of meaning, the large impact of international investment arbitration on domestic and global public interest operates a massive power-shift from sovereign states to the investment arbitration community transferring in practical terms a broad law-making authority from the former to the latter.[82]

And second, the patterns described and the way they are produced are highly problematic in terms of the rule of law ideal for, no matter what the personal ethics or beliefs of arbitrators, they actually serve to advance a particular politics as 'non-politics' which makes international investment arbitration virtually impervious to other views of the world, society and human life characterizing investment arbitration as a technology for the implementation and legitimation of such politics.

Within the broader context of CIL, this research shows how the state-centred narrative of public international law actually masks and supports the power politics of global financial operators behind the screen of traditional international legal positivist categories and beliefs, helping the advancement of global elite interests and neo-colonial domination. Against this backdrop, critical international legal scholarship not only exposes and repudiates the traditional view of the state as the exclusive centre of power, law and politics; it also aims to open up new places for political engagement, refusing the fantasy of serving the state, and turning to local, private (or privatized), and unconscious politics.[83]

Yet, as mentioned above, such type of legal work deals with discourses, beliefs, practices and actors in constant transformation and, thus, requires permanent updating. This highlights the importance of the essentially 'empirical' orientation of CIL pointed out in previous chapters. As it delves into what law does to society beyond the mainstream narrative of state-centred international liberal legalism, critical legal research cannot fully ignore empirical inquiry into these questions.[84]

3 Examples of Legal Deconstruction in Practice

The previous section offers a general description of legal deconstruction as the main style in critical legal work. But how does deconstruction in international law work in practice? The analysis of legal doctrine and argument as a type of rhetoric implies that each legal discipline can be understood as a specialized language that is meaningful inside a particular community of speakers—mostly practitioners and academics. This specialized language is the rhetorical matrix within which particular

[83] Kennedy (1988), pp. 9-10.

[84] About the possible use of empirical legal research in critical legal scholarship, see chapters on "Legal Method in the Context of Social Thought" and "Third World Approaches to International Law (TWAIL)".

[85] ICJ Reports 1974, p. 253.

[86] David Kennedy (1987), pp. 56-66.

legal discourses are possible; both the matrix and the discourses produced within it are the object of critical legal deconstruction.

In the main, deconstruction proceeds in two stages that consist of: (1) identifying the argumentation structures that underpin a particular doctrine or argument; and (2) exposing the political choices advanced by that particular discourse (and the community of speakers that produced it) as well as the interests furthered by these choices and their consequences for the oppressed and disenfranchised members of society. Such choices are exposed as non-objective, non-neutral political preferences to which the critics may propose alternative choices.

This section presents and comments in detail on two examples of international legal deconstructive practice. The first (Sect. 3.1) analyses David Kennedy's deconstruction of the 1974 *Nuclear Tests Case* (Australia v. France)[85] as an instance of how unilateral declarations reveal the structural argumentation patterns within the doctrine of international legal sources.[86] In this classic example, Kennedy construes a matrix of conceptual oppositions (hard/soft) within which the discourse of sources and the 1974 *Nuclear Tests Case* are deconstructed. The second example presented in this section (Sect. 3.2) explains in some detail the critical rhetorical analysis of the European Court of Human Rights' (ECtHR) judgment in *Garib v The Netherlands* (2017).[87] The analysis of this example shows a different approach to legal deconstruction that delves into the use of different rhetorical modes of persuasion and the value-preferences they reveal.

3.1 Deconstruction and the Structure of International Legal Argument

3.1.1 The Rhetoric of Sources in Unilateral Declarations

In this example of legal deconstruction, Kennedy begins by sketching a conceptual opposition that helps to structure sources discourse. The opposition consists of two metaphoric terms—*hard* and *soft*—that represent familiar, yet radically different ways of grounding legal obligation: *hard* arguments about legal sources ground the bindingness of rules in the 'consent' of the state; *soft* arguments resort to 'some extraconsensual notion of the good or the just'.[88] These two terms of argumentation are incompatible and mutually exclusive; they cannot be simultaneously used in a coherent manner. Yet, they are also dependent on each other. That is, 'neither set of arguments can be convincing by itself and neither can trump the other', which forces

[87] Garib v The Netherlands [GC] no. 43494/09, judgment, 6 November 2017. Section 3.2. comments and expands on Garcia Blesa (2024).

[88] Kennedy (1987), p. 29. David Kennedy calls them 'rhetorical or persuasive styles'.

[89] Ibid, p. 31.

[90] Ibid, p. 32.

[91] Ibid, pp. 33-53.

[92] Ibid, p. 32.

anyone arguing in favour of a rule to 'continually switch from one rhetoric to the other'.[89] Resulting from these constraints, the pattern of argumentation within sources discourse projects the image of an international normative order that binds states who nevertheless remain sovereign and autonomous. However, this image of separation (freedom) combined with equality and mutual respect (order) must simultaneously rely on the rhetoric of two opposed normative sources: normative autonomy (sovereign freedom) and normative authority (social order).[90]

Thus, sources discourse needs to resort to different 'rhetorical strategies of inclusion' that combine both *soft* and *hard* terms in order to retain the normative autonomy of the legal order and manage the resulting internal tension.[91] Since no logical, coherent solution is possible, the outcome is a doctrinal and argumentative practice of continuous movement between the two terms that produces 'an image or a feeling of resolution'.[92] However, due to the fundamental incompatibility of *soft* and *hard* arguments, the image of non-conflictual inclusion and compatibility is always unstable and threatened by its internal tension making it necessary to permanently re-elaborate their relation in an endless argument without definitive resolution. This internal tension is reproduced inside all traditional sources (treaties, custom, general principles, etc.) and is managed through different rhetorical strategies. Kennedy illustrates this idea by examining unilateral declarations in international law.

The *hard/soft* rhetoric of sources is reproduced within discussions about the bindingness of unilateral declarations. For *hard*, consensualist views, all declarations and acts based on state will (consent) are binding and, thus, unilateral promises are individual obligations; for *soft*, systemic views, on the other hand, the bindingness of state acts and declarations is predicated upon mutual reliance and the expectations of other states (order).[93] In order to verify whether a unilateral act or declaration is legally binding, the literature generally relies on either the intention of the declarant alone or on intention combined with some systemic element—e.g. reliance or third state expectations. The pure intent of the declarant state as a sufficient basis for bindingness is a *hard* rhetorical position, whereas the systemic requirements of reliance and third state expectations are inspired on *soft* rhetoric.[94] Following Jack M. Balkin's dyadic representation of the conceptual oppositions that structure legal discourse,[95] Kennedy's analysis of the *hard/soft* rhetorical structure of unilateral declarations could be depicted like this (see Fig. 1):

[93] However, this association can be flipped to make the *hard* argument about unilateral declarations be based on the acceptance (consent) of third states and the *soft* argument rely on the systemic importance of respecting sovereign authority as a condition for all legal obligations. In other words, any position can be (re)interpreted in both *hard* and *soft* terms, see ibid, pp. 54-55.

[94] Ibid, p. 55.

[95] Balkin (1986).

[96] Kennedy (1987), p. 56.

[97] Ibid.

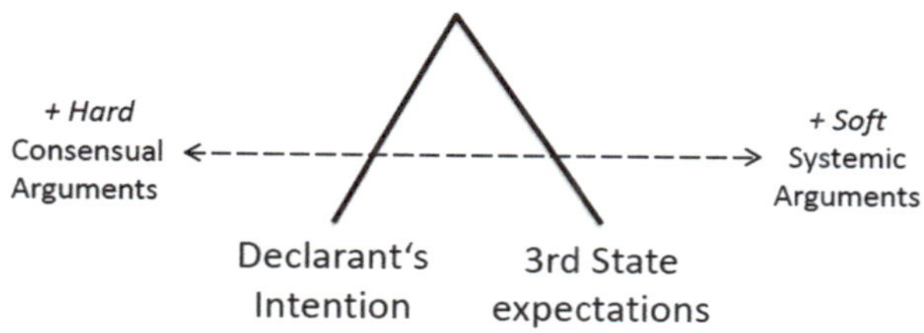

Fig. 1 The hard/soft rhetorical structure of unilateral declarations

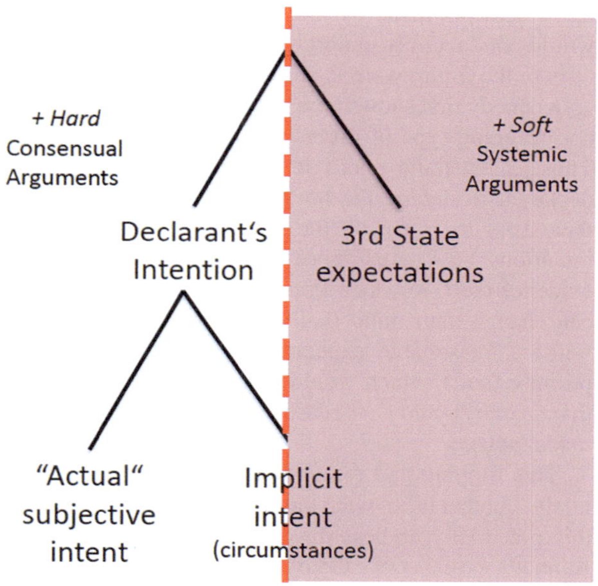

Fig. 2 Implicit intent (hard) comes 'closer' to the *soft* rhetoric of sources

These two basic positions about the same issue can be developed into further, more refined sub-positions which, despite their difference with the primary terms described above (intent vs. intent and systemic requirements), reproduce the same *hard/soft* rhetorical dichotomy that structures the whole sources discourse. Each of these terms will be 'relatively' *harder* or *softer* in relation to the originally chosen opposition. The hard strand has two sub-positions: a *harder* one (only actual subjective intention of the declarant can ground legal obligation); and a *softer* one (intention can be construed or implied from the circumstances).[96] Despite its being derived from the intent argument (*hard*), the sub-argument of implicit intent comes 'closer' to and is tainted by the *soft* argument as it relies on factors external to the will of the declarant (Fig. 2).

Sources rhetoric privileges *hard* arguments, yet the *hard* rhetoric of sources needs always to be complemented by *soft* arguments and, therefore, the most extreme

[98] *Nuclear Tests* Case (Australia v. France), para 34-41.

[99] Kennedy (1987), p. 57.

consensualist position (i.e., only the declarant can know their subjective intent), which leaves no room for *soft* arguments or arguments about evidence and proof, usually seems unacceptable.[97]

3.1.2 Analysis of the 1974 *Nuclear Tests Case* (Australia v. France)

Within this framework, Kennedy analyses the rhetorical structure and rhetorical strategies of mediation in the International Court of Justice's (ICJ) judgment on the *Nuclear Tests* case (Australia v France), where the Court had to decide whether the statements made by the President of France in 1974 to the effect that France would conduct only underground nuclear tests and refrain from further atmospheric tests in the future were legally binding for the French Republic.[98]

Kennedy first shows how the rhetorical possibilities open to both parties allow for a zigzagging type of discussion moving from hard to soft arguments and back.[99] Thus, if Australia opens its argumentation by relying on the sole intent of the declarant to defend the bindingness of the French declaration (hard), France can then deny its intent on the grounds that only the declarant can know their own intentions (hard). Australia can then retort that intent must be assessed against factual evidence (soft) to which France can counter that, if intent alone binds, the declarant can change their mind (hard). Australia may reply that the systemic principles of fairness, reasonable expectations or mutual reliance require France to keep its promise (soft), which would force France to respond on similar grounds by stating that no one should have reasonably relied on the declaration because no promise was made (soft).

This flipping and reinterpreting of each other's arguments could go on indefinitely, but that is not what the ICJ does because '[t]he aim of argument is to terminate this potentially endless dialogue in a persuasive fashion'.[100] To accomplish this, Kennedy explains, the Court repeatedly switches between the two incompatible and contradictory rhetorical poles when considering whether and under what circumstances the French declaration might be binding.

The ICJ begins its argumentation by stating the principle that unilateral declarations may be binding upon the declarant state '[w]hen it is the intention of the State making the declaration that it should become bound according to its terms'.[101] In such case, 'intention confers on the declaration the character of a legal undertaking'.[102] In other words, the Court opens its argumentation by taking the hard, intent-based view that the basis of unilateral legal obligations, their very binding nature, stems from the mere intent of the declarant. Yet, given that France is denying its own will to be bound by its declarations of 1974, the hard principle alone

would force the ICJ to reject the bindingness of France's declarations –and in fact to

[100] Ibid, p. 58.

[101] *Nuclear Tests Case* (Australia v. France), para 43.

[102] Ibid.

[103] Ibid, para 46.

leave the validity of all unilateral obligations in the hands of the declarant, threatening their legal nature as a whole. Consequently, the Court needs to close its opening examination of unilateral declarations as a source of legal obligation by referring to soft, systemic principles of law:

> One of the basic principles governing the creation and performance of legal obligations, whatever their source, is the principle of good faith. Trust and confidence are inherent in international co-operation, in particular in an age when this co-operation in many fields is becoming increasingly essential. Just as the very rule of *pacta sunt servanda* in the law of treaties is based on good faith, so also is the binding character of an international obligation assumed by unilateral declaration. Thus interested States may take cognizance of unilateral declarations and place confidence in them, and are entitled to require that the obligation thus created be respected.[103]

As Kennedy shows, the ICJ seems first to rely on the declarant's intent to ground the bindingness of unilateral declarations; but, if taken to the extreme, this approach implies that the declarant could as well change its mind, denying the bindingness of its unilateral declaration. The extreme form of the hard argument could also make necessary the acceptance of third states, turning unilateral into bilateral obligations. But this is denied by the Court when it states that 'nothing in the nature of a *quid pro quo* nor any subsequent acceptance of the declaration, nor even any reply or reaction from other States, is required for the declaration to take effect, since such a requirement would be inconsistent with the strictly unilateral nature of the juridical act'.[104] As a result, 'intent alone cannot support the idea of obligation'.[105] The hard, intent-based rule precludes the very legal bindingness of the unilateral acts it purports to sustain; bindingness requires the soft, systemic support supplied by the principles of predictability, legal certainty, good faith and *pacta sunt servanda* (Fig. 3.).

However, soft principles can also be incompatible with the principle of intent and the bindingness of unilateral acts, if they are interpreted to require acceptance and exchange of consent to be 'registered' by the community.[106]

The ICJ, therefore, cannot fully rely on only one of these two principles, but relying on both confronts the Court with a rhetorical problem: depending on how they are presented, each principle can appear as both compatible and incompatible with each other. If they are not presented in a manner that appears compatible, the Court's opinion would expose unilateral undertakings' potential for rhetorical contradiction and indeterminacy and would threaten their very legal nature –the Court, thus, needs to blend the two terms.[107] Yet, in order to manage the inherent tension

[104] Ibid, para 43.
[105] Kennedy (1987), p. 60.
[106] Ibid, p. 61.
[107] Ibid, p. 59.
[108] Ibid, p. 61.
[109] Ibid, p. 62.

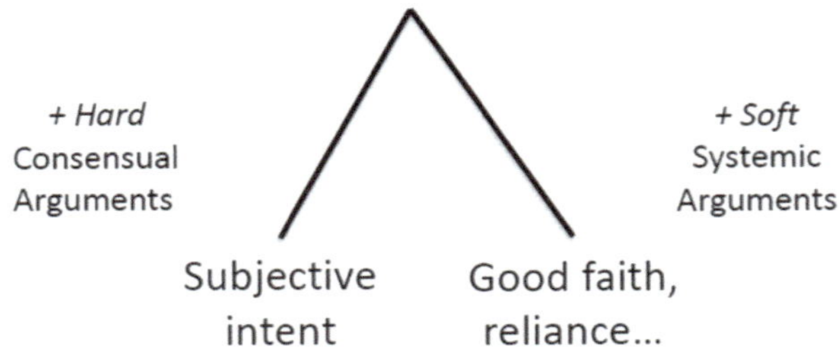

Fig. 3 Hard arguments require the support of *soft* systemic arguments

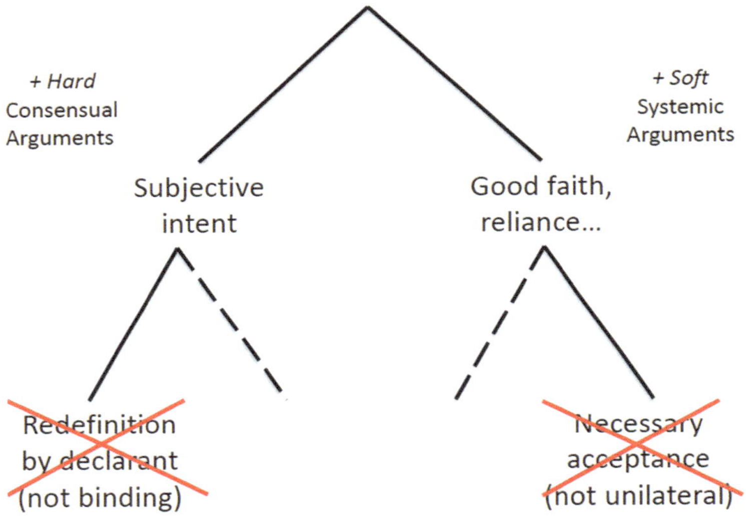

Fig. 4 Rhetorical management avoids extreme versions of *hard* and *soft* rhetoric

between these two principles, the Court needs to avoid extreme versions of both hard and soft rhetoric showing the side of each rule that is compatible with unilateral obligations (Fig. 4.).

This is achieved 'by expressing each in a way which affirmed its opposite and denied itself.'[108] The Court plays with different rhetorical possibilities to accommodate the opposing principles. First, it emphasizes elements of both that support the binding nature of unilateral obligations presenting the hard principle in a soft fashion. The Court then suggests that good faith, predictability, etc. (soft) support the exercise of sovereign free will (hard) by protecting the ability of third states to rely on the declarations of others and, thus, the ability of the declarant state to create legal obligations (Fig. 5). In other words, the hard principle is embraced and justified

[110] Ibid, p. 63.

[111] Ibid, p. 64.

Fig. 5 The *hard* principle is justified in *soft* terms

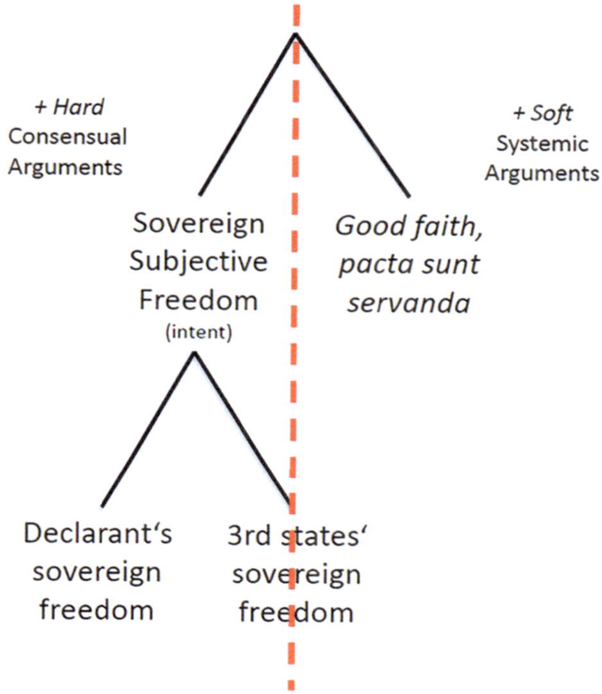

in soft terms.[109] The reference to the subjective freedom of third states safeguards reliance on the hard principle of state will, while allowing for binding declarations.

This tends to avoid the purely hard, extreme position of intent that would allow France to redefine its obligations at will; yet, the redefinition of an intent-based system of unilateral obligations needs to be grounded in the requirement that intent be measured against objective criteria (soft) that must be assessed by the ICJ (soft). The subjective intent on which a binding unilateral declaration is based could be derived either from the declarant's interpretation of its own declaration (hard) or from the wording, the 'actual terms' of the declaration as ascertained by an external interpreter (soft).[110] Whereas the first purely 'subjective' option would be incompatible with the idea of legal obligation; the ICJ chooses the 'objective' alternative (soft) in order to further limit the potentially self-defeating consequences that the subjective intent principle could have for the bindingness of unilateral obligations (Fig. 6.).[111]

---

[112] Ibid, pp. 64-65.

[113] *Nuclear Tests Case* (Australia v. France), para 48.

[114] Kennedy (1987), p. 64.

[115] Ibid, p. 66.

Fig. 6 *Hard* sovereign subjective freedom is reinterpreted in *soft* objective terms

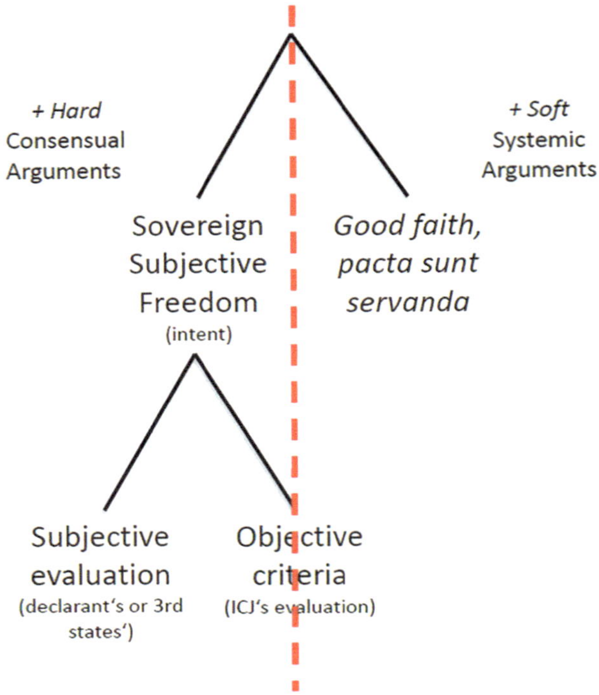

The Court further stresses the compatibility of its objective measurement approach with the subjective intent principle by insisting on the protection of the true intention of France from the subjective, 'politicized' interpretation of third states, like Australia.[112]

> The Court must however form its own view of the meaning and scope intended by the author of a unilateral declaration which may create a legal obligation, and cannot in this respect be bound by the view expressed by another State which is in no way a party to the text.[113]

This objective and soft approach to the subjective principle of intent is limited, in turn, by the adoption of the rule that only restrictive interpretation (hard) –never extensive (soft)– should be allowed in order to protect 'true' intent (Fig. 7.).[114]

It is easy to appreciate the zigzagging movement of the Court's elaboration from harder to softer arguments and back in order to produce an image of blend and compatibility. The blend of objective and subjective approaches allows the ICJ to merge hard and soft principles reinterpreting intent in soft terms. The move to objectivity is justified by the defence of the subjective intent, the 'true' reflection of subjective will and interests of states. The possibility of conflict of interests between France and Australia is explained away by the ICJ's role.[115] The mediation

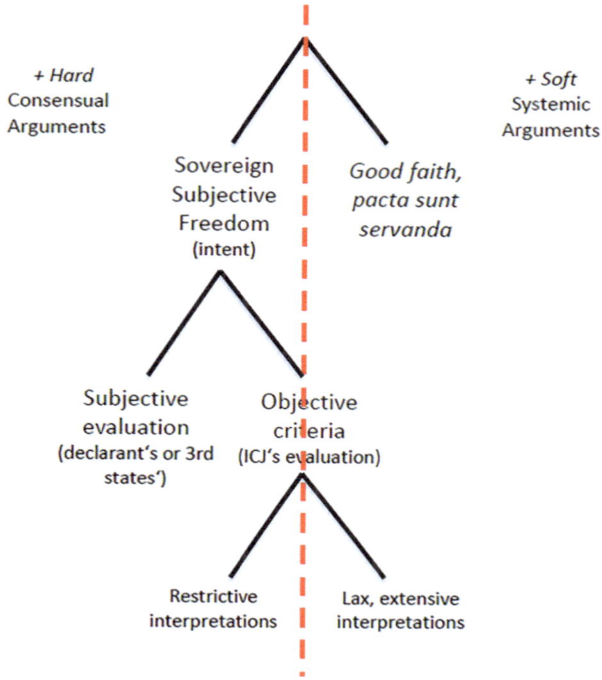

Fig. 7 The *soft* objective argument is tempered with appeals to *hard* restrictive interpretations

and apparent stabilization of hard and soft rhetoric of sources is thus achieved in this case.

3.1.3 Exposing Political Preferences and 'Blind Spots' in the ICJ's Discourse

With the analysis above, Kennedy offers a deep insight into the structure of the ICJ's argumentation that exposes the preference for certain terms and arguments as well as their mutual dependence, which opens the door to reconsidering current preferences as terms that are somehow 'interchangeable' and can be replaced by new terms. This opening-up of new alternatives, however, needs to be made against the backdrop of an in-depth study of the political, social, economic, cultural, historical and other structural circumstances of the case. Such a background study would allow unearthing interests that have been either neglected or just ignored by the ICJ's narrative.

As mentioned above, Kennedy's deconstruction style does not include this type of contextualization. Instead, it aims to show the lack of normative determination in the Court's argumentation in the hope that, by unsettling the doctrinal discourse, it will expose it to political critique and reconfiguration by others.

Although the ideological critique of the *Nuclear Tests* case is beyond the scope of this chapter, perhaps some tentative guidance to explain how such critique could proceed is in order. For instance, based on the previous destabilization of the ICJ's discourse, one could pay special attention to the interests of the weakest groups and individuals involved (like the interests of the peoples inhabiting the Pacific islands who live in a political status of neo-colonial domination by France and other Western states or the interests of the environment and the rights of plant and animal beings) that are simply left out of the debate by the dominant legal argumentation (both hard and soft). Admittedly, in this case such interests were protected in an indirect manner, yet they were never part of the discussion nor were they taken duly into account, which opens the door to further neglect.

Furthermore, optimism about the ability of the dominant rhetorical terms examined above to protect interests outside the realm of sovereign state politics and interest should be avoided. The Court does not consider the legality at large of atmospheric tests—which was the original purpose of Australia's claim; it limits itself to deal with France—and only with respect to the South Pacific. Atmospheric tests by other states would still be allowed according to the Court's Opinion. Moreover, underground tests end up being somewhat legitimized, implicitly presented as a less harmful, 'clean' option. Yet, their destructiveness for both human life and environment are beyond any doubt.

As explained above, it is at this evaluative second step of legal critique where CIL scholarship splits and develops into several strands of thought depending on the perspectives and interests that critical researchers prefer to focus on. Indeed, the divergencies at this point lead to a large diversity of approaches, movements and perspectives, like race and international law, feminist international law, Third World approaches, post-colonial studies or transnationalism.[116] Some of these approaches are presented in other chapters of this volume.

3.2 Critical Rhetorical Analysis of Law

This section excerpts and elaborates on another example of deconstructive critique. It features the rhetorical analysis of law (RAL) applied to a judgment of the European Court of Human Rights (ECtHR) and explores how the *pathos* and *ethos* appeals supporting the highly indeterminate structure of the Court's reasoning in social rights cases (especially, through proportionality reasoning) reveal not only the attitudes of the Court vis-à-vis both the state policies assessed and the applicant herself, but also the socio-economic rationality within which the whole rhetorical construction of the judgment makes sense.[117]

[116] See e.g., Singh and Meyer (2014), and chapters "Critical International Law" and "Feminist Approaches to International Law" below.

[117] This part of the chapter comments and expands on Garcia Blesa (2024).

[118] Although the example analysed here features the rhetorical analysis of one single judgment as a case-study, examples of diachronic studies of several cases can be found, e.g., in Garcia Blesa (2023), or Ervo (2016).

[119] Unger (1977), pp. 250-252, Trubek (1984), p. 604.

The example of RAL presented here starts by mapping the main *topoi* that structure the Court's discourse in cases dealing with conflicts between indirectly protected social rights and the economic and social policies of the Member States. In a second stage, it tracks how specific instances of *ethos* and *pathos* supplement the argumentative development (*logos*) of the topical structure -and to what practical effect- in a particular case, *Garib v The Netherlands* (2017). Finally, the analysis turns to the political economic rationality giving meaning to that legal discourse and its broader socio-political outcomes.[118]

3.2.1 Main *topoi* in the ECtHR's Social Rights Cases

In order to map the *topoi* used by the Court in similar cases, the rhetorical analysis of law relies on the notion of clusters. As interpretivist approaches to social research show, specific beliefs hinge upon broader systems of beliefs shared by an interpretive community. These systems are groupings of interrelated ideas that cluster together according to certain principles of meaning to produce meaningful wholes. As such belief systems, legal ideas are not isolated from each other. They organise according to different principles of meaning. Legal interpretivism studies these clusters and principles to explain how they are connected to each other and to other legal and extra-legal codes forming larger and evolving semantic systems and visions of life.[119]

As inconclusive commonplace ideas, legal *topoi* build clusters that tend to structure judicial discourse in so-called 'trees of arguments'.[120] Generally, some of the main topic clusters used by the ECtHR are the applicability and scope of rights protected in the Convention and its Protocols, the *prima facie* infringement of those rights, the legality of the restrictive measures, the legitimacy of the public aims pursued by them, and their proportionality. But in the case of indirectly protected socioeconomic rights, these clusters develop into other subtopics more specific to this subject-area.

In particular, the legitimacy of the aims pursued by state authorities and the proportionality of the means chosen to achieve such aims are governed by the opposition of two subtopics. The first subtopic is the states' wide margin of appreciation (MoA) that expresses the Court's high degree of deference towards the social and economic policies and proportionality assessment of national authorities. The second term of the opposition is the Court's own power of review—as states act only 'in principle' within the MoA, this must be verified by the Court (Fig. 8).

The extent of judicial control, however, is modulated by the idea that in social rights cases the Court's function is merely subsidiary or supervisory, which allows only for a low-intensity scrutiny of the public aims and the measures adopted under the umbrella of the MoA. That weaker control is expressed in the 'manifestly without reasonable foundation' (MWRF) test (Fig. 9).

In opposition to the MWRF's weaker review, the 'special situations' or 'suspect grounds' cluster comprises a number of subtopics that can lead to a stronger scrutiny

[120] von Schlieffen (2005), p. 422.

Fig. 8 The basic rhetorical structure of the ECtHR's scrutiny

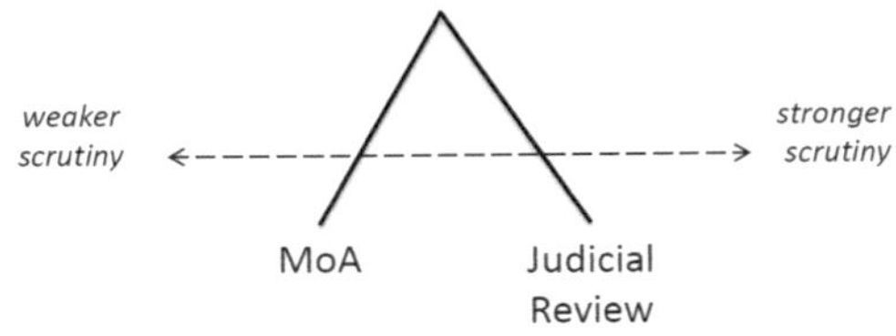

Fig. 9 The weaker MWRF test tempers judicial review

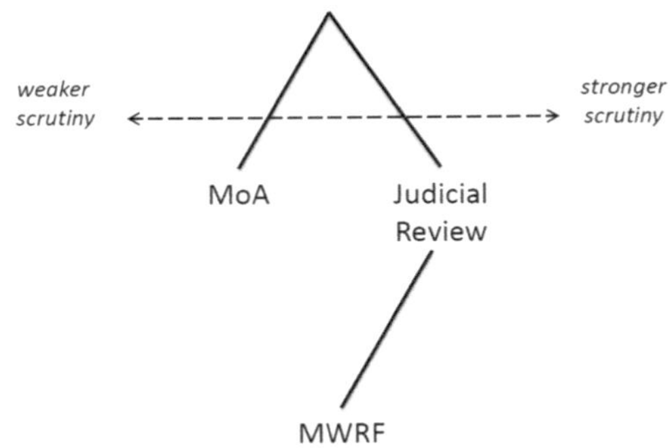

Fig. 10 The VWR test allows for an alternative, stronger scrutiny of the Court

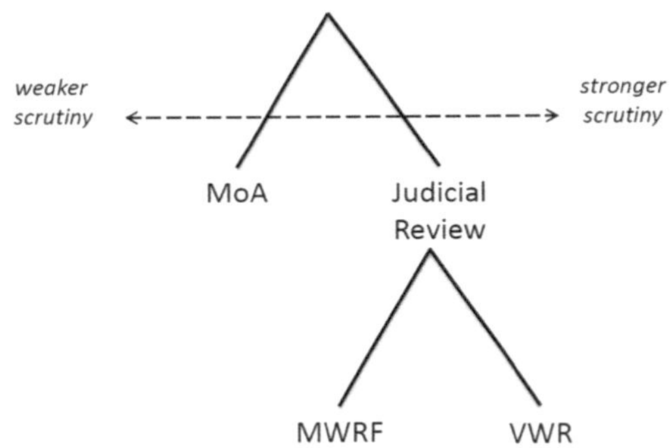

by the Court and a narrower MoA. These subtopics include state measures that involve (1) a differentiated treatment related to gender, nationality, race, etc.; (2) a negative impact on a particularly important facet of a person's existence or identity; (3) children's best interest; or (4) vulnerable groups. In such situations, states are requested to prove 'very weighty reasons' (VWR) to justify the contested restrictions (Fig. 10.).

Finally, there is an important cluster of 'particular circumstances' that modulates the previous subtopics making the determination of their meaning and scope even more flexible. The 'particular circumstances' cluster of subtopics includes aspects such as the timing of measures, possible compensatory measures, the essential content of rights, the threat to the applicant's subsistence by the rights' deprivation or the excessive individual burden of the applicant as opposed to the society or other groups in similar circumstances.

All the topics and subtopics described above can be mobilized to reduce or increase the MoA and, thus, intensify or weaken the Court's scrutiny of the public aims' legitimacy and the proportionality of the measures assessed. That is, the combination and recombination of these argumentation building blocks in the chain of reasoning is not based on *logos* alone. Rather, the driving force behind the choices involved is revealed by the *ethos* and *pathos* appeals that support these choices. These appeals tend to shed light not simply on the attitudes of the Court towards a particular case, but also on broader tendencies vis-à-vis the victims of socioeconomic rights violations, their life and their interests in the context of social and economic public policy-making.

3.2.2 Tracking the *Ethos* and *Pathos* Supplements

The rhetorical analysis of the *Garib* case revolves around two main issues. First, the indeterminacy of the Court's proportionality reasoning—and how the Court actually performs no *stricto sensu* proportionality test as far as the specific circumstances of the applicant's case are concerned. And second, the guiding role played by the Court's empathy (and the lack of it) towards the parties' conflicting interests and positions expressed in the *ethos* and *pathos* interwoven in the judgment.

Regarding the general background of the case, Mrs. Garib—an unemployed mother of two children with a migratory background who lives in the centre of Rotterdam—is not allowed by local authorities to move into a better apartment within the city centre and is expelled to the suburbs in application of normative measures that prohibit unemployed people from taking up residence in impoverished areas of the city centre as a means to promote economic activity and safeguard public order in those areas. The ECtHR's Grand Chamber (GC) construes the case as a conflict between the freedom to choose one's residence according to Article 2 of Protocol No. 4 (A2-P4)—which in this case protects the social right to housing indirectly– and the respondent state's economic and social policies.

Yet, a decision based on the open confrontation of these conflicting terms would reveal clearly political choices. Thus, in its decision, the Court manages the rhetorical tension by making a series of rhetorical moves that tend to augment the credibility and weight of the state's position while diminishing the position and interests of the applicant almost to the point of her personal effacement in the crucial proportionality balancing of the interests in conflict. The following explains the rhetorical analysis of four of these moves, how they are identified and examined in terms of their embeddedness in *logos* argument, the feelings and attitudes they appeal to and their general effect on the overall discourse.

3.2.2.1 The Guiding Role of *Pathos* in the Construction of the Problem

As mentioned before, the *pathos* and *ethos* elements of legal discourse tend to surface at the weakest points of the chain of *logos*. The analysis, thus, begins by reading carefully the rational argumentation and paying special attention to the links between the different topics and arguments it presents. In the *Garib* judgment, the first weak spot in the reasoning appears very early on in the description of the public

[121] *Garib* case, para 20-79.

policy background.[121] The explanation of the problem assessment and the purposes of the national authorities mixes a number of issues and policy aims without establishing any explicit or clear link between them. Behind a heap of details, the submission of the public authorities presenting their policy aims is obscure about the very problem they intend to address.

The contested national legislation gives local authorities the power to prohibit unemployed and low-income workers from moving into certain city areas as a means to solve 'inner-city problems.' But under that label, a hodgepodge of issues, like the quality of life, poverty, public order, the promotion of economic activity, immigration and crime, are thrown together without openly explaining their connections—e.g., whether and how poverty is a problem of public order or low-income immigration is related to crime rates. The legal and policy framework examined relies on conventional wisdom about implicit causes and solutions to an amalgam of social issues.

Yet, the GC seems to work out the links between these problems and their possible causes and solutions despite the lack of any rational explanation. In other words, the Court shares or sympathizes with the implicit assumptions of the national authorities about these broad issues and the vague and controversial relations between them. This is rhetorically conveyed, among other things, by the prolific use of figures of emphasis and euphemisms in the summary of facts,[122] metaphoric personifications,[123] and intensifying language to support the authorities' pessimistic assessment about the 'quality of life' in a district with high rates of recipients of social benefits, low-income workers and migrant population who create a 'very severe stress' for that area.

In contrast, the critical opinion submitted by the Dutch Equal Treatment Commission is presented with a tedious and distanced tone in a summary of data that shows the percentage and total numbers of persons actually prevented from taking up residence or indirectly displaced by the prohibition. This tone gives the impression that, all in all, the hundreds of persons affected by the measures are a small price to pay for the policy's promises of prosperity. The judgment uses the same tone to summarize the critical 2015 report of the University of Amsterdam confirming the lack of overall positive impact and causal connection between the measures adopted and social changes occurred in the selected areas.

In sum, the opening delimitation of the problem targeted and the aims pursued by national authorities is based on hidden meanings about unstated causal connections between immigration, low-income workers, crime and social benefits that signals

[122] The legislative and regulatory measures in question do not expel poor workers, immigrants and unemployed people or induce gentrification; they 'stem the influx of socioeconomically deprived house-seekers' and aim at 'increasing population diversity', *Garib* case, para 29.

[123] One of the key figures of the judgment is the personification of the central district of Rotterdam so it appears almost human and in need of help –for instance, the downtown needs to 'breathe', *ibid*, para 31.

[124] Ibid., para 85-92.

[125] *Garib* case, para 95-102.

from the outset an empathetic attitude towards the perceptions and solutions of the national authorities.

3.2.2.2 The *Ethos* of Comparative Law

The judgment builds upon different *ethos* appeals. One of them is a comparative law analysis under the heading 'Practice Elsewhere' that borrows authority from Danish law.[124] Its reproduction in the judgment construes a cross-European paradigm suggesting the reasonability of such legislation. More specifically, Danish law creates the possibility for public authorities to exclude some groups of people from taking up residence in certain districts to eliminate 'ghetto areas' and increase the quality of housing. 'Ghetto areas' are defined as social housing areas of more than 1000 residents and a social makeup of, e.g., 50% of non-Western (sic) immigrants and their descendants, 2.7% of ex-convicts, 40% of unemployed, 50% of uneducated or people earning less than 55% of the average income. The tacit association of criminality, race and low-income workers is evident.

3.2.2.3 The Use of Metonymy to Discard the Applicant's 'Special Situation' and the VWR Test

The way the ECtHR declines the application of the VWR test is also interesting in the context of this chapter.[125] The Court rules out the applicability of Article 14 of the Convention (the prohibition of discrimination on grounds of gender, race, social origin, etc.) on formal procedural grounds. Yet, the VWR test can be triggered by 'suspect grounds' other than the discrimination covered by Article 14 (e.g. negative impact on the applicant's personality or their belonging to a vulnerable group). That is, the Court's choice to omit the VWR test does not logically follow from the procedural inapplicability of Article 14. To support this decision, the judgment resorts to metonymy (substituting a part for the whole) supported by concession and the emphatic evocation of logical language.

First, the Court takes notice of the compelling argument presented by the applicant in favour of the substantive application of Article 14 based on the power of the Court to define the legal nature of the facts. The Court could directly reject those arguments on procedural grounds (as it eventually does), but it would run the risk of looking too formalistic and unfair. Instead, it includes a fragment of counter-discourse in its judgment as a typical appeal to the *pathos* of fairness.[126] This fragment also helps introduce the figure of concession (it concedes one point to make the opposite argument stronger), equally connected to the *pathos* of fairness. The judgment emphatically accepts the applicant's argument that the Court is the master of the characterization to be given in law to the facts of the case, but it immediately dismisses the consequences of this point by dissociating the freedom to characterize the facts in legal terms and the freedom to accept submissions without regard to the 'procedural context'.

[126] See also Ervo (2016), p. 226.

[127] *Garib* case, para 136-141.

Inadvertently, this discussion supports the use of silence or omission in dealing with the central issue of the VWR test. By focusing on Article 14, the attention of the reader is diverted from the fact that the higher intensity/VWR review can be triggered by other aspects of the case. The Court, thus, remains silent about the plausible characterization of the facts as one of those suspect grounds that would require enhanced review.

3.2.2.4 Rhetorical Augmentation and Diminution Strategies

In the final part of the judgment, the Court turns to the question of '[w]hether the restriction was "justified in a democratic society"', which should entail the review by the GC of the Chamber's proportionality assessment of the measures contested, including the balancing of the measures' beneficial effects for society against their negative impact on the life of the applicant. The operation of balancing is not based on logical reasoning, but the Court arranges this final section in the shape of an apparent syllogism to support its value-choices with the strongest possible appeal to logical cogency. Thus, in a short summary of precedents, the Court first recounts the principles and standards upon which its proportionality balancing will proceed next.[127]

Interestingly, this is accompanied by the Court's emphatic appeal to the neutral and technical *ethos* of both the Chamber, whose assessment must be reviewed, and the GC, who is conducting that review. The Court finds it necessary to stress that it aims to examine 'carefully' whether a 'fair balance' exists between public and individual interests, which evokes feelings of trust in its own attitude and good will as the most indeterminate part of the judgment is about to unfold.[128]

After thus presenting itself, the Court performs a separate evaluation of the 'inner-city problems' legislative and policy framework on one hand and the particular circumstances of the applicant on the other. Already this arrangement has the effect of suggesting that both aspects need to be assessed in different terms and disconnected from each other, placing the broader framework at the front of the discussion and somewhat conditioning the weight of the individual circumstances' assessment.

As the Court refuses to evaluate the means-ends adequacy or whether less restrictive measures were available, its proportionality assessment is reduced to the legitimacy of the aims pursued and the proportionality balancing. The role of *pathos* and *ethos* in the construction of these two argumentative steps turns out to be decisive. The Court's assessment reveals not only sympathy and trust, but also unwavering faith in the public authorities' measures; while, on the other hand, it shows not simply lack of sympathy, but the total illegibility for the Court of the applicant's situation.

[128] Ibid, para 138.

[129] Ibid, para 142-157.

[130] Ibid, para 142.

Sympathy, Trust and Faith in the Legislative and Policy Framework's Evaluation

The first part of the assessment supports the proportionality of the permit system as a whole.[129] This is based on the confirmation of the hidden ideas about the 'inner-city problems' described before, buttressed by a partial evocation of the benevolence of the system and the personification of the city centre.

First, almost in passing, the Court assumes the vague link between unemployment, social benefits, low-income work, antisocial behaviour, crime and illegal immigration argued by the national authorities. In fact, the Court even paraphrases the Government's explanatory memorandum to the Parliament. Thus, for the Court, it requires no further explanation that 'the domestic authorities found themselves called upon to address increasing social problems' resulting from 'impoverishment caused by unemployment and a tendency for gainful economic activity to be transferred elsewhere'.[130]

Within this mindset, the legitimacy and coherence of the system simply feel unquestionable. That is, as underpaid workers and social benefit recipients are linked to crime, antisocial behaviour, etc., it is obvious that '*bona fide*' economic activity and a higher income average are the only plausible solution. For that purpose, the notion that local authorities would seek to improve the economy and reduce unemployment by physically removing unemployed and other poor people needs no further elaboration.

Reinforcing these assumptions, the judgment resorts to the personification of the inner-city areas as it reminds us that the intention of the authorities was 'to foster diversity and counter the stigmatisation of particular inner-city areas as fit only for the most deprived social groups. It is for this purpose that the Inner-City Problems (Special Measures) Act was called into existence.'[131] As a result, it is the city centre whose stigmatization should be reversed, instead of that of low-income workers, social benefit recipients or immigrants. It is the city centre that requires our pity and empathy, not the persons targeted by the measures.

This sympathetic appraisal is reinforced by the emphatic repetition of a selective account of 'particular circumstances' that aim to shed a positive light on the system. The judgment insists on the safeguard clauses, the temporal and geographic limitation of the restrictions, the individual hardship clause and the availability to potential victims of two levels of judicial review that fully respect fair trial requirements, all of which leads the Court to assert that the national authorities made 'adequate provision for the rights and interests of persons' potentially affected.[132] Yet, the Court had enough information to dismiss at least some of these arguments. For instance, when it comes to the time limitation to which the measures are subjected, it is clear from

[131] Ibid.

[132] Ibid, para 150-156.

[133] In 2012 the regime is extended for a period of 20 years, ibid, para 72, 77-78.

[134] Ibid, para 146-149.

[135] Ibid, para 158-166.

the file that the measures can be and actually are being extended for long periods of time.[133]

This part of the judgment also shows how the Court's argumentation eventually turns the discussion into a matter of faith in both the authorities and the measures discussed, whose virtue becomes an unfalsifiable truth. Thus, in the face of empirical evidence disputing the positive effects or causal relation between the measures and potential social improvements, the Court simply dismisses the facts and embraces faith in the regime. For instance, the applicant's argument based on different surveys reporting that the measures are actually ineffective or that their effectiveness cannot be empirically demonstrated or linked to social facts is dismissed because those surveys had been conducted some years after the Inner-City Problems legislation was passed and 'with the benefit of hindsight'—an argument that ignores the continuing existence and effects of those measures.[134]

The Rhetorical Effacement of the Applicant

Once it has presented the whole legal regime in such terms, the Court announces that it is going to weigh the interests of the applicant considering her particular circumstances (family needs, financial resources, etc.) against the general interest of local communities as envisaged by national legislation.[135] Yet, the Court's attitude towards the applicant's situation is quite different from that displayed in relation to the national authorities, the legal regime and the city centre area.

First, all the applicant's submissions concerning her good behaviour—her having been a resident in the area for more than 5 years and the state of disrepair of her first dwelling that would have caused her and her children health problems—are dismissed as irrelevant vis-à-vis public interest or for lack of evidence.[136] Then, the Court asks why Mrs. Garib did not stay in her original apartment and wanted to move instead to a new one within the same area; the Court also wonders why she did not move back once she found work and qualified for living in the city centre area. Finding no answer that it wants to take into consideration, the Court deduces that the only reason for her seeking a change of residence was 'personal preference', which projects a whimsical *ethos* on Mrs. Garib. Thus, given this supposed lack of information, the Court decides that Mrs. Garib had experienced no disproportionate hardship that could outweigh the general interest.

The Court's argumentation shows a clear contrast between the empathy expressed previously towards the authorities' narrative and the sheer lack of it towards the applicant's situation. Even if the applicant's submissions had been dismissed for compelling reasons, the apparent gaps in her situation could be easily filled by

[136] Ibid., para 158-160. For example, the applicant's submission about the state of disrepair of her first dwelling is rejected due to her landlord's decision not to request a building permit.

[137] To learn more about intersectionality, see chapter on "Feminist Approaches to International Law" below.

[138] *Garib*, para 95–102.

inference from what is known about her life with a modest amount of empathy and effort to understand her circumstances. Here arises the question of intersectionality.[137] Taking into account even the most abstract aspects of the applicant's situation, it is not hard to see why a single mother of two children, unemployed and belonging to a minority group would want to stay in the same area where they had lived, gone to school, created a social network, become familiar with the available services, etc. for more than five years. From this viewpoint it is also easy to understand why she did not want to move back to the city centre eight months later, after qualifying for residence in that area. This is obvious to anyone having experienced a change of residence with two children or little financial resources. The fact that the applicant is a single parent and that she finally found work in her new area of residence would make the rationale of her decision even clearer.

But the Court seems unable to grasp even the most obvious practical difficulties for the applicant. It adopts a tone of reproach about the lack of sufficient information concerning her situation, which betrays the Court's inability or unwillingness to read the individual circumstances and the socio-political context that would have required special legal protection and a high-intensity scrutiny against public measures overwhelmingly affecting the euphemistically called 'migrant population'—mostly persons of African and Middle-Eastern origin.[138] Such illegibility sharply contrasts with the effortless decipherability of the legislative and policy framework, whose nature and rationale remain hidden under a heap of fragmentary references to vague problems and policies (e.g. about the role of public order aims).

The stark contrast between the attitude and tone displayed in the treatment of the Government's position on one hand and the disqualifying tone vis-à-vis Mrs. Garib's interests and persona on the other produce an effect of rhetorical augmentation of the former and a diminution of the latter. At the end, the applicant stands as an abstract and almost anonymous subject who has experienced a minor limitation or a mere inconvenience, against the backdrop of the general interest of the economy validated in the previous part of the judgment.

3.2.3 The Critique of Ideology: Exposing Institutional Neoliberal Rationality in Europe

The rhetorical analysis excerpted here shows how the rationality and the persuasiveness of the ECtHR's discourse are not predicated upon proportionality reasoning. Ultimately, the Court performs no actual proportionality balancing of the interests involved at all. As the person and the interests of the applicant fade away in the final part of the judgment, the comparison becomes purely rhetorical—i.e., it is devised to give the impression of measurement despite the complete lack of it.[139] This figure (rhetorical comparison) is key to the construction of proportionality discourse as it conceals that the Court, rather than comparing, is simply deciding. And the deciding

[139] Rhetorical comparisons are defined by the lack of terms of reference, Perelman and Olbrechts-Tyteca (1971), p. 242.

[140] *Garib* case, para 142, 159.

can only be based on *a priori* value preferences which are revealed by the strongly varying degrees of legibility (or illegibility) of the contending positions and interests involved. In other words, the discourse itself is not irrational or unpersuasive if examined from the perspective of a particular value programme. The final step of this rhetorical analysis consists precisely of studying the *Garib* case's rhetorical construction in relation to broader systems of belief in order to understand possible deeper meanings.

This requires, first, synthesizing the topical and emotional threads that structure the judgment. In the main, the absence of sympathy for the applicant and persons like her, who experience this humiliating stigmatization and the expulsion from their area of residence is connected to the faith in economic growth as paramount policy goal and its promises of 'prosperity for all'. These promises are embraced as the solution to an indeterminate number of controversial issues that outweigh the interests of the persons negatively affected. From this viewpoint, it appears logical that the unemployed and immigrant population left behind who are presented as the roots of the impoverishment of an area must be physically replaced by responsible entrepreneurs and professionals who have a 'gainful economic activity of their own'. Moreover, in the name of 'fostering diversity', this understanding of social policy also denigrates dependency and social rights altogether.[140]

From this summary, the critical rhetorical analysis presented here links these threads with several features and themes that have been described as part of contemporary forms of neoliberal rationality. For this operation, the analysis relies on previous studies about neoliberal rationality and its supporting discourses. For instance, the work points out how the *Garib* case re-elaborates the theme of *entrepreneurial reason* in public affairs performing a contemporary version of the 1990's entrepreneurial urbanism described by Peck as neoliberal 'urban creativity strategies'.[141] Similarly, it connects the judgment's *ethos* and *pathos* appeals regarding the applicant to the *responsibilization* of individuals for the collective consequences of neoliberal social policies.[142] And finally, it tracks within the *Garib* case several elements of the rhetoric of social *sacrifice*, a central aspect of post-austerity neoliberal political and legal discourses.[143]

4 Optional Exercises

This section offers four exercises that invite the reader to apply the approach (es) presented in this chapter to a few small tasks. The goal of the exercises is to facilitate the active learning of these approaches and their transfer to the reader's own research work.

[141] Peck (2010).

[142] Dardot and Laval (2017), and Harvey (2005).

[143] Brown (2015), and Wang (2020).

Exercise 1

Read pages 373-375 of the *Dissenting Opinion of Judge de Castro* to the *Nuclear Tests case* (Australia v France), *I.C.J. Reports 1974, p. 253.*

In what is Judge de Castro departing from the opinion of the majority of the Court presented above? How is his reasoning structured as opposed to that of the majority? What different rhetorical moves does he make and to what effect? What would have been the impact on the Court's decision had this been the position of the majority?

Exercise 2

Read pages 20–30 of the Advisory Opinion of the ICJ in the *Reservations to the Genocide Convention case, I.C.J. Reports 1951, p. 15.*

Using David Kennedy's appraisal of sources rhetoric summarized above, analyse the Opinion of the Court. Can you identify hard and soft arguments? How are they presented in relation to each other? What new oppositions are presented by the Court? What are the choices made by the Court in respect to these arguments? What are the purpose and the effect of these choices? What is the impact on the development and implementation of the Convention?

Now read the *Dissenting Opinion by Judges Guerrero, McNair, et al.*, pp. 31–47.

How does this opinion depart from the Court's majority in terms of its argument structure? What different arguments and choices do the dissenting Judges make? What is the result in terms of their conclusions? What could have been the impact on the development and implementation of the Convention had this been the Opinion of the majority?

Exercise 3

Read the UN General Assembly *Declaration on Principles of International Law concerning Friendly Relations and Co-operation among States* (UN GA Res. 2625 (XXV), of 24 October 1970).

How does it reproduce liberal political thought? Can you identify the so-called 'domestic analogy'? What are considered to be the constituent parts of this social system and why? How is the relation between the constituent parts of this society and the social order articulated? Who and why is left out of this social system?

Exercise 4

Select a court decision you are familiar with. Try to choose one whose background (socio-political, economic, cultural, etc.) you are well-acquainted with. Now, conduct a rhetorical analysis of that decision.

First, analyse the 'tree of arguments' (von Schlieffen, 2005). Start by identifying the opening topic of the argumentation; then, trace other topics that develop from the first. Study how the topics are elaborated and the connections between them. Try to identify how the decision relies on the different modes of persuasion (*logos, ethos, pathos*—see sections on the rhetorical analysis of law above).

Based on the previous analysis and on your knowledge about the political discourses and struggles that make out the context of that decision, try to identify the ideological tendencies and preferences revealed by your analysis.

References

Alexy, R. (1989). *A theory of legal argumentation: The theory of rational discourse as theory of legal justification*. Clarendon Press.

Aristotle. (1991). *The art of rhetoric*, (H.C. Lawson-Tancred, Trans.). Penguin Books.

Balkin, J. M. (1986). The crystalline structure of legal thought. *Rutgers Law Review, 39*(1), 1–110.

Balkin, J. M. (1996). A night in the topics: The reason of legal rhetoric and the rhetoric of legal reason. In P. Brooks & P. Gerwitz (Eds.), *Law's stories: Narrative and rhetoric in the law* (pp. 211–224). Yale University Press.

Baumeister, R. F., & Vohs, K. D. (2007). *Moral emotions. Encyclopedia of social psychology* (Vol. 1, pp. 588–589). SAGE Publication.

Behn, D. (2015). Legitimacy, evolution, and growth in investment treaty arbitration: Empirically evaluating the state-of-the-art. *Georgetown Journal of International Law, 46*, 363–415.

Brabazon, H. (Ed.). (2017). *Neoliberal legality: Understanding the role of law in the neoliberal project*. Routledge.

Brown, W. (2015). *Undoing the Demos: Neoliberalism's stealth revolution*. Zone Books.

Carty, A. (1986). *The decay of international law? A reappraisal of the limits of legal imagination in international affairs*. Manchester University Press.

Carty, A. (1991). Critical international law: Recent trends in the theory of international law. *European Journal of International Law, 2*, 1–27.

Cohen, A. J. (2009). Dispute systems design, neoliberalism, and the problem of scale. *Harvard Negotiation Law Review, 14*(1), 51–80.

Coombe, R. J. (1989). Room for manoeuver: Toward a theory of practice in Critical Legal Studies. *Law & Social Inquiry, 14*, 69–121.

Cooper, F. (2012). Social rights and human rights in the time of decolonization. *Humanity, 3*, 473–492.

Cotterrell, R. (1996). *Law's community: Legal theory in sociological perspective*. Oxford University Press.

Dardot, P., & Laval, C. (2017). *The new way of the world: On the neoliberal society*. Verso.

Derrida, J. (2001). Structure, sign and play in the discourse of the human sciences. In *Writing and difference* (pp. 351–370). Routledge.

Desautels-Stein, J., & Rasulov, A. (2021). Deep cuts: Four critiques of legal ideology. *Yale Journal of Law & the Humanities, 31*(2), 435–519.

Ervo, L. (2016). *The hidden meanings in the case law of the European Court for Human Rights*. Semiotica: 209–230.

Farber, D. A., & Sherry, S. (1996). Legal storytelling and constitutional law: The medium and the message. In P. Brooks & P. Gerwitz (Eds.), *Law's stories: Narrative and rhetoric in the law* (pp. 37–53). Yale University Press.

Faure, M., & Ma, W. (2020). Investor-state arbitration: Economic and empirical perspectives. *Michigan Journal of International Law, 41*(1), 1–61.

Garcia Blesa, J. J. (2022). Indeterminacy, ideology and legitimacy in international investment arbitration: Controlling international private networks of legal governance? *International Journal for the Semiotics of Law, 35*, 1967–1994.

Garcia Blesa, J. J. (2023). Proportionality rhetoric and neoliberal rationality in the 'fundamental social rights' adjudication of the Court of Justice of the European Union. *London Review of International Law, 11*(2), 159–194.

Garcia Blesa, J. J. (2024). Neoliberal rationality and the rhetoric of sacrifice in the construction of proportionality discourse: A case-study from the European Court of Human Rights. *The International Journal of Human Rights.*, 1–26.

Geuss, R. (1981). *The idea of a critical theory*. Habermas & the Frankfurt School, Cambridge University Press.

Golder, B., & McLoughlin, D. (Eds.). (2018). *The politics of legality in a neoliberal age*. Routledge.

Goodrich, P. (1987). *Legal discourse. Studies in linguistics, rhetoric and legal analysis*. MacMillan Press.
Haidt, J. (2013). *The righteous mind*. Penguin Books.
Harvey, D. (2005). *A brief history of neoliberalism*. Oxford University Press.
Hunt, A. (1985). The ideology of law: Advances and problems in recent applications of the concept of ideology to the analysis of law. *Law & Society Review, 19*(1), 11–37.
Hunt, A. (1986). The theory of critical legal studies. *Oxford Journal of Legal Studies, 6*(1), 1–45.
Kairys, D. (1998). Introduction. In D. Kairys (Ed.), *The politics of law. A progressive critique* (3rd ed., pp. 1–20). Basic Books.
Kelman, M. (1987). *A guide to critical legal studies*. Harvard University Press.
Kennedy, D. (1973). Legal formality. *Journal of Legal Studies, 2*, 351–398.
Kennedy, D. (1979). The structure of Blackstone's commentaries. *Buffalo Law Review, 28*, 205–382.
Kennedy, D. (1987). *International legal structures*. Nomos.
Kennedy, D. (1998). *A critique of adjudication: fin de siècle*. Harvard University Press.
Kennedy, D. (2001). A semiotics of critique. *Cardozo Law Review, 22*, 1147–1189.
Kennedy, D. (1988). A new stream of international law scholarship. *Wisconsin International Law Journal, 7*, 1–49.
Kennedy, D. (2005). Challenging expert rule: The politics of global governance. *Sydney Law Review, 27*(1), 5–28.
Keter, V. (2012). Economy or law? In M. Stone, I. r. Wall, & C. Douzinas (Eds.), *New critical legal thinking: Law and the political* (pp. 167–177). Routledge.
Koskenniemi, M. (2005). *From apology to Utopia. The structure of international legal argument*. Cambridge University Press.
Koskenniemi, M. (2007). Methodologies of international law. In: *Max Planck Encyclopedia of International Law, Oxford Public International Law*. Oxford University Press, 2015. http://opil.ouplaw.com
Levine, A. (1981). *Liberal democracy. A critique of its theory*. Columbia University Press.
MacCormick, N. (2005). *Rhetoric and the rule of law: A theory of legal reasoning*. Oxford University Press.
MacNaughton, G., & Frey, D. F. (Eds.). (2018). *Economic and social rights in a neoliberal world*. Cambridge University Press.
Marks, S. (2001). Big brother is bleeping us: With the message that ideology doesn't matter. *European Journal of International Law, 12*(1), 109–123.
Marks, S. (2009). False contingency. *Current Legal Problems, 62*(1), 1–21.
Nicol, D. (2011). Business rights as human rights. In T. Campbell et al. (Eds.), *The legal protection of human rights: Skeptical essays* (pp. 229–243). Oxford University Press.
Norton, P. M. (2018). The role of precedent in the development of international investment law. *ICSID Review, 33*(1), 280–301.
Odumosu, I. T. (2007). The law and politics of engaging resistance in investment dispute settlement. *Penn State International Law Review, 26*(2), 251–287.
Paso, M. (2012). The Court of Justice of the European Union as a rhetorical actor. *Maastricht Journal of European and Comparative Law, 19*(1), 12–36.
Peck, J. (2010). *Constructions of neoliberal reason*. Oxford University Press.
Perelman, Ch., & Olbrechts-Tyteca, L. (1971). *The new rhetoric: A treatise on Argumentation*, (J. Wilkinson and P. Weaver, Trans.). University of Notre Dame Press
Pinho, F. (2018). On logos, pathos and ethos in judicial argumentation. In L. Huppes-Cluysenaer & N. M. M. S. Coelho (Eds.), *Aristotle on emotions in law and politics* (pp. 133–153). Springer.
Prieto-Rios, E. (2015). Neoliberal market rationality: The driver of international investment law. *Birkbeck Law Review, 3*(1), 55–76.
Roberts, A. (2010). Power and persuasion in investment treaty interpretation: The dual role of states. *American Journal of International Law, 104*(2), 179–255.

Schlag, P. (1988). Cannibal moves: An essay on the metamorphoses of the legal distinction. *Stanford Law Review, 40*(4), 929–972.
Shalakany, A. A. (2000). Arbitration and the third world: Plea for reassessing bias under the specter of neoliberalism. *Harvard International Law Journal, 41*(2), 419–468.
Singh, P., & Meyer, B. (Eds.). (2014). *Critical international law: Postrealism, postcolonialism and transnationalism*. Oxford University Press.
Slobodian, Q. (2018). *Globalists: The end of empire and the birth of neoliberalism*. Harvard University Press.
Sobota, K. (1991). System and flexibility in law. *Argumentation, 5*, 275–282.
Sobota, K. (1994). Logos, ethos, pathos: A quantitative analysis on arguments and emotions in law. In Retorik & Rätt (Eds.), (pp. 155–171). University of Uppsala.
Trubek, D. M. (1984). Where the action is: Critical legal studies and empiricism. *Stanford Law Review, 36*(1/2), 575–622.
Trubek, D. M., & Santos, A. (Eds.). (2006). *The new law and economic development: A critical appraisal*. Cambridge University Press.
Unger, R. M. (1977). *Law in modern society. Toward a criticism of social theory*. The Free Press.
Ureña, R. (2014). Of precedents and ideology. Law making by investment arbitration tribunals. In P. Singh & B. Mayer (Eds.), *Critical international law: Postrealism, postcolonialism, and transnationalism* (pp. 276–303). Oxford University Press.
von Schlieffen, K. (2005). Zur topisch-pathetischen Ordnung juristischen Denkens: Resultate empirischer Rhetorikforschung. In K. D. Lerch (Ed.), *Die Sprache des Rechts: Recht Verhandeln. Argumentieren, Begründen und Entscheiden im Diskurs des Rechts* (pp. 405–448). Walter de Gruyter.
Wang, K. (2020). *Legal and rhetorical foundations of economic globalization: An atlas of ritual sacrifice in late-capitalism*. Routledge.
White, J. B. (1985). Law as rhetoric and rhetoric as law: The arts of cultural and communal life. *The University of Chicago Law Review, 52*, 684–702.
Wittgenstein, L. (2009). *Philosophical investigations* (G.E.M. Anscombe et al., Trans.), 4 Wiley-Blackwell

Further Reading

Cass, D. Z. (1996). Navigating the newstream: Recent critical scholarship in international law. *Nordic Journal of International Law, 65*, 341–384.
Kennedy, D., & Tennant, C. (1994). New approaches to international law: A bibliography. *Harvard International Law Journal, 35*(2), 417–460.
Munger, F., & Seron, C. (1984). Critical legal studies versus critical legal theory: A comment on method. *Law & Policy, 6*(3), 257–297.
Paul, J. (2001). CLS 2001. *Cardozo Law Review, 22*, 701–720.
Schlegel, J. H. (1984). Notes toward an intimate, opinionated, and affectionate history of the conference on critical legal studies. *Stanford Law Review, 36*(1/2), 391–411.
Tushnet, M. (1991). Critical legal studies: A political history. *Yale Law Journal, 100*, 1515–1544.

Feminist Approaches to International Law

Cristina Zamora-Gómez, Alazne Irigoien, and Elena Ghidoni

Contents

C. Zamora-Gómez (✉)
University of Alicante, Faculty of Law, Alicante, Spain
e-mail: cristina.zamora@ua.es

A. Irigoien
University of the Basque Country, Faculty of Law, San Sebastian, Spain
e-mail: alazne.irigoyen@ehu.eus

E. Ghidoni
University of Deusto, Pedro Arrupe Institute of Human Rights, Bilbao, Spain
e-mail: elena.ghidoni@deusto.es

J. J. Garcia Blesa (ed.), *Contemporary Methods in International Legal Research*, Springer Textbooks in Law, https://doi.org/10.1007/978-3-031-69522-3_5

1 Introduction

In order to explain feminist approaches to international law, it is important to begin by outlining some general traits that will allow us to understand what it means to analyse the law from a feminist epistemology that encompasses diverse theories and methods. Feminism is generally understood as a social and political movement, as well as a continuously evolving philosophy and critical theory that has developed at least over the past three hundred years. Contributions within feminist thought share some common concerns and themes. Historically, feminist strategies for transforming social reality have revolved around issues such as advocating for the rationality and subjectivity of women as human beings, the struggle for civil, political, social, economic, and cultural rights, the promotion of individual and collective awareness and empowerment, women's access to the public sphere and the reconfiguration of the false public-private divide, among many others. When translated into the analysis of international law these feminist concerns have often pivoted around the androcentric nature of the configuration of the different sectors in international law, the critical study of human rights, and so on. The ongoing debates surrounding the subject of feminism and the influences of new philosophical currents have broadened the concerns and themes that feminism addresses. Recent debates include questioning the gender binary,[1] challenging the socially constructed nature of both gender and sex, critiquing the homogenous and totalizing representations of women's experiences by white feminists in earlier works, and acknowledging diverse oppressive categories that shape women's lives, such as race, class, religion, national status, age, and many others. In the context of international law, these debates have translated, for instance, into feminist analyses of the construction of gendered identities in international law discourses, including intersectional analysis.

This extensive array of topics covered by feminist research reflects a diversity of approaches and perspectives within feminist epistemology. Some feminist ideas may exist in opposition to each other, while others complement or add various dimensions to feminist analyses. This attests to the complexity of the feminist theoretical corpus. Depending on the feminist approach adopted, analyses and outcomes will vary providing different insights into the same reality. This yields

[1] The term 'gender binarism' has been especially developed by postmodern feminisms, and it is understood as the classification of gender into male and female, which in most societies and cultures translates into the categorization of individuals as boys/men or girls/women, Nadal, Kevin (2017), p. 401. Note of the Authors: to ensure that women's contributions to knowledge production are made visible throughout the text, the chapter follows the feminist citation style and include authors' full names.

[2] See, for example, Banu, Roxana (2017), Keyes, Mary (2019), and McKenna, Miriam B and Arvidsson, Matilda (2024).

huge analytical richness and the dynamic, vibrant character that defines feminist perspectives. Notably, feminist contributions are currently positioned as one of the most recognized streams of critical thought.

Feminists have analysed various domains of life and delved into diverse fields of knowledge, including the field of law. Since the 1970s and 1980s, feminist legal studies have grown into a wide and diverse theoretical corpus. These feminist analyses of law have been framed as 'legal theory', 'feminist jurisprudence', or 'feminism'. Feminist legal theories (henceforth FLTs) produce critical studies of the law where the analysis of power is central. In this regard, the theoretical foundations of feminism are essential to understanding FLT's analysis of the law, including international law.

Therefore, this chapter aims to provide the reader with a concise but sound account of the basic traits of feminism and the foundations of FLTs as applied to international law. This contribution deals with the main feminist methodologies applied to public international law and, more specifically, to the field of International Human Rights Law (henceforth IHRL). This decision is motivated by two reasons: first, the intense development of the feminist methodologies in public international law to the detriment of private international law[2]; and second, the academic training of this chapter's authors, who have developed their work and research in the field of IHRL applying FLTs.

Acknowledging that law is both a tool and a site of struggle (and of reproduction of inequality),[3] this chapter takes the view that feminist theory in its transformative endeavour cannot neglect law as a powerful tool for transformation.

The chapter is structured as follows. The first section sets out the **theoretical roots** of FLTs by introducing the main concepts and the common tenets of the feminist critique. The subsequent section introduces the **feminist epistemology and methods** developed by FLTs in order to reveal, challenge and transform gendered laws and methods. Moving from the general to the specific, this introductory part concludes zooming in on the specific contributions of **FLTs to IHRL**. After this overview of theories and methods, the chapter presents three practical examples of how feminist methods are deployed to carry out research in three different domains: legal doctrine, judicial reasoning, and socio-legal research. The last section is devoted to **practical exercises** and indications as to the concrete steps that could be taken to design and carry out a research project following feminist approaches.

2 Theoretical Contributions of Feminist Legal Theories

FLTs have been characterised by both a critique of the law and the production of proposals for alternative legal arrangements. Critique has focused on both the **content** of laws, their normative underpinnings, and their consequences for the reproduction of women's oppression, as well as **legal structures, methods and**

[3]Conaghan, Joanne (2013).

[4]Conaghan, Joanne (2013).

[5]Rubin, Gayle (1975).

reasoning.[4] Like feminist theory in general, FLTs share a deep connection between theory and practice.

This first section delves into (1) the **key concepts** of feminist theory (gender, patriarchy, and intersectionality), before introducing (2) the common **tenets of feminist critique** vis-à-vis the pillars of legal positivism (e.g. the belief in law's neutrality and objectivity, and the universal legal subject), which form the backdrop for introducing feminist methodologies in international law.

2.1 Gender, Patriarchy and Intersectionality

Challenging the intrinsic nature of sexual difference, the **concept of 'gender'** (or the 'sex-gender system'), first coined by the anthropologist Gayle Rubin,[5] was an attempt at explaining women's oppression while simultaneously overcoming biological determinism (the belief that women and men are biologically different, therefore women's subordinated position is justified as a fact of nature).[6] Challenging theories that relegated sexism to an afterthought or secondary aspect to other inequalities, gender claimed a space for theorising about women's oppression as a separate phenomenon.

Rubin defines gender as the 'systematic social apparatus which takes up females as raw materials and fashions domesticated women as products'.[7] The concept of gender, thus, explains women's subordinate condition as a social construct, rather than a natural *status quo*. If women's subordination is not natural but socially constructed, then the social structures and mechanisms sustaining it should be criticised and dismantled, including the law.

The distinction sex-gender, as mirroring the nature-culture one, has later been questioned from many scholars challenging the biological nature of sex, as opposed to gender (e.g. Butler). This critique can be found already in the work of the French sociologist Christine Delphy, who argued that sex acquired its meaning because of gender, therefore establishing a prior relevance of the latter on the former, and the social construction of sex too.[8]

The definition of sex and gender remains highly contested in recent debates, while radical feminism used gender as an analytical tool to understand women's oppression and emancipate them from biological destiny, the **emergence of gender as**

[6]Biological determinism, realism, essentialism or reductionism are used as synonyms in this chapter.

[7]Rubin, Gayle (1975), p. 158.

[8]Delphy, Christine (2009[1970]).

[9]Butler, Judith (1990).

[10]In Butler's words, 'gender proves to be performative -that is, constituting the identity it is purported to be. In this sense, gender is always a doing, though not a doing by a subject who might be said to preexist the deed', ibid, p. 25.

[11]Ibid.

[12]Mouffe, Chantal (1992).

performance and sexual difference exemplify how gender has become richer in its meanings and uses. Postmodern feminism has prompted a critique of ontology, challenging the notion that 'woman' is a being that precedes all socio-historical discourses that have constructed her.[9] Judith Butler's theorization on the socio-cultural construction of gender and sex, wherein she questions the invariable nature of sex and contends that sex is as culturally constructed as gender, is arguably her most significant contribution. The idea of gender as performative, being created and reinforced through repetitive practices, is yet another way of suggesting its unstable nature and the possibility of change.[10] Butler does not especially focus on the law, but her ideas lay the theoretical groundwork for later research on it. For example, she points at how legal frameworks and structures contribute to the construction of gender and enforce normative views of sexuality and gender (as heteronormative and binary).

Butler[11] as well as prominent postmodern author Chantal Mouffe[12] question monolithic identities and contemplate the consequences of framing feminist demands based on them. Thus, extending these observations to the legal realm, Mouffe[13] argues that thinking of subjects homogeneously and as a foundation for articulating and organizing legislative or rights claims conceals the complex relations of subordination that exist in reality. Although some feminist scholars warned against disintegrating the subject 'woman', postmodern feminist proposals provide key ideas for the analysis of the legal realm.

The concern with the risks of essentializing 'women' into homogeneous categories is common to different feminist positions, beyond postmodern feminism. For example, Elizabeth V. Spelman, renowned exponent of critical race feminism, has argued against the view that women have some feature in common that makes them women, which she refers to as 'gender realism'.[14] Spelman argues that gender is socially constructed and intertwined with other aspects of identity like race and class, rather than having an inherent essence. Her critique of gender realism challenges the idea that gender identity is fixed and separable from other factors, therefore pointing at the relevance of an intersectional perspective. While her views are widely accepted in feminist philosophy, some scholars suggest that Spelman's arguments may not entirely discredit gender realism.[15]

Beyond gender performance, for example, feminist scholars influenced by Lacan

and psychoanalysis have stressed the relevance of sexual difference and its development at the level of subjectivity and the unconscious, adding a layer to the concepts

[13] Ibid.

[14] Spelman, Elizabeth V. (1988)

[15] Mikkola, Mari (2006).

[16] Lamas, Marta (2000).

[17] Ibid, p. 5.

[18] Walby, Silvia (1990), p. 20.

of sex and gender.[16] According to Lamas, the use of the concept of gender led to ignore the role of unconscious in shaping sexual difference. Thus, sexual difference was relegated to the anatomy of bodies, neglecting its psychoanalytic dimension.[17] Feminist scholars influenced by psychoanalysis believe that sexual determination lies in the unconscious, and that sex is built there, rather than in anatomy.

The concept of **patriarchy** or **patriarchal order**—and its various theorisations, mainly by radical feminists and dual-system theorists—refers to the phenomenon of women's oppression as 'a system of social structures and practices in which men dominate, oppress and exploit women'.[18] Men and women are understood as social groups, and the systemic understanding of patriarchy allows to 'sum-up' individual instances of women's oppression, which stop being perceived as isolated accidents and become parts of a broad inequality system embedded in everyday practices. Patriarchy recognizes women's oppression as an independent status, thus challenging the idea that it could be subsumed into other political fights. To understand the notion of social system that patriarchy lies upon, it is necessary to move outside the legal field and look for contributions in other social sciences. The concept of 'oppression' described by I.M. Young, as the 'everyday practices of a well-intentioned society', perpetuated by 'unquestioned norms, habits, and symbols, in the assumptions underlying institutional rules and the collective consequences of following those rules' sheds light on the meaning of patriarchy.[19] Additionally, Walby revisited the concept of social system to theorise the existence and relationship between different systems of oppression (e.g. patriarchy, racism, capitalism), therefore accommodating the concerns of intersectionality.[20] In the context of antidiscrimination law, Barrère has coined the term 'subordiscrimination', to integrate the notion of subordination in the legal definition of discrimination. Subordiscrimination seeks to capture the reality of group discrimination. It identifies the individual manifestations of a system of oppression, portions of a phenomenon that the legal system apprehends only through individual complaints, but that are symptoms of a broader system.[21]

Beyond debates on sex-gender and patriarchy, feminist theory has problematized the complex interaction of gender with other inequalities based on race/ethnicity, class, disability, etc., through the concept of **intersectionality**. The concept was first

---

[19] Young, Iris Marion (1990), p. 41.

[20] Walby, Silvia (2007).

[21] Barrère, María Ángeles (2014).

[22] Crenshaw, Kimberlé (1989, 1991).

[23] Eisenstein, Zillah R. (1979), Hartmann, Heidi I. (1978), Vogel, Lise (1983), Delphy, Christine (1980, 2006), Guillaumin, Colette (1992), Anthias, Floya and Yuval-Davis, Nira (1983, 1992). A brief overview of the predecessors of intersectionality in materialist feminism can be found in Conaghan, Joanne (2009) and Lutz, Helma et al. (2011).

[24] Davis, Angela (1981), Hull, Gloria T et al. (1982), Combahee River Collective ([1977]1997), Collins, Patricia H. (1990).

[25] Lugones, María (2008), Mohanty, Chandra T. (2013), Spivak, Gayatri C. (1988).

[26] Crenshaw, Kimberlé (1989), p. 139.

developed within feminist theory but has progressively travelled away from sex-gender, to explore intersections among other groups. While the term was coined in the 1990s by the feminist legal scholar Kimberlé Crenshaw,[22] it had already a long trajectory among materialist and socialist feminists,[23] as well as racialised and lesbian feminists.[24]

Decolonial feminist thought also contributed to unravelling the complexity of multiple inequalities of race, class and gender, from the perspective of the coloniality of power, with a critique towards West-centred feminist hegemonic discourse.[25]

While it is crucial to acknowledge the legacy of this field of study, Crenshaw remains a reference for her contribution in legal theory. Her critique exposed that the way antidiscrimination law conceived of sex-gender or race discrimination systematically erases the experiences of Black women who are discriminated against. This is because both categories of discrimination are meant to protect only a subgroup of privileged individuals among women (white women) and among the Black population (Black men). In other words, law constructs gender and race as 'mutually exclusive categories of experience and analysis'.[26] When Black women sought to build a case of discrimination, they found out that neither of these categories allowed them to represent their own experiences.[27] Crenshaw successfully exposed the shortcomings of the existing legal categories when it comes to addressing intersecting inequalities. Thus, intersectionality expanded the critique against the neutrality and objectivity of law, shedding light on yet another pitfall of law's structure and tools.

Despite its success, intersectionality remains a contested and indeterminate concept, difficult to translate into practice, particularly in law and policymaking. Two main uses of intersectionality can be identified nonetheless, which correspond to different answers to the question 'what is intersecting?': the focus on the intersection of multiple identity traits or multiple structures of power.[28] As argued by Crenshaw herself, intersectionality can point at the experience of an intersectional group (e.g. Black women) as qualitatively different from the sum of race and sex oppression. But it can also move away from identities, and focus directly on the source of their inequalities at the intersection between systems of oppression. This second understanding is called 'structural intersectionality'.

Crucially, for feminist legal theory, the aim of intersectionality is not to get rid of categories and concepts, which are fundamental in law, but rather to problematize their meaning and use, exposing the partiality and privileges they overshadow. As

---

[27] *Emma DeGraffenreid v. General Motors* 413 F Supp 142 (E D Mo 1976). In this case, a group of Black women had challenged the 'last hired-first fired' layoff policy enacted by the GM company, as discriminatory towards Black women. Due to past discrimination in hiring, the layoff disproportionately affected them as the last hired. However, because the relevant comparator groups (black men and white women) did not reveal any discriminatory treatment based on sex, race, or a combination of these factors, they could not succeed in their claims.

[28] Barrère, María Ángeles (2016), and Bilge, Sirma (2010).

[29] Crenshaw, Kimberlé (1989), p. 140.

[30] Bello, Barbara G. and Mancini, Letizia (2016), p. 16.

Crenshaw argued, the problem intersectionality raises cannot be resolved by creating new categories, or by including Black women 'within an already established analytical structure', because their experience was 'greater than the sum of racism and sexism'.[29] Instead, we should rethink 'the analytic commitments of antidiscrimination law altogether'.[30]

2.2 Common Tenets of Feminist Legal Critique

Following Carol Smart's classic distinction, FLTs have moved through different phases and approaches to law. The 'law is sexist' approach reflects how law actively disadvantage women by neglecting their experiences, judging them by inappropriate standards, or maintaining structures that oppress them (e.g. sexual division of labour). 'Law is male', instead, provides an empirical observation that most people producing, interpreting and applying laws are male, carrying certain values, perspectives and criteria. Being both of these approaches limited and likely to be criticised for biological determinism, Smart proposed the concept of 'law as gendered', which instead focuses on the processes and practices that produce inequality. Such understanding does not require adopting a fixed category of man and woman, and does not assume that whatever law does 'exploits women and serves men'.[31]

Despite a wide variety of positions and methods, there are some tenets of critique to law that FLTs have in common. These common tenets stem from the critique of positivist legal theory and its assumptions, which Nicola Lacey singled out as being: the neutral framework of legal reasoning; law's autonomy and discreteness; law's neutrality and objectivity; law's centrality; law as a system of enacted norms or rules; law's unity and coherence.[32] For matters of space and relevance, this chapter focuses on two main tenets: the false neutrality of law and the critique of the universal legal subject. These arguments have been broadly explored not only among feminists, but also among other critical legal scholars (e.g. in Critical Legal Studies, Critical Race Theory, etc.).[33]

Feminisms that emerge especially from the 1990s are linked to postmodern and queer theories, drawing on the philosophical contributions, among others, of Jacques Lacan and Jacques Derrida, Michel Foucault, or Julia Kristeva. These authors challenged premises of modern or Enlightenment thinking, such as rationality, truth, or dichotomous dualisms. Attention to language, discourses, knowledge, and power is characteristic of postmodernism. For example, Foucault's theorizations on

---

[31] Smart, Carol (1992), p. 33.

[32] Lacey, Nicola (1998), p. 7 ff.

[33] Minda, Gary (1995).

[34] Levit, Nancy and Verchick, Robert R. M. (2006), p. 37.

[35] Costa, Malena (2016), p. 238.

[36] Garbay Mancheno, Sussy (2018), and Smart, Carol (2000), p. 69.

power are well-known and have greatly influenced postmodern feminist analyses of the Law. Power, instead of being something that a sovereign and autonomous subject possesses, is interwoven through relations and mechanisms—also referred to as 'dispositifs' in the Foucauldian language. In that regard, the Law would constitute part of the dispositifs of power and elements shaping discourse. In the field of postmodern legal theory, attempts are made to challenge entrenched concepts in dominant legal thinking, such as the immutability of the Rule of Law and the concealment of the political biases of norms.[34] For feminist legal scholars aligned with this tradition, the law constitutes a 'social discourse that operates by prescribing what corresponds legitimately with duty and what does not, qualifying behaviors, and therefore, as a mechanism for the institution of subjectivity'.[35] In other words, the Law is a set of discourses that do not question sexual difference or, rather, assimilate sexual difference (male/female) with the social construct (man/woman) and becomes a power mechanism that establishes and shapes the production of gender meanings.[36]

2.2.1 The False Neutrality of Law

Whereas the positivistic doctrine presents law as the realm of neutrality and objectivity, FLTs have exposed how law is constructed to mirror men's experiences and needs and systematically erase women's. This exclusion is historically marked by the late recognition of women's rights to vote, to exercise certain professions, to retain their income, and to see the harms done against them recognised as forms of discrimination. As Mackinnon argued, gender equality laws have not traditionally included sexual assault or reproduction, because these are not experienced by men as a group.[37] Women's experiences of discrimination, like pregnancy discrimination, gender-based violence, reproductive injustice, are treated as exceptions, for they are incomparable to men's experiences of discrimination.

Feminist strategies moved from claiming inclusion into men's rights (or assimilation to them) to demanding recognition of women's specific needs and rights (or claiming difference from them). The tension between equality vs difference, or assimilationist strategies (e.g. emphasising similarities with men to access their world and rights) and claims for the recognition of women's differences from men (e.g. feminism of difference and an alternative feminine culture)[38] revealed at some point the existence of a male standard that was never questioned. As Mackinnon put it:

---

[37] Mackinnon, Catharine A. (1991b), p. 14.

[38] E.g. Gilligan, Carol (1982).

[39] Mackinnon, Catharine A. (1991a), pp. 1285–1287.

[40] Minow, Martha (1990), p. 50. Five unstated assumptions underpin the way difference is attributed to social groups, and the role power hierarchies play in it: (1) difference is intrinsic, not relational; (2) the norm need not be stated; (3) the observer can see without a perspective; (4) other perspectives are irrelevant, (5) the status quo is natural, uncoerced and good.

[41] MacKinnon, Catharine A (1991a).

> Why should anyone have to be like white men to get what they have, given that white men do not have to be like anyone except each other to have it?[39]

An example of how the false neutrality of law can be examined is through the so called 'dilemma of difference'. The 'dilemma of difference' refers to the stigmatization of a social group that comes from either ignoring their difference or noticing it. What the dilemma makes evident is that equality and difference are predicated in relation to an unstated standard that is not external to the terms under comparison, which is the male norm. Being equal or different is not relational anymore but an intrinsic and absolute characteristic defined by disalignment with the male norm. Hence, it is the male norm that defines which differences become inequalities.[40] The treatment of pregnancy discrimination is a clear example of how the male unstated norm works: in US antidiscrimination law, pregnancy discrimination was assimilated to discrimination against a sick worker. Women's experience of discrimination was defined as an exception compared to men's experiences of discrimination.[41]

2.2.2 The Universal Legal Subject

FLTs have problematized the way law builds gendered subjectivities through dichotomous constructions, while claiming a 'universal legal subject'. Legal positivism builds on the assumption of a universal legal subject, an individual who is rational, autonomous and free of needs. The legal concepts of 'worker', and 'citizen', for example, rest on a set of gendered assumptions that are left implicit and that systematically leave women at the margin. The 'worker' of labour laws, for example, is a male individual employed full-time in work for wages, with no care responsibilities, white, and able-bodied. These gendered and intersectional assumptions are not explicit, but operate to frame those subjects outside of the norm as exceptions to the norm.

Looking at the relationship between law and gender, Rikki Holtmaat argues that the law works through the same elements involved in the social construction of the relationships between the sexes, as theorised by Joan W. Scott.[42] Namely, law uses binary pairs to describe people and situations, thus reproducing cultural symbols ('strength/weakness, autonomy/dependence, objectiveness/subjectiveness, rationality/emotionality, general/ specific, public/ private, rights/needs etc.')[43] but also separates what is regulated by law and what is not, or what is relegated to special branches of the law. Cultural symbols are then fixated and crystalized in normative concepts that represent yet other binary oppositions. Social institutions participate in reproducing and reinforcing these binary gender representations as if they were

[42] Her work combines Joan W Scott's theorisation with Carol Smart's concept of 'law as gendered'. See Holtmaat, Rikki (2001).

[43] Ibid, p. 167.

[44] Spivak,Gayatri C. (1988).

[45] Butler, Judith (1990).

timeless and objective (political system is male; family is female; the law is gender-neutral). Moreover, the law itself constructs subjective gender identities through legal discourse: the unmarried mother, the good/bad mother, the female criminal, the prostitute, the welfare mother, the 'true' victim of sexual violence, etc.

Similar arguments are developed by postmodern and decolonial feminist approaches, analysing the construction of othered-subjects, particularly the Western and 'third-world' women subjectivities.[44] On one hand, postmodern feminisms denounce the construction of a falsely universal and neutral subject, raising concerns as to the ways in which femininities and masculinities are constructed as well as for the intersections of gender with other power structures, such as those imposed by class and race. In this regard, the contributions of Judith Butler,[45] have been pivotal in the evolution of contemporary feminist thought. On the other hand, decolonial feminists have precisely exposed the Western-centrist discourses evoked by some feminist scholars that have contributed to 'speaking for' Others, resulting in the maintenance of power positions even within the feminist approaches to international law. Queer legal analyses of international law have exposed that the majority of feminist work on international (human rights) law understands sex as a natural biological fact.[46] Challenging the core of international law's roots, queer thinking upholds that, for example, human rights do not necessarily 'need to operate within binaries (such as local/international, civil-political/social, etc.)'.[47]

3 Feminist Epistemology and Methods in International Law

Contrary to legal positivism, feminist epistemology has embraced the theory of **situated knowledge** by Donna Haraway, suggesting a more nuanced understanding of knowledge production, which takes into account the situatedness of knowledge and the diverse perspectives that shape it. In this sense, knowledge is always situated and local, associated with a specific place or position.

Applied to international law, situated knowledge enabled the critique of disembodied scientific objectivity and an emphasis on the embodied nature of knowledge.[48] Haraway also emphasizes the importance of partial perspectives and the need to see together with others, without claiming to be other. Haraway's ideas on situated knowledge highlight the limitations of traditional approaches that prioritize the role of the human in knowing the human.[49] The concept of situated knowledge can be further refined to elucidate the manners in which legal knowledge is moulded by power dynamics, social structures, and historical contexts. This conceptual framework serves as a valuable tool for unveiling the inherent biases and limitations ingrained in legal knowledge, promoting a more critical and reflexive

[46] McNeilly, Kathryn (2019), p. 430.

[47] Ibid, p. 431.

[48] Haraway, Donna (1988).

[49] Kurki, Milja (2015).

[50] Mossman, Mary Jane (1992).

approach to legal analysis and decision-making. By acknowledging the situated nature of legal knowledge, we open the door to considering alternative perspectives and voices that have traditionally been marginalized or excluded from legal discourse. This shift in perspective holds the potential to contribute to a more inclusive and transformative approach to law, one that takes into account the diverse experiences and knowledge systems of different individuals and communities.

According to Mossman, throughout history, there have been limited opportunities within the legal domain to scrutinize the processes involved in delineating issues of interest to the law, the selection of pertinent premises, and what ought to be excluded from its purview.[50] Put differently, discussions regarding the methodologies employed in legal practice and juridical research are inadequately represented in legal literature. Acknowledging legal methodology as a potent source of legal authority, some feminist scholars have ventured into the task of interrogating the production of legal knowledge. In so doing, they have laid bare the fallacy of neutrality and sought a transformative perspective. Feminist epistemologies have undertaken a critical examination of legal methodology, surpassing the discourse merely advocating for the inclusion of 'women's experiences' in law school curricula.[51]

This section overviews the most relevant feminist methodologies or approaches, understood as 'sets of ontological and epistemological premises, which shape any intellectual enterprise'.[52]

3.1 Feminist Legal Analysis

Katharine Bartlett's main contribution to the feminist method was exploring the aspects of feminist analysis and its relation to the content of feminist analysis using Martha Fineman's lecture on dependency as a focus. Feminist legal analysis, as proposed by Katharine Bartlett, involves incorporating a gender perspective into the evaluation of policies and programs. It requires a multidisciplinary approach to understand the problems and analyse the effectiveness of implementation. Bartlett's methodology aims to analyse the incorporation of gender perspective in legal texts and assess if it is being done adequately. This approach is part of the broader feminist legal movement, which seeks to challenge and transform the patriarchal nature of the legal system. By applying posthuman feminist theory, feminist legal analysis can be used to examine various areas of international law, such as the regulation of military technologies and environmental law.[53] Overall, feminist legal analysis aims to bring about legal change and address the inequalities and exclusions present in the legal

---

[51] Campos Rubio, Arantza (2008).

[52] González Hauck, Sué, Kahl, Verena, Etkin, Başak, Green, Alex, Paige, Tamsin P and Bagchi, Kanad (2024), p. 64.

[53] Jones, Emily (2023).

[54] Bartlett, Kathrine T (1990), Bartlett, Katharine T and Kennedy, Rosanne (1991).

system. Bartlett criticizes non-feminist methods in the field of international law as those that combine rules and assumptions that shape and limit our perspectives on the exclusion of women's experiences in this discipline. To overcome this exclusion, she proposes a feminist method of legal analysis structured in three sections: **asking the woman question; feminist practical reason; and the principle of 'Consciousness-Raising'.**[54]

Asking the Woman Question

The application of the 'asking the woman question' method, as advocated by feminists like Bartlett, represents a distinctive approach integrated into legal analysis. This method is predicated on scrutinizing the law for biases in its treatment of women and, subsequently, proactively suggesting alterations to rectify these biases. Through the employment of this method, feminists have engendered substantial insights and analyses within the realm of law, bringing to the forefront previously overlooked facets of gender dynamics embedded in legal systems. This method is intricately interwoven with the broader feminist endeavour, aiming to challenge and rectify gender bias within legal frameworks. It functions as a mechanism for meticulous examination, elucidating how the law interacts with and impacts women. Its overarching goal is to pinpoint areas where systemic improvements can be instituted to advance the cause of gender equality. In essence, 'asking the woman question' serves as a critical tool in the ongoing pursuit of reshaping legal landscapes to be more equitable and just for all genders.

Feminist Practical Reasoning

Feminist practical reason, as proposed by Bartlett, involves critiquing the concepts of practical reason and autonomy in Kantian philosophy from a feminist perspective.[55] Bartlett argues that these concepts assume a male-centred, monological and disembedded subject, which excludes women from fully exercising their practical reason and autonomy. Bartlett suggests that the limitations of Kant's philosophy lie in its teleological assumptions about the realization of morality in history. She emphasizes the importance of interaction and communication for the use of practical reason and the exercise of autonomy. Applied to international law, this approach holds the potential to address the political concerns associated with acknowledging and valuing women's differences, while concurrently confronting the deeply ingrained masculinist biases inherent in Western reason in general, and in international law specifically. By promoting interaction, communication, and consensus-building in decision-making processes, feminist practical reasoning aspires to

---

[55] Nobus, Dany (2017).

[56] See also MacKinnon, who defined consciousness raising as: 'the major technique of analysis, structure of organization, method of practice, and theory of social change of the women's movement. In consciousness raising, often in groups, the impact of male dominance is concretely uncovered and analyzed through the collective speaking of women's experience, from the perspective of that experience" Mackinnon, Catharine A. (1982), p. 520.

engender more inclusive and equitable outcomes within the framework of international law.

The integration of feminist practical reason into the realm of international law is not merely theoretical; it has practical implications. This application can contribute substantially to the formulation of practical guidelines for feminist research, particularly in fields such as nursing. In doing so, it offers the potential to inform nursing practices and elevate the quality of care provided to historically oppressed groups. In essence, the infusion of feminist practical reason into international law represents a transformative force, fostering greater inclusivity, equity, and sensitivity to diverse perspectives.

Consciousness-Raising
The third component within Katharine Bartlett's feminist legal analysis is referred to as 'Consciousness-Raising'.[56] This approach stems from the examination of common patterns observed in the diverse individual experiences of women. The transformative potential of this method lies in its capacity to influence the interpretation and application of laws, prompting modifications in legislation and practices. To harness the insights generated by this approach, it becomes imperative to employ tools beyond the conventional ones within the legal domain. A comprehensive understanding of women's experiences is necessary, necessitating the utilisation of multidisciplinary approaches.[57] Disciplines like sociology or psychology, for instance, can be invoked to fulfil this requirement.

3.2 Contextual Feminist Legal Theories

Among the FLTs that we can call 'contextual' are the authors Martha Minow and Elizabeth V. Spelman. Martha Minow's contributions to feminist legal theories demonstrate a commitment to understanding the complexities of power, identity, and justice within legal systems. Her work has influenced discussions on how the law can better address the needs of diverse and often marginalised groups, including women. It emphasises the importance of a sustained ethical engagement with marginalised groups and critiques the intrusiveness of traditional research methods.[58] Minow's work has explored the idea of legal pluralism, recognizing that individuals often navigate multiple legal systems simultaneously. This is particularly relevant for women, who may seek justice through both formal state law and informal community norms. By acknowledging the existence of diverse legal orders, Minow's contributions encourage a more inclusive understanding of how justice is sought and achieved. Traditional notions of autonomy often emphasize individual independence. Martha Minow introduces the concept of 'relational autonomy',

[57] Selim Alkan, Yavuz (2012).
[58] Minow, Martha (1988).

arguing that autonomy is shaped not only by individual choices but also by social relationships and contexts. In feminist legal theory, this perspective challenges simplistic views of autonomy and highlights the importance of considering the impact of social structures on women's ability to make choices. For example, Minow's exploration of restorative justice offers an alternative to punitive legal approaches. She emphasizes the need to address the needs of victims and promote healing, rather than focusing solely on punishing offenders. In the context of feminist legal theories, this approach aligns with efforts to provide justice for survivors of gender-based violence and challenges traditional punitive models.

3.3 Deconstruction and Other Postmodern Approaches

The postmodernist contributions have extensively theorized about methodologies. The methods of the so-called 'deconstruction' and 'discourse analysis' may perhaps be the most recognized. The 'deconstruction' method—originating from Derrida's work[59]—involves unveiling the contradictions and assumptions present in texts and language, challenging the notion that language can provide objective and stable representations of reality. Discourse analysis—originating from Foucault's ideas—focuses on how power and knowledge are intertwined in discourse, revealing how language constructs social realities and shapes power relationships.[60] Michel Foucault also refers to the method of 'problematization', as the necessity of abandoning certainties, turning into problematic that which, up to that point, was clear, evident, and undisputed. In policy analysis, Foucault's work has inspired Carol Bacchi's approach called 'what's the problem represented to be', which proposes a set of questions to unveil unquestioned assumptions.[61]

Other methods within the postmodern epistemology focus on the 'voice' of often made-invisible or subaltern subjects,[62] and put in the centre the experiences of those subjects as the primary source of knowledge. Feminist postmodern approaches apply these methodologies. For example, legal postmodern feminists tend to look at the hidden contradictions and assumptions and the intertwined gendered power dynamics in legal discourses, such as those found in legislations and jurisprudence, including those at the international level.

[59] Derrida, Jacques (1976).

[60] Michel Foucault also refers to the method of 'problematization''. He alludes to the necessity of abandoning certainties, turning into problematic that which, up to that point, was clear, evident, and undisputed. This 'problematizing' task transforms the analytical exercise into a disturbance, not only for the researcher but, above all, for the power systems that benefit and legitimize themselves based on evidence and the 'irrefutability' of their principles, Foucault Michel (1991), cited in Macaya Andrés Laura (2013), p. 61.

[61] Bacchi, Carol (2012a, 2012b).

[62] Spivak, Gayatri Chakravorty (1988).

4 Feminist Legal Theories in International Law

4.1 Mainstream Feminist International Law Scholarship

Charlesworth and Chinkin significantly impacted feminist methodology in international law through their seminal 1991 article, 'Feminist Approaches to International Law'. This influential work emerged from their dissatisfaction with the noticeable absence of female perspectives at a conference, prompting them to critically examine why gender had been largely overlooked within the discipline. The article, born out of this frustration, not only questioned the conventional structure of international law but also sought to uncover potential avenues for integrating feminist theory into its framework.

Their ground-breaking contribution was marked by a challenge to the traditional norms of the discipline, introducing a feminist lens to explore possibilities within international law. This venture stirred both controversy and intrigue, eliciting reactions from prominent scholars in the field. Charlesworth and Chinkin's contribution lie in their exploration of feminist approaches to international law, striving to bridge the gap between theory and practice. Importantly, they leveraged feminist theory not only to analyse but also to advocate for legal change, emphasizing the transformative potential of feminist perspectives in reshaping the landscape of international law.

Professors Charlesworth and Chinkin highlighted the crucial recognition of gendered imbalances in societal power, influencing outcomes for women involved in international efforts to address violence against them. During the 1990s, they emphasized the need for transformative change, advocating for a profound restructuring of existing gender relations. The vision of legal feminists at that time extended beyond mere formal inclusion, urging strategic initiatives that would bring about substantive equality rather than a superficial 'add women and stir' approach.

By the 1990s, Charlesworth and Chinkin had already identified the limitations of approaches that superficially included women in international forums without fostering genuine integration or prompting a radical reconsideration of policies and gender awareness. During this period, feminist scholars predominantly critiqued specific areas of international law, such as International Human Rights Law, International Humanitarian Law, and International Criminal Law, while leaving the bulk of international law, including state responsibility and the law of treaties, unexamined.

Despite this, a notable exception emerged in the form of 'The Boundaries of International Law: A Feminist Analysis'[63] which engaged with international law as a whole. This scarcity of comprehensive exploration was partly a result of the increasing fragmentation of international law itself, marked by diversification and

---

[63] Charlesworth, Hilary and Chinkin, Christine (2000).

[64] Yearbook of the International Law Commission, 2006, Vol II, Part two, Chapter XII: Fragmentation of international law: difficulties arising from the diversification and expansion of international law.

[65] The concept emerged during the United Nations Third World Conference on Women of 1985 in Nairobi, and was explicitly endorsed in the 1995 Conference and in the Beijing Platform for Action.

expansion. The International Law Commission recognized this phenomenon as posing the risk of conflicting rules, principles, and institutional practices.[64] The implications of this process for the feminist project in international law remain relatively unexplored.

The connection between gender and discrimination against women has, to some extent, diminished. The prevalent terms in international initiatives concerning women now often emphasize 'gender equality' in the context of formal equality or 'gender neutrality', while the acknowledgment of a gender hierarchy has become less frequent. This shift in the usage of gender-related terminology is proving problematic for women, as there is a growing resistance not only within legal initiatives but also more broadly, including the provision of humanitarian assistance, against efforts to enhance protections for women.

Gender mainstreaming, adopted as a major strategy within the United Nations and its institutions, aimed to advance women's empowerment by assessing the implications of any policy, program, or legislation for men and women.[65] Originally seen as promising, it was designed to address the issue that women's concerns were often relegated to the margins when handled by specialized bodies. However, there is a perception that the application of this policy has undermined the goal of achieving true equality between men and women. The limitation of its effectiveness stems from the assumption within international institutions that 'gender' exclusively refers to 'women'. This assumption fails to recognize that substantive equality necessitates changes not only for women but also for men, involving the dismantling of the gender hierarchy.

International law feminists remain divided on the interpretation and use of the terms 'women', 'sex', and 'gender', and there is ongoing debate about the need to dismantle the masculine/feminine binary to broaden feminism's scope beyond women alone. This intense focus has led to increasing concerns about the widening gap between theory and practice, prompting reflection on the failures of feminist strategy and its underlying reasons.

It is defined as 'the process of assessing the implications for women and men of any planned action, including legislation, policies or programmes, in all areas and at all levels. It is a strategy for making women's as well as men's concerns and experiences an integral dimension of the design, implementation, monitoring and evaluation of policies and programmes in all political, economic and societal spheres so that women and men benefit equally and inequality is not perpetrated. The ultimate goal is to achieve gender equality", UN Women (2014) Gender Mainstreaming in Development Programming, p. 7. Available at: https://unsdg.un.org/sites/default/files/gender-mainstreaming-issuesbrief-en-pdf.pdf.

[66] Otto, Dianne (2006).

[67] Ibid, p. 320.

4.2 The Neutrality of International Human Rights Law and Its Universal Legal Subject

FLTs developed a critique of the universal subject of IHRL, showing how it erases women's experiences, and produces gendered subjectivities.[66] In particular, Dianne Otto finds three female subjectivities in International Human Rights Law: the wife and mother; the woman who is 'formally equal', and the 'victim' subject. Each of these subjectivities is paired by an opposed male subjectivity which sets the standard of rights bearer (the male protector, the right bearer, and the civilised rescuer).[67]

According to Otto, women were present in IHRL since its inception, mostly as implicit or 'other' compared to the standard male legal subject. Early instruments regulating war were concerned with (male) combatants, and addressed women indirectly, establishing duties to respect 'family honour and rights'. Through these arrangements, IHRL contributed to reify the division between **public and private sphere**, and the notion of the nation-state. Crimes against women were framed as violations of the rights of the male family member, relegating women to the status of objects, rather than subjects of rights.

FLTs deployed different strategies to realise the promise of emancipation embedded in human rights. These strategies reflect the tension between equality (understood as assimilation) and difference (as the recognition of specificity) exposed above, and echo the debate on universality and specificity in human rights law.

The first strategy is the **promotion of women's specificities** in the Universal Declaration of Human Rights (UDHR),[68] mainly exemplified by the work of the Commission on the Status of Women (CSW) in its struggle for the recognition of women's rights.[69] The second strategy in the adoption of a **specialised women's human rights instrument** (CEDAW),[70] which expands the boundaries of human rights to substantive equality, and the 'de facto' realisation of women's rights, challenges the public vs private division, and reconstitute the subject of human rights as a woman.[71] Pitfalls in this strategy led back to the first strategy, in the form of the **'women's-rights-are-human-rights' claim**. This time, the strategy combined the recognition of gender-specific rights, with the 'mainstreaming' of women's

[68] Universal Declaration of Human Rights (adopted 10 December 1948), UN General Assembly Resolution 217A(III) (UDHR).

[69] Otto, Dianne (2006), pp. 330 ff.

[70] Convention on the Elimination of All Forms of Discrimination Against Women (adopted 18 December 1979), UN General Assembly 34/180 (CEDAW) UNTS 1249, p. 13.

[71] Otto, Dianne (2006), pp. 338–339.

[72] HRC, General Comment n. 28 ICCPR (29 March 2000), UN Doc. CCPR/C/21/Rev.1/Add.10; CESCR, 'General Comment 16' (13 May 2005), UN Doc. E/C.12/2005/3; CERD, 'General Recommendation XXV' (20 March 2000), as contained in UN Doc. HRI/GEN/1/Rev.5. See Otto, Dianne (2006), p. 343.

[73] Otto, Dianne (2006), p. 344.

[74] Ibid, pp. 344–345.

[75] Ibid, p. 356.

human rights in different human rights instruments.[72] It is identified starting from the late 1980s and in particular with the 1995 Fourth World Conference on Women ('Beijing Conference') and its reference to the 'indivisibility of women's human rights'.[73] As a way out of the dilemma of difference, Otto proposes a fourth strategy based on '**re-scripting sex as shifting and multiplicitous**'. This approach encompasses different strategies, such as reframing the universal in a 'double subjectivity', creating two sets of sexually specific rights; codifying injuries inflicted upon men as a result of gender hierarchies; and reversing existing gender stereotypes so that men are represented as nurturers and carers and women as breadwinners. Finding limitations to all these strategies, Otto concludes that gender should be re-defined away from a dichotomy, as multiplicitous and detached from bodily parts.[74] Drawing on Ratna Kapur's peripheral subjects, she argues that feminist human rights strategies should be built 'on the normative challenges presented by such disruptive subjects', thus, taking the perspective of the marginalised ones.[75]

4.3 Postcolonial Feminist Approach

Charlesworth and Chinkin are emblematic of mainstream feminist international law scholarship, characterized by a reluctance to delve into the intricate connection between the fundamental structures of capitalism, imperialism, and international law. As conventional scholars, they refrain from extensively exploring the 'logic of capital', as noted by Chimni.[76] This approach diminishes the depth of their analysis of international law. Neglecting to examine the interplay between patriarchy and capitalism or the phenomenon of imperialism omits a crucial discussion of the structural influences that have significantly moulded the evolution of international law over the past four centuries. Chimni advocates for the adoption of a socialist feminist approach to international law that integrates the perspectives offered by postcolonial theory. The argument for a postcolonial socialist feminist approach to international law is based on the premise that patriarchy's ideology, institutions, and practices in the modern era have been significantly influenced by the 'logic of capital'. This influence, while impacting various social formations differently, has led to distinct articulations in metropolitan, colonial, and postcolonial spaces. While recognizing that global capitalism and imperialism do not encompass all aspects of patriarchy, the argument asserts that critiquing both is crucial for promoting women's emancipation, whether in the Global South or the Global North. For example, Mohanty advocates for an anti-imperialist, anticapitalistic, and context-specific feminist project to unveil and highlight the diverse, overlapping forms of women's subjugation.[77]

[76] Chimni, Bhupinder S. (2017).

[77] Talpade Mohanty, Chandra (2013).

[78] Kapur, Ratna (2002).

[79] Engle, Karen (2005), and Engle, Karen et al. (2022).

Ratna Kapur criticizes both radical and liberal feminism for portraying the third-world woman as the 'authentic victim subject', particularly through their emphasis on violence against women (VAW).[78] According to Kapur, this focus within the VAW campaign reinforces gender and cultural essentialism in the realm of international women's human rights. She rejects the notion of a universal sisterhood based on shared experiences of victimization, arguing that such a construction fails to make room for diversity or the empowerment of women as active subjects. Kapur is troubled by the stereotypical portrayal of women as weak and helpless, fearing that it aligns with conservative, right-wing agendas that are protective rather than liberating. From Kapur's perspective, feminists should articulate their politics without subjugating other subjectivities through claims to a 'true self' or a singular truth about all women.

Similarly, according to Karen Engle, in the years leading up to September 11, Third World feminists, including those in the United States, were actively involved in critiquing both international law and Western feminist perspectives on international law.[79] This critique primarily targeted the First World feminist understanding and deployment of culture, urging for transformative changes in the lives of women in the Third World. These critics argued that First World feminists frequently engaged in the essentialization of culture, reducing Third World women to a stereotypical cultural essence. In doing so, First World feminists were accused of negating the agency of Third World women within or in resistance to their own cultural contexts.

Within the feminist framework of Third World Approaches to International Law (TWAIL), Vasuki Nesiah has made a significant contribution by exploring the intersection of international law with the histories of slavery and colonialism. Nesiah argues that unravelling the racial and capitalist history of international law requires an expansive and heterodox approach to legal interpretation and legal sources. She proposes a methodological intervention focused on the **intertextual reading of international law**.[80]

Regarding the question of whether there can be a feminist approach that does not exclusively centre on women, Nesiah suggests that feminist legal research may need to challenge its own assumptions to revitalize its intellectually and politically radical approach. This involves distancing oneself from conventional power structures and taking greater political risks. Nesiah advocates for critically examining the universalization of analytical prisms, such as the public/private dichotomy, and exploring the conditions of their formation to ensure that feminist research agendas are intellectually robust and subversive.

In contrast to many other areas of feminist research that have challenged the category of 'woman', Nesiah highlights that feminist research on international law

[80] Nesiah, Vasuki (2023).

[81] Ibid.

has surprisingly kept this category largely intact. She proposes that revitalizing critical feminist traditions requires the courage to challenge and question the closed acceptance of this fundamental issue. Nesiah advocates for a critical feminist approach that does not always initiate its analysis from gender as the central point but adopts a broader and politically engaged perspective to understand and question the enabling conditions and distributive implications of international law in an intellectually versatile and politically relevant manner.[81]

4.4 Governance Feminism

With Janet Halley the concept of **governance feminism** was born to talk about how the international legal order increasingly welcomes feminist discourses in its power elites and how feminist legal reform is emerging as a new and formidable source of legal ideas. Drawing on the work of Prabha Kotiswaran, governance feminism is understood to encompass several foundational principles. Firstly, it involves a concerted effort to challenge and reshape prevailing power structures within organizations and institutions, striving for more equitable and inclusive decision-making processes. Secondly, it places a strong emphasis on intersectionality, acknowledging the intricate connections between gender and other social categories such as race, class, and ethnicity. Thirdly, feminist governance advocates for the politics of presence and self-organization, pushing for the active representation and participation of marginalized groups in decision-making. Additionally, it engages in a critical examination and reimagining of traditional notions and practices related to accountability, strategy, and risk, with the goal of establishing more inclusive and compassionate organizational frameworks. Finally, scholarship in feminist governance underscores the importance of adopting feminist epistemology in research methods, incorporating intersectionality and decolonial perspectives, and recognizing the researcher's own power and positionality.[82]

Prabha Kotiswaran's work highlights the intricate dynamics between national and international Governance Feminism. It reveals how these spheres collaborate to mobilize international law, particularly in the service of dominant forces. While the international domain does not dictate the national one, it significantly influences and shapes national agendas by endorsing hegemonic discourses. This collaboration, akin to the collaboration among capitalist classes transcending national borders, as posited by Marxists, prompts reflection. Kotiswaran points out that Governance Feminism often understates its power dynamics, neglecting to acknowledge its substantial impact on global distribution. Despite its significant influence, Governance Feminism tends to position itself as the underdog, a stance that demands scrutiny from feminists to prevent inadvertent alignment with existing power structures.

[82] Halley, Janet et al. (2018).

5 Examples of Feminist Approaches to International Law in Practice

5.1 Feminist Approach to Classical International Scholarship in International Refugee Law

This section will address the practical application of two FLTs' methodological approaches to the academic literature on International Refugee Law (IRL): situated knowledge and feminist legal analysis. Following the application of both approaches, the doctrinal consequences of this analysis will be presented: the androcentrism of the 1951 Geneva Convention and the treatment of women as 'non-subjects' in IRL literature.

When approaching the feminist critique of the academic literature produced around IRL, as a first step, **I 'situate' myself as a researcher,** so that whoever approaches my research can understand the context and place from which I write. Thus, this study is situated research that arises from a political stance in relation to scientific research: it is neither impartial nor objective.[83] Knowledge is a shared good and is influenced not only by the historical and cultural context in which the research is carried out, but also by the personal perspective of the researcher. Therefore, recognizing the subjectivity of research is considered a value in the face of supposed academic neutrality. The humanization of international law is contingent upon the acknowledgment of the agency and perspectives inherent in individuals and communities affected by international legal norms and processes. By embracing the concept of situated knowledge, the trajectory of international law can deviate from a top-down, state-centric approach and, instead, engage with the diverse experiences and knowledge systems of various actors within the international system.

In the first stage of analysis, the incorporation of feminism into the IRL implies directing attention to the way in which this legal framework has been configured. In this context, this examination entails analysing the rationality, objectivity and neutrality of the legal method. In this initial task of evaluation, Professor Bartlett suggests a fundamental methodological question: **where are the women?** The answer involves investigating how the international legal field of refugee protection fails to take into account women's experiences, or how existing legal standards and concepts may adversely affect them. From the critique of these questions, general premises are derived that serve as a starting point for the initial gendered study of IRL and the subsequent formulation of regulatory proposals *de lege ferenda*[84]:

[83] Haraway, Donna (1988).

[84] Charlesworth, Hilary and Chinkin, Christine (2000).

[85] Campos Rubio, Arantza (2008).

[86] Bartlett, Katharine T (1990), pp. 849–863, and Campos Rubio, Arantza (2008), pp. 208–214.

- Women have been systematically excluded from the axioms to be protected by the IRL.
- They have been represented in a homogeneous manner, ignoring their diversity and perpetuating this homogenization also in jurisprudence.
- The subject 'women' has been conceptualized as a deviation from the norm, which is the subject 'men'.

The second component that Bartlett introduces is **feminist practical reasoning**. To counter the male perspective that affects IRL, Bartlett's feminist practical reasoning involves, as Campos Rubio puts it, 'broadening conventional notions of what is legally relevant, so that the legal decision-making process is more responsive to the particularities of a case that have not yet been addressed by legal doctrine'.[85] The aim is to prevent the practical aspects of daily life from being underestimated in favour of an abstract notion of justice.[86] Miguel Juan points out that by recognizing 'the importance of gender and women's experiences, the question arises as to what is the position of women and whether it is taken into consideration in universal norms and in the elaboration of social responses to these problems'.[87]

Finally, in accordance with the above reasoning, **consciousness-raising** arises, which implies a deep understanding of the extent to which legally accepted paradigms are truly valid. This principle seeks to generate knowledge through the study of common experiences and patterns that emerge from similar life stories. What was initially experienced as personal wounds suffered at the individual level is revealed as a collective experience of oppression, thus allowing to rectify errors and build more equitable paradigms of protection.[88] To identify, document and evaluate these wounds, 'awareness-raising' is based on a combination of methods: on the one hand, it will be necessary to resort to empirical qualitative legal research, as detailed in chapter 5. On the other hand, it is also necessary to resort to interdisciplinary research. In this case, a sociological approach is taken to understand the system of domination over 'the others', in our case study: the refugee women. Resort to statistics, furthermore, completes the picture as it substantiates in quantitative terms the magnitude of the absences presented in the classic literature on violence against refugee women. In the application of the feminist method to IRL scholarship, we extend this consciousness-raising to the gender-based violence experienced by refugee women as a reason for persecution absent in the letter of the Geneva Convention. It consists of generating a collective awareness of the legal elements that oppress women and others because of their gender, or, as Jiménez Sánchez mentions, it involves 'reconstructing (intellectually) society and the law with a gender perspective'.[89]

---

[87] Miguel Juan, Carmen (2016).

[88] Bartlett, Katharine (1990), pp. 863–867.

[89] Jiménez Sánchez, Carolina (2015), p. 6.

[90] Beyani, Chakola (1995), p. 29.

The Androcentrism of the Geneva Convention

The definition of 'refugee' according to the 1951 Geneva Convention (GC) relating to the Status of Refugees is androcentric. Neither sex nor gender is considered a defining element in the definition of a refugee. Chaloka Beyani, a prominent jurist and professor committed to making women and their experiences visible in refugee claims, points out that the category of sex is not included among the grounds of persecution under the GC. Despite the fact that in many other IHRL instruments sex is listed as a reason to prohibit discrimination, this oversight means, according to Beyani, that women's claims for protection from persecution related to their sex or gender can never be adequately addressed within the GC framework.[90] In addition, he stresses that the category of sex is also omitted as a ground for prohibition of discrimination against refugees under Article 3 of the GC. In his perspective, this creates a 'theoretical and practical gap' between the protection of refugees and the fulfilment of human rights, manifested in the lack of adaptation of the normative instrument to protect the human rights of refugees, especially female refugees.

In the historical study of the context in which the promulgation of the GC took place, Professor Arenas Hidalgo argues that in the drafting of the GC 'the liberal and Eurocentric paradigm in which the concept of refugee emerges was imposed'.[91] The representative of Yugoslavia, during the preparatory meetings for the Convention, suggested adding the word 'sex' to Article 3 of the GC, which prohibits discrimination on the basis of race, religion or country of origin. This proposal reflected an attempt to at least mention women in a context where they were still not given much attention. However, the proposal was rejected by UN High Commissioner Van Heuven Goedhart, who expressed doubts about the existence of cases of persecution based on the sex of the victims.[92]

The interpretation of this omission in the GC has highlighted how the IRL and its traditional doctrine adopt a masculine discourse that is considered neutral, which contributes to the reproduction of sexism as a system of domination within the universal regulation of refugees. This approach has led to the interpretive framework of the refugee definition being shaped by patriarchal structures, leading to the standardization and generalization of male refugee experiences to other refugee experiences.[93] Feminist legal scholarship supporting this position argues that the principles of objectivity, neutrality and impartiality underpinning the IRL have been

[91] Arenas Hidalgo, Nuria (2005), p. 77.

[92] UN High Commissioner for Refugees (UNHCR), The Refugee Convention, 1951: The *travaux préparatoires* analysed with a Commentary by Dr. Paul Weis, 1990, available at: https://www.refworld.org/docid/53e1dd114.html.

[93] Charlesworth, Hilary (1994), p. 60.

[94] Jiménez Sánchez, Carolina (2017), p.12, and Charlesworth, Hilary and Chinkin, Christine (2000), pp. 640–643.

[95] Musalo, Karen (2005), pp. 12–14.

[96] Miguel Juan, Carmen (2016), pp. 17–19.

developed from the predominant male perspective, which masks the alleged lack of universality or partiality of rights.[94]

As a result of the above, many human rights violations committed against women have not been identified as acts of persecution that would provide protection under refugee status.[95] This is also due in part to the way in which signatory states to the GC interpret the definition of a refugee, focusing on the male experience as a typical model. Miguel Juan adds that this paradigm has been based on the persecution of men in the public sphere by state agents, a model that does not fit the majority of the experiences of women, whose predominant persecution does not follow the same pattern. The author suggests that the problem with this interpretation lies in applying an egalitarian standard that does not take into account the specific characteristics of other groups that do not fit the male model. Miguel Juan proposes that the application of an 'egalitarian principle of difference' could address this bias by considering the particularities of the persecution faced by women.[96]

The Treatment of Refugee Women Under the IRL Doctrine

Refugee women have gone from being considered vulnerable subjects to being conceptualized as 'subordiscriminated' subjects in the IRL literature. Key to this evolution has been the introduction of FLTs.[97]

Women are in a position of greater vulnerability than men in situations such as leaving their countries of origin in search of refuge. Part of the international doctrine has approached the protection of women in the field of human rights, especially in the regulation of access to refuge, from a classic protectionist perspective. This has led to frame the protection of women in the belief that they are particularly vulnerable subjects. The vulnerability that has characterized women in the international normative sphere of the right to refuge derives from the conviction that they face specific problems in their search for international protection simply because they are women. Professor Martín Arribas identifies three main challenges that refugee women face: the sexual subjugation they suffer in a wide variety of manifestations, such as rape, sexual exploitation or forced prostitution; their particular needs linked to their female genital apparatus and reproductive capacity; and a whole set of responsibilities they carry out in domestic and educational spheres.[98] The 'specific problem' faced by women has been interpreted by more traditional doctrine as the 'particular set of circumstances that make them especially vulnerable to fear of persecution'. The author noted that while the problems and obstacles faced by refugees are similar, for women they are compounded by their gender, with additional challenges specific to their sex and gender. This consideration has become the

[97] Barrère Unzueta, María Ángeles (1997).

[98] Martín Arribas, Juan José (2000), pp. 98–99.

[99] Ibid.

[100] Indra, Doreen (1987), pp. 3–4.

[101] The sociology of gender plays a fundamental role in the practical application of this approach and will therefore be elaborated upon in Sect. 5.3, which explains the sources from which these borrowings are drawn and how to integrate them into feminist legal research.

basis for demanding, according to Professor Martín Arribas, 'specially differentiated treatment in the context of refugee status determination both for reasons of physical security and to break down systematic discrimination, as well as to avoid their sexual exploitation'.[99]

The feminist current, represented mainly by Professors Meijer in the Netherlands and Indra in Canada in the 1980s, has emphasized the importance of making 'refugees' visible on the international agenda. Indra highlights two crucial factors for contextualizing and understanding the particularities of women's refugee experiences.[100] The first factor is related to the different ways in which men and women relate to their state, according to gender sociology.[101] While men tend to occupy the public space and make decisions, women tend to make the private sphere of their homes their primary sphere. Indra highlights the public interpretation of the motives indicated by the GC, pointing out that this, together with the two factors she mentions, explains why resistance activities from every day and private spaces are not considered politico-public. On the other hand, Professor Meijer reflected on the social and sexual positioning of those seeking refugee protection and how this sexual status is reflected in the universal definition of a refugee person.[102] In the context of the October 2001 Global Consultations, the third expert roundtable was held in San Remo, where a number of issues were addressed, including gender-based persecution. As a result of this work, UNHCR published in 2002 its Guidelines on International Protection: Gender-Related Persecution in the Context of Article 1A(2) of the 1951 Convention relating to the Status of Refugees and/or its 1967 Protocol. Professor Santolaya Machetti, who participated in the UNHCR Global Consultations in San Remo in 2001, endorses the proposals of the feminist doctrine and goes a step further in delving into this issue by speaking of the need for 'an approach to the study of asylum law from the perspective of the sex or gender of the applicants, inasmuch as not only a significant percentage of them are women, but, above all, because they seem to present specific gender features that cannot be understood from the supposed gender neutrality of the GC categories with which we normally face the phenomenon of refugees'.[103]

These academic proposals mark a transformation in the perception of women refugees: from being considered as vulnerable subjects to being recognized as individuals with specific protection needs attributable to the 'gender' factor: 'most of the applications filed by women cannot be considered directly related to their gender; on the contrary, they are similar to those of men and are based on the same grounds of persecution provided for in the GC'.[104] This statement was accompanied by a precise observation on the need to always consider the applicant's status as a woman 'even when presenting allegations substantially identical to those of her male compatriots'. This approach seeks to overcome discrimination based on sex and

[102] Meijer, Marika (1985), p. 37.
[103] Santolaya Machetti, Pablo (2000), p. 583.
[104] Ibid, p. 568.

gender, and even through affirmative measures, to avoid the repetition of discriminatory treatment.

All these positions highlighted how the IRL doctrine has also adopted the apparently neutral male discourse and, therefore, falls into the reproduction of sexism as a system of domination within the interpretative sphere of refuge by protecting women refugees because they are considered 'especially vulnerable'. There is evidence of an effort on the part of academic research to overcome the discourse that naturalizes the vulnerabilities of women, seeking a social foundation for the oppressive power that places them in a position of subordination and discrimination. In this doctrinal evolution, it stands out how the FLTs contribute to leave aside the presumed intrinsic vulnerability of women, naming their specific experiences as gender violence, i.e., caused by a factor external to themselves.

5.2 A Feminist Approach to the CEDAW Committee's Decisions

An example of feminist legal approach to IHRL, Loveday Hodson's analysis[105] of the case *Alyne da Silva Pimentel Teixeira v Brasil*[106] allows us to delve into the practical application of a number of approaches identified above. In her 2020 chapter, Hodson provided a feminist critique of the decision taken by the CEDAW Committee (the UN treaty body that monitors the implementation of the Convention on the Elimination of All Forms of Discrimination Against Women) in the case of Alina da Silva Pimentel, a pregnant Afro-Brazilian woman who died as a result of inadequate reproductive health care. After a brief overview of feminist approaches in IHRL, the chapter moves on to illustrate the facts of the case under analysis, highlighting the different arguments brought forward by the author, the state, and the conclusions drawn by the Committee, with reference to the specific violations of the Convention.

After setting the stage, Hodson engages with the feminist critique of the decision in four steps, **combining different feminist approaches analysed above**. She first explains how the Committee used the technique of 'contextualisation' to change the narrative of the events that took place. Within contextualisation, she also looks at the extent to which the Committee adopts an intersectional analysis of the facts. Second, she examines the Committee's ability to identify and challenge dichotomous constructions embedded in the case. The chapter then widens the gaze to explore other cases in IHRL that deal with reproductive rights, with the aim to grasp the general trends in adjudicating these rights and how they are represented. The chapter closes with a more pragmatic consideration about the effects (and efficacy) of the Committee's decisions on both the individual rights of the claimant and the structural issues the case stems from.

In sum, the analysis proceeds as follows:

---

[105] Hodson, Loveday (2020).

[106] *Alyne da Silva Pimentel v Brasil*, CEDAW/C/49/D/17/2008 (27 September 2011).

1. Overview of feminist approaches to IHRL
2. Facts of the case under analysis
3. Feminist critique:
   a. Contextualisation
      i. Intersectional analysis
   b. Challenging gender dichotomies (or binaries)
   c. Challenging the public/private division in IHRL
   d. Effects (and efficacy) of the decision

Contextualisation

Hodson's analysis sets out with *contextualisation*, understood as a way of 'telling the story differently', by adopting equality, power and justice as lenses of her analysis. She looks at whether the Committee did or did not successfully contextualize the facts of the case. The result was positive, since the Committee was able to tell the story differently and shifted the narrative on maternal mortality from fatality or accident to an issue of human rights and social justice that could be prevented. As Hodson argued, the Committee's argumentative turn was made possible by recognising the role that inequalities based on poverty, race and gender played in exposing Alyne da Silva to poor obstetric care, which led to her death. Contextualisation, in this case, is described as the exercise to focus on the individual victim, while acknowledging the broad structural inequalities that exposed her to harm. The individual is seen through the lens of the vulnerable group she belongs to. Not as an isolated victim of misfortune, but as a person made vulnerable by inequalities of race, gender and class. Contextualisation also allowed the Committee to go beyond individual perpetrators, to grasp the institutional responsibilities and question how access to health care is hampered by structural and institutional barriers.

Contextualisation was made possible also thanks to the participation of non-governmental organizations (NGOs) in the procedure. NGOs provided evidence to locate the individual woman's situation within the broader picture of maternal deaths in Brazil. Such evidence was essential to challenge the government's narrative and bring forward a contextualized understanding of the facts.

Intersectional Analysis

Within contextualisation, attention to the intersectional perspective should also be paid. Hodson analyses this aspect of the Committee's approach, raising some concerns. 'Addressing the intersection of multiple discriminations points to structural causes', Hodson argues.[107] However, in this case, the Committee did not perform well in its intersectional analysis, as it should have recognised how race and gender interacted in her experience of neglect by the health care system. Because

[107] Hodson, Loveday (2020), p. 54.

[108] Templeton Dunn, Jennifer, Lesyna, Katherine and Zaret, Anna (2017).

she was a woman of African descent, her life was of lesser value, and this understanding underpinned and justified the treatment she received from the hospital ('she was left haemorrhaging and abandoned in the hallway for hours until she died a she was not considered worthy of priority in treatment').[108]

While intersectionality is key to correctly frame the facts of the case, Hodson clarifies the limits of this notion, which risks overshadowing the individuality and agency of Alyne by overemphasizing the role of structural inequalities in directing her destiny. Hodson maintains that a balance should be struck between these two dimensions.

Challenging Gender Dichotomies

A feminist approach to the arguments of judicial and quasi-judicial bodies requires engaging with the law's role in reproducing gender dichotomies (or binaries). In this case, Hodson critically analyses how the Committee frames reproduction and reproductive rights as 'sex-specific' rights, missing the social construction of reproduction. In particular, while the Committee recognises reproductive rights as human rights, it adopts an ambiguous approach when it comes to abortion. By taking a restrictive approach to abortion, and recognising the state a wider margin of appreciation, the Committee contributes to entrench gender inequalities. A feminist approach identifies and challenges the tension between women's autonomy vs state margin of appreciation. It asks what is behind this ambivalence, why the problem is framed in these terms, and what is the effect of such understanding on the construction of reproductive rights as human rights. If reproductive rights are human rights, why abortion is submitted to the state's appreciation? Why is abortion defended only in specific circumstances (rape, incest, threats to the life of the woman, etc.)? Why is women's autonomy not recognised regardless of the circumstances above? Beyond the discursive level, it asks what is the effect of this problem on women's lives.

In examining how reproductive rights are represented and adjudicated, the author looks beyond the practice of the CEDAW Committee and maps how other UN treaty bodies and regional courts address this issue. It locates the CEDAW's practice within the broad trends in human rights adjudication.

Challenging the Public/Private Division in IHRL

Feminist legal approaches are characterized by their expansion of state's positive obligations regarding issues that are generally framed as external or alien to the scope of IHRL, namely those belonging to the private sphere of sexuality, reproduction, family life, etc. In claiming the relevance of these matters, FLTs aim at dismantling the public/private division that impairs the protection of women's human rights. As it was exposed above, IHRL entrenches this division. By exposing

[109] Hodson, Loveday (2020), p. 61.

these underlying normative boundaries of IHRL, FLTs not only seek to challenge it, but also to change IHRL itself.

Effects (and Efficacy) of the Decision

Hodson argues that it is important for feminist approaches to ask about the individual and structural impact of a decision or judgment.[109] Namely, she asks what changes did the decision produce both for the individual victim who seeks redress, and at the level of the root causes of these human rights violations. The question is not only formal (e.g. about the practical implementation of the decision and the mechanisms to ensure compliance), it is substantive in nature. When adjudicating individual communications, upon the finding of a violation, the UN treaty bodies deliver recommendations to the defendant state, which can be more or less specific, therefore, offering guidance as to the concrete actions needed for the state to meet its obligations under the CEDAW Convention. Recommendations are therefore crucial to shape a state's positive obligations, but they also have an important diagnostic role. Acknowledging that a thorough and gender-aware diagnosis is crucial to formulate transformative solutions, a feminist approach must enquire the extent to which the recommendations correctly identify the issues in terms of power, inequality and justice. Moreover, the analysis should focus on what is left unproblematic, or silenced, and the structural causes that hinder women's access to reproductive health care.

5.3 Feminist Socio-Legal Approaches to International Law: The Example of Feminist Judgments in International Law

In this section, we analyse an example of 'feminist judgment projects' or, in other words, the feminist rewriting of key judgments of international courts as a feminist socio-legal approach and method to examine international law.

Socio-legal studies (also known as law and society studies or research) engage with diverse theoretical and methodological approaches, constituting a highly interdisciplinary area. They converse with other disciplines such as sociology, anthropology, psychology, politics, history, international relations, economics, philosophy, and cultural studies, among others.[110] The body of work that exists in this field makes it very difficult to define, so a broad understanding of socio-legal studies might be more suitable for a first introduction. Socio-legal studies have been defined as 'a way of seeing, of recognising the mutually constitutive relationship between law and society'[111] and as 'disciplines and subjects concerned with law as a social

[110] Feenan, Dermot (2013), and Creutzfeldt, Naomi et al. (2020).

[111] Creutzfeldt, Naomi et al. (2020), p. 4.

[112] Feenan, Dermot (2013), p. 4.

[113] Creutzfeldt, Naomi et al. (2020), p. 3.

[114] Ibid, p. 18.

institution'.[112] Socio-legal approaches have influenced legal scholarship, mainly challenging assumptions on the nature of law, legal thought, the relations between law and morality, religion, governments, and on legal institutions and culture.[113] They first emerged as a reaction to legal formalism and positivist approaches to law as the dominant paradigm in legal thought and practice. Today, they are a fluid and continuously evolving area of legal scholarship, and equally, they use a variety of methods.[114]

International law has also been analysed through the lenses of socio-legal approaches, resulting in a vast variety of research. An example of the long relationship between international law and socio-legal approaches is the early journal *International Journal of Law in Context* (1970) which was established as the first truly international law and society journal,[115] already more than fifty years ago.

When looking at feminist scholarship in law, much of it (though by no means all) has taken a socio-legal approach,[116] and it has been argued that feminist legal scholars have been those who have most prominently promoted sociological research on law, especially since the 1980s.[117] Feminist legal scholars have often been appealed by socio-legal approaches, due to their attention to how law both reflects (or fails to reflect) and constructs women's experiences of gendered lives, and their understanding of law as not being autonomous, but on the contrary, well entrenched in societal power dynamics, relations and structures.[118] Hunter divides the feminist socio-legal critique into two strands. The first strand criticizes the law's failure to recognize gender differences and women's lives and sees law as an institution that excludes women. The second strand criticizes the ways in which law's gender constructions produce limiting effects on women, drawing from post-modern scholarship which sees law as a discourse.[119] Both strands have applied to

[115] Ibid. Currently, Cambridge University Press edits the journal, and it presents itself as the journal providing 'a forum for interdisciplinary legal studies and offers intellectual space for ground-breaking critical research. It is not committed to any particular theory, ideology or methodology and invites papers from a variety of standpoints, ideologies, perspectives, and methods. It publishes contextual work about law and its relationship with other disciplines including but not limited to science, literature, humanities, philosophy, sociology, psychology, ethics, history and geography. The journal aims to explore and expand the boundaries of law and legal studies'. More information https://www.cambridge.org/core/journals/international-journal-of-law-in-context.

[116] Hunter, Rosemary (2020), p. 260.

[117] Baxi, Pratiksha (2008), p. 79.

[118] Hunter, Rosemary (2013), p. 205.

[119] Ibid. The feminist author Rosemary Hunter, interestingly examines a variety of socio-legal publications, showing 'a mixed picture when it comes to recognizing the socio of socio-legal studies as gendered and understanding the processes by which that gendering occurs', ibid., p. 218. That means that feminist socio-legal approaches are only one part of all the socio-legal work that is being done, leaving still a significant body of socio-legal contributions ignoring or refusing to acknowledge the gendered and intersectional nature of the 'social' they analyse.

[120] Hodson, Loveday and Lavers, Troy (2019).

[121] Berger, Linda et al. (2018).

feminist analysis of international law and have often used socio-legal methodologies, as shown in the following paragraphs.

One of the most prominent examples of feminist socio-legal approaches—and recent developments in legal methodology—is the so-called 'feminist judgments projects' or, the feminist rewriting of key judgments.[120] The first feminist judgment projects focused on national jurisdictions and mainly from common law countries (from Canada, England and Wales, Ireland and Northern Ireland, Australia, the USA, and New Zealand). However, the efforts to rewrite court decisions from a feminist standpoint have broadened to other national jurisdictions (for example, India, Mexico, and Argentina[121]) and to international and regional jurisdictions (for example, the International Court of Justice and Court of Justice of the European Union[122]). The majority of feminist judgments introduce well-constructed social frameworks and materials in order to place the case or its particular facts, as well as the legal issues involved, in a broader context.[123] Feminist legal scholars are well aware that incorporating social science research and common feminist knowledge about women's lives can significantly influence judicial decision-making in various ways,[124] and thus, feminist jurists have developed **methods for rewriting case-law** (judgments and other court decisions) from feminist perspectives.

Feminist judgment projects show their socio-legal character in various ways.[125] First, they understand judging as a socially engaged practice and point at the particular form of authoritative performance that writing as a judge involves.[126] Second, they connect with the social more broadly, because when a story needs to be told differently, it often requires the introduction of 'contextual' or 'social framework' material (see previous example in Sect. 5.2) to gain a full understanding—especially of the facts.[127] Following this approach will often call for challenging the facts that a court decided to take into account and finding new facts through socio-legal research in order to reveal new gendered dimensions that had been overlooked. Third, Feminist judgment projects unveil the institutional practices behind each judgment. This implies showing the judge as a relational subject who engages in conversations with others in a shared enterprise of production rather than as an

[122] McCall-Smith, Kasey et al. (2019), and Carneiro, Marta et al. (2019).

[123] Hunter, Rosemary (2013), p. 209.

[124] Ibid, p. 210.

[125] Ibid, pp. 264–267.

[126] Davies, Margaret (2012), p. 174.

[127] Hunter, Rosemary (2020), p. 265.

[128] Ibid, p. 266.

[129] Hodson, Loveday & Lavers, Troy (2019), p. 9.

[130] Besides Part I of the introduction and Part V of the conclusions, the book is divided into three more parts, each composed of several judgments rewritten by feminist international legal scholars. Part II focuses on 'General International Law' and it encompasses key judgments from the Permanent Court of International Justice, the International Court of Justice, and the Court of Justice of the European Union. Part III focuses on 'Human Rights' and includes feminist rewritings of well-known judgments of the European Court of Human Rights. Finally, Part IV focuses on

isolated thinker.[128] This applies especially to international law, where judgments of international courts are mainly written in a collective voice and the views of individual judges are not identified.[129]

Feminist judgment projects might be one the finest methodological contributions of FLTs to contemporary legal research today. In international law, the work of Hodson and Lavers *Feminist Judgements in International Law* (2019) constitutes a major contribution to the field of feminist approaches to this area of law. It encompasses no less than 15 individual and collective contributions analysing and undertaking in various forms the task of rewriting international judgments from feminist approaches.[130] In this work, the reflections and contributions on method are remarkable. Decision-making and writing in international case-law traditionally prioritises abstract logic and formal law.[131] Contrarily, the process of rewriting from feminist approaches involves bringing the facts and the laws to be applied to the ground.

On the other hand, the authors that have engaged in feminist case-law rewriting processes point at various practical challenges, such as revealing how power—including the author's own situatedness—shapes the research process, the knowledge formation and the judgment-writing itself.[132] Some of them even conclude that the very nature of writing and delivering a judgment might have several incompatibilities with feminist methodology.[133] For example, some felt uncomfortable about the fact that the nature of judgment-writing seems to look for a 'single truthful narrative'[134] or a 'singular and universal position'.[135]

Hodson and Lavers point out that they are part of a growing number of feminist scholars who aim to push the discipline in a new direction, and that in rewriting key international judgments, they have aimed to demonstrate possible alternatives to the structural inequalities of traditional international law in accessible and meaningful ways.[136] When looking at that contribution, all feminist judgments have been rewritten following a specific socio-legal methodology adapted to the international law field. Beyond the innovation of its international jurisdictional context, in this work authors have been encouraged to **adopt a reflexive instance and a collaborative approach**.

The first element, the reflexive instance, is presented in the last section of the structure under the title 'reflections' section. All feminist judgments follow the same structure, which is divided into three main parts. It begins with an 'Author's Note' to

'International Criminal Law', rewriting judgments from the Special Court for Sierra Leone, the International Criminal Court, and the International Criminal Tribunal for the Former Yugoslavia.

[131] Ibid, p. 6.

[132] Ibid, p. 9.

[133] Ibid, p. 9.

[134] Ibid, p. 9.

[135] Greenman, Kathryn and Lavers, Troy (2019), p. 114.

[136] Hodson, Loveday and Lavers, Troy (2019), p. 7.

introduce the key objectives and legal context and make the rewritten judgments accessible. This is followed by the rewritten judgment. The judgment is rewritten following the structure typically used by each court. After indicating the general information about the judgment (the name of the case and its code, the date, the name of the chamber and the judges…), the rewritten judgment often starts with the analysis of the facts, then focuses on the legal discussion (legal foundations) and then explains the court's conclusions. Finally, in the 'reflections' section, the authors gather their thoughts on the judgment-writing process and their experiences with the methodology.

This last part is particularly interesting due to its methodological particularities and the specific challenges it poses. In this section, some authors have chosen to answer a few key questions, for instance, 'How was the process of delivering a judgment experienced?' or 'What did the experience reveal about the structures and norms of international law?'.[137] For example, for Zoi and Yahyaoui, the experience of rewriting feminist judgments revealed various tensions about the international structures and norms, such as the ontological and political tensions existing between law and time and the scientific and political tensions existing between judging and doing historical work.[138] But, more generally, they highlight that the experience has made them realize that despite their resolutely feminist stance, the structures and norms of international law had quite a strong grasp on them, and thus, they acknowledge that they might have contributed albeit unwittingly to the perpetuation of norms and structures of the very international law they were attempting to transcend.[139] Other contributions, for example in Chinkin et al., the authors question whether law—and particularly, a judgment- can be feminist.[140] They concluded that it can be feminist but that it can only go so far, as going beyond would mean to go beyond the law itself in order to find satisfactory legal transformations.[141] Buckner et al. make also interesting observations when they reflect upon their experience rewriting a CEDAW Committee's decision.[142] They ask if CEDAW's decision was not already feminist, what sort of feminism is revealed and, in line with what has been mentioned in the previous section (Sect. 5.2), they reflect on the necessity to make intersectionality truly central to the decision. However, they note the difficulty of this endeavour: 'The very form of a legal decision constrained our ability to write about harms intersectionally. The fact that legal opinions –including CEDAW

[137]Zoi Aliozi, Bérénice K. Schramm and Yahyoui Krivenko Ekaterina (2019), pp 140–146, and Bengston, Sara; González-Salzberg, Damian; Hodson, Loveday and Johnson, Paul (2019), pp. 198–201.

[138]Zoi Aliozi, Bérénice K. Schramm and Yahyoui Krivenko Ekaterina (2019), p. 143.

[139]Ibid, p. 144.

[140]Chinkin, Christine; Heathcote, Gina; Jones, Emily and Jones, Henry (2019), pp. 48–49.

[141]Ibid.

[142]Buckner Inniss, Lolita; Hohmann, Jessie and Tramontana, Enzamaria (2019), pp. 365–368.

[143]Ibid, p. 366.

[144]Charlesworth, Hilary (2019), pp. 491–493.

views- are organised on an issue-by-issue analysis, that proceeds sequentially through the violation of each individual article of the relevant law, meant that the ability to write about the totalising effect of the operation of the law over an indigenous single woman subject to violence in the home, and unable to assert her legal rights before the courts, kept slipping from our grasp'.[143]

Additionally, considering that all these reflections show the contradictions, emotions, conflicts, and uncertainties of rewriting the judgments, Charlesworth notes that these act to 'destabilize the authoritative voice in which the judgments have typically been re-written'.[144]

The second element, the collaborative approach, is expressed in the fact that the judgments in Hodson and Lavers' work were written by chambers composed of two to four judges, as it was anticipated that this way of collective working would enable the authors/scholars to 'experience more closely the "real-world" nature of international judgment writing'.[145] Some authors offer some reflections on the collaborative process.[146] For some, working and writing the judgment collaboratively has 'developed with great ease'[147] or 'relatively smoothly'.[148] Others have worked out the reflection part individually in order to listen to each other's voices, also because they thought it was impossible to write in a sole voice in the judgment which they found so particularly challenging.[149]

Although, to some extent, Hodson and Laver's contribution touches on the question of what other differences would follow if gender parity were achieved in international courts' benches,[150] the work seeks to adopt feminist approaches to international law self-consciously, focusing on the content, processes, and results of undertaking feminist approaches beyond the author's gender. Four main conclusions arise from the analysis of the feminist rewritten judgments of Hodson and Laver's contribution. First, all of them have **widened the judicial lens**. They have resisted the abstract and relied on a greater range of (socio-legal) materials than the original judgments to build a fuller account of the background of the case.[151] Second,

[145] Hodson, Loveday and Lavers, Troy (2019), p. 9.

[146] For example, Hodson, Loveday and Lavers, Troy (2019), p. 112, and Zoi Aliozi, Bérénice K. Schramm and Yahyoui Krivenko Ekaterina (2019), pp. 140–141.

[147] Carneiro, Marta; Ketscher, Kristen and Semanda, Freya (2019), p. 166.

[148] Choudhry, Shazia and Herring, Jonathan (2019), p. 275.

[149] Alghrani, Amel; Ali Amal and Marshall, Jill (2019), pp. 226–230, and Zoi Aliozi, Bérénice K. Schramm and Yahyoui Krivenko Ekaterina (2019), pp. 142–146.

[150] To illustrate the lack of gender parity in international courts, in 2018 just three out of fifteen elected members of the Court of Justice were women, and that number has been the highest to date. Charlesworth notes that the presence of women judges has symbolic significance, and explains some of the challenges that feminist women judges face, e.g., if they use feminist ideas or vocabularies, they are faced with backlash stating that are biased and prejudiced against men or that they introduce unpredictability into the judicial process, Charlesworth, Hilary (2019), p. 485.

[151] Ibid, p. 486.

[152] Ibid, p. 489.

[153] Ibid, p. 491.

feminist judgments **have heard and accorded prominence to women's and other outsiders' voices**. Third, they have taken the **politics of law into account, expanding judicial agendas** and 'blurring the traditional separation of law from politics.[152] Fourth, and in line with what was mentioned before, **feminist judgments have unsettled the determinacy of law** by introducing reflections on the writing process. In some way, the author's diverse acknowledgments on the judging process have helped **redefine the nature of judging as one engaging emotions (like sympathy), as much as detached reasoning.**[153]

6 Optional Exercises

Exercise 1: FLTs on Academic Commentary and Research

As a practical exercise related to the application of FLTs to the analysis of academic commentary and research, we propose the literature developed in the field of International Humanitarian Law. This area of international law has been dealt with in a vast body of research that, in recent years, has undergone a feminist re-reading. The culminating moment of this trend was the approval by the United Nations Security Council of Resolution 1325, a key element of the 'Women, Peace and Security Agenda'.[154] In order to complete the exercise, we propose that you take the following steps:

1° **Selection of literature**. The first step is the selection of a piece of academic commentary on International Humanitarian Law. For the exercise to be more meaningful, try to find a piece of research that reflects classical views on the subject.

2° Secondly, apply to the piece chosen **Haraway**'s **theory of situated knowledge** discussed above**.** In the analysis of the selected texts, it will be important to gain knowledge of the context: e.g. who is the author (in terms of **social categories**—class, political orientations, national origin, culture, etc.); and in what **year** was the text written. This information will provide us with some knowledge about the position from which the work was produced.

3° Thirdly, we propose to apply the **feminist analysis of law** posing the three key questions to the text analysed (Sect. 3.1).

We suggest that you focus on gender assumptions and what is excluded or left outside of the piece analysed. The conclusions to this exercise will be useful later to compare them with examples of current research, elaborated after the approval of Resolution 1325 in 2000, and draw some further conclusions about the state and evolution of the discipline through time.

[154] UN Security Council Resolution 1325 (2000, October 31). On Women and Peace and Security (S/RES/1325). Retrieved from http://www.refworld.org/docid/3b00f4672e.html.

Exercise 2: FLTs on Judgements and Other Legal Decisions
To help researchers engage with FLTs in the analysis of legal reasoning in judgements and decisions of judicial and quasi-judicial bodies, this exercise proposes two types of activity: the problematisation and the re-writing of judgments. The reader can complete one or both of them.

The first step is the selection of the **case-law** that will be analysed. In the activities below, we propose some cases that can be used for the exercises. However, we encourage the reader to conduct their own case salection. For a general overview of how to approach case-law selection, it might be useful to have a look at different sources, like the series of posts on methodology published on the *Strasbourg Observers*'s blog.[155] Readers might also want to guide their selection based on existing academic literature, or the search for key words, and/or specific article violations on IHRL databases (e.g. HUDOC for the European Court of Human Rights, OHCHR Juris Database for decisions of the UNTBs, etc.). Not all databases allow for advanced search so it is always useful to check existing scholarly analysis to identify the most relevant and recent cases in any given field. Needless to say, case-law commentaries are also found in legal journals. Regarding women's rights, specialized repositories of judgements are usually compiled by NGOs and associations, for example, Women's Link Worldwide (WLW),[156] and the Women in Refugee Law Network (WiRL).[157]

Note that the **feminist legal methods** proposed can be also combined with **critical discourse analysis**, **deconstruction**, and **critical approaches to human rights law**.[158]

Option 1: Problematization One way of conducting a feminist analysis of judgements and extract hidden gendered assumptions from the arguments set forth is to use the approach of **problematization**. In this section, we use the set of questions that constitute the WPR approach ('What's the problem represented to be'), designed by Carol Bacchi.[159] This set of questions helps reveal the underlying assumptions behind the different parties involved in the trial, as well as the arguments developed by the courts to support their final decisions. The WPR approach asks how an issue is problematised and what are the effects of this problematization, what underlying assumptions are present, what is left unquestioned, and under which conditions such problematization emerged. WPR also urges

[155] Smet, Stjin (2015), Van den Eynde, Laura (2015) and Peroni, Lourdes (2015).

[156] On their webpage, there is a 'Gender justice observatory' with a list of relevant case law from different jurisdictions. https://www.womenslinkworldwide.org/en/gender-justice-observatory/court-rulings-database.

[157] The WiRL network has its own database: https://wirl.org.uk/database/?_type=case-law.

[158] Peroni, Lourdes (2015). See also chapters "Legal Method in the Context of Social Thought" and "Critical International Law" in this volume.

[159] Bacchi, Carol (2012a, 2012b).

the researcher to be mindful of their own inner assumptions, to avoid perpetuating biases in their way of looking at problems and doing research.

The case we propose for the judgment problematisation option is M.E.N. v Denmark (2013), of the CEDAW Committee.

CEDAW Committee, *M.E.N. v Denmark*, CEDAW/C/55/D/35/2011 (26 July 2013).

M.E.N. is a Burundian woman who claimed asylum in Denmark on grounds of gender-based persecution for her political affiliations. The Committee found she failed to substantiate her allegations for the admissibility of the case.

Questions:

- What is gender-based persecution represented to be in this case?
- What is the political action represented to be in this case?
- What are the gendered assumptions implicit in the representation of both issues? Look for binary representations, they indicate the presence of hidden assumptions.
- What is left unquestioned in the case? Look for the silences, the missing issues and the effects of such silences on the case. In doing so, remember to: ask the woman question

  Assume the perspective of the 'other', the perspective of M.E.N., as a way to unveil the partiality of the viewpoints presented as objective or 'true' in the judgment.[160]
- How has this representation of the 'problem' come about? Look for the broader context of doctrinal and judicial development. How is gender-related persecution shaped in IHRL, is it the same in other international jurisdictions? What is an alternative way of framing the issue that would take into account women's experiences?
- What effects are produced by this representation of the 'problem'? Beyond the effects on the individual applicant (e.g. being denied protection), what are the effects on women as a group, on their legal representation, and on the legal categories of gender-based persecution and political affiliation as grounds for asylum.
- How/where is this representation of the 'problem' produced, disseminated and defended? How could it be questioned, disrupted and replaced?
- What are the legal mechanisms that sustain this representation or the tools used to silence women's experiences?

[160] Martha Minow (1989) suggests engaging in a permanent assessment of hidden points of view.

Option 2: Re-writing Following the examples of the 'feminist judgment projects', rewrite one or more of the following international and European court's recent judgments:

- European Court of Justice: *CJ v. TGSS*. 24 February 2022 (C-389/20).
- European Court of Human Rights: *J.L. v Italy* 27 May 2021 (Application no 5671/16).
- ICC, Warrant of Arrest for Omar Hassan Ahmad Al Bashir in the case of The Prosecutor v. Omar Hassan Ahmad Al Bashir ('Omar Al Bashir'), March 4, 2009.

We encourage the reader to follow two steps in their re-writing process: (1) setting a feminist and intersectional approach; and (2) building a structure for the new/rewritten judgment. In the first part, a set of statements and questions are formulated.[161] In the second part, some structure examples are provided. These steps break down into smaller actions that are detailed below for the sake of clarity and support.

Setting a feminist and intersectional approach:

- Understand judging as a socially engaged practice. Writing as a judge involves a particular form of authoritative performance.
  1. How is judging perceived and developed in the society or community in which the court operates?
  2. Are there, and if so, what are the social, political, and economic... expectations of judging in that court and with regard to that case?
  3. What mechanisms does the judge use to perform its authority in the written judgment?[162]
- Connect with 'the social' more broadly.
  1. What sociological data and information are relevant to the case?
  2. Can the victim or subject/object of the judgment/decision be located within a larger social group or in relation to a particular social group? Does that information help understand the complexity of the issue to be resolved?
  3. What was the context?
- Unveil the institutional practices behind the judgment.
  1. Can the voices of the different judges be heard in the judgment/decision, or, on the contrary, do the judges need to debate and agree to one specific argumentation and conclusion or resolution to the case collectively?

---

[161] These questions constitute only some of many possible questions and formulations that could be applied to the judgment rewriting process from a feminist perspective. The field is vast and the options it offers are too many to be included in this exercise. We have selected this two-step structure for our proposal.

[162] About legal rhetoric in the construction of judgments, see chapter "Legal Method in the Context of Social Thought".

2. What other subjects and institutions might the judge or judges be in contact with when writing the sentence?
3. What is the process or what are the specific steps, the written or unwritten rules that the judge might have had to follow to write the judgment within that court?

Building a structure for the new/rewritten judgment:
The aim of adopting a structure for the new/rewritten judgment is to provide for both a 'reflexive instance' and a collaborative approach. Of course, different structures are possible for rewriting feminist judgements. Here are two examples:

- Hodson et al. (2019):

This is explained more extensively in Sect. 5.3.

1. Author's Note: it introduces the key objectives and the legal context, and makes the rewritten judgments accessible.
2. The rewritten judgment: it follows the traditional structure and form of the court's judgments but introduces feminist approaches in the judgment.
3. Reflections: in this part, the authors gather their thoughts on the judgment-writing process and their experiences with the methodology. They show the contradictions, emotions, conflicts, and uncertainties of rewriting the judgments that the authors have been through.

- Hunter et al. (2010)[163]:
    1. A 'commentary': It offers a short explanation on the original decision and some details of the original conflict, the contemporary reactions to the original judgment, and subsequent developments. It also incorporates some reflections on the feminist judgment that immediately follows.[164]
    2. The judgment: In this example, the authors attempt to mirror some judicial writing practices, language, and format style. For example, the font style, page layout, the changing practices of paragraph format, with or without numbers or headings, and the use or prohibition of footnotes. They also try to follow the writing customs of courtesy within the judiciary, such as, 'My noble and learned friends',[165] 'My Lords, I have had the advantage of reading'[166] and

[163]Note that the cases chosen in this book are significant decisions in English law across a broad range of substantive areas, and not international judgments. Hunter, Rosemary; McGlynn, Claire and Rackley, Erica (2010).

[164]Moran, Leslie J. (2012), p. 288.

[165]Hunter, Rosemary; McGlynn, Claire and Rackley, Erica (2010), p. 159.

[166]Ibid, p 338.

[167]Ibid, p 106.

[168]Rackley, Erika (2010), p 56.

'I must respectfully disagree'[167]. . .Rackley analyses in depth the 'art and craft of writing judgments' while making references to the various rewritten (feminist) judgments that are included in the work. One of the key issues is that 'judgments and judgment-writing retain a unique power and status', and thus, feminist judgment projects seek to harness and exploit those dimensions by putting feminist theory into judgment form.[168]

References

Alghrani, Amel, Ali, Amel, & Marshall, Jill (2019). Leyla Şahin v Turkey. In Hodson, Loveday & Lavers, Troy (Eds.), *Feminist judgements in international law* (pp. 203–230). Hart Publishing.

Anthias, Floya, & Yuval-Davis, Nira (1983). Contextualizing feminism: Gender, ethnic and class divisions. *Feminist Review, 15*, 62–75.

Anthias, Floya, & Yuval-Davis, Nira (1992). *Racialized boundaries: Race, nation, gender, colour and class and the anti-racist struggle*. Routledge.

Arenas Hidalgo, Nuria (2005) Mujeres refugiadas: entre el silencio jurídico y la aplicación de las perspectivas de género. Gallego Durán, Mar y García Guitiérrez, Rosa (Eds.), El legado plural de las mujeres Alfar, , pp 76-116

Bacchi, Carol (2012a). Introducing the 'What's the problem represented to be? Approach. In Bletsas, Angie & Beasley, Cris (Eds.), *Engaging with Carol Bacchi: Strategic interventions and exchanges* (pp. 21–24). The University of Adelaide Press.

Bacchi, Carol (2012b). Why study problematizations? Making politics visible. *Open Journal of Political Science, 2*(1). https://doi.org/10.4236/ojps.2012.21001

Banu, Roxana (2017). A relational feminist approach to conflict of laws. *Michigan Journal of Gender and Law, 24*, 1–52.

Barrère Unzueta, María Ángeles (1997). *Discriminación, Derecho antidiscriminatorio y acción positiva a favor de las mujeres*. Civitas.

Barrère Unzueta, María Ángeles (2014). *El Derecho Antidiscriminatorio y sus límites. Especial referencia a la perspectiva iusfeminista*. Grijley.

Bartlett, Katharine T (1990). Feminist legal methods. *Harvard Law Review, 103*, 829–888. https://doi.org/10.2307/1341478

Bartlett, Katharine T, & Kennedy, Rosanne (1991). *Feminist legal theory: Readings in law and gender*. Avalon Publishing.

Barrére Unzueta (2016) Maggy Derecho antidiscriminatorio, interseccionalidad y categorías sistémicas:análisis y propuestas con proyección legislativa, en La Barbera, MC. y Cruells, M. (coords.) Igualdad de género y no discriminación en España: evolución, problemas y perspectivas, Centro de Estudios Políticos y Constitucionales, Madrid, cap. 19, pp. 455–479.

Baxi, Pratiksha (2008). Feminist contributions to sociology of law: A review. *Economic and Political Weekly, 43*(43), 79–85.

Bello, Barbara Giovanna, & Mancini, Letizia (2016). Talking about intersectionality. Interview with Kimberlé W. Crenshaw. *Sociologia del Diritto, 2*, 11–21. https://doi.org/10.3280/sd2016-002002

Bengston, Sara, González-Salzberg, Damian, Hodson, Loveday, & Johnson, Paul (2019). Christine Goodwin v the United Kingdom. In Hodson, Loveday & Lavers, Troy (Eds.), *Feminist judgements in international law* (pp. 175–202). Hart Publishing.

Berger, Linda, Crawford, Bridjet J, & Stanchi Kathryn, M. (2018). Methods, impact, and reach of the global feminist judgments projects. *Oñati Socio-Legal Series, 8*(9), 1215–1223.

Beyani, Chaloka (1995). The needs of refugee women: A human-rights perspective. *Gender and Development, 3*(2), 29–35.

Bilge, Sirma (2010). Recent feminist outlooks on intersectionality. *Diogenes, 57*(1), 58–72. https://doi.org/10.1177/0392192110374245

Buckner Inniss, Lolita, Hohmann, Jessie, & Tramontana, Enzamaria (2019). Cecilia Kell v Canada. In Hodson, Loveday & Lavers, Troy (Eds.), *Feminist judgements in international law* (pp. 333–372). Hart Publishing.
Butler, Judith (1990). *Gender trouble: Feminism and the subversion of identity*. Routledge.
Campos Rubio, Arantxa (2008). Aportaciones iusfeministas a la revisión crítica del Derecho y a la experiencia jurídica. En Astola Madaragiaga, Jasone (Ed.) *Mujeres y Derecho. Pasado y presente* (pp 167–226). Universidad del País Vasco.
Carneiro, Marta, Ketscher, Kirsten, & Freya, Semanda (2019). Gómez-Limón Sánchez-Camacho v Instituto Nacional de la Seguridad Social (INSS) and others. In Hodson, Loveday & Lavers, Troy (Eds.), *Feminist judgements in international law* (pp. 149–174). Hart Publishing.
Charlesworth, Hilary. (1994). Women and international law. Australian Feminist Studies, 9(19), 115–128. https://doi.org/10.1080/08164649.1994.9994728
Charlesworth, Hilary (2019). Prefiguring feminist judgemnt in international law. In Hodson, Loveday & Lavers, Troy (Eds.), *Feminist judgements in international law* (pp. 479–494). Hart Publishing.
Charlesworth, Hilary, & Chinkin, Christine (2000). *The boundaries of international law: A feminist analysis*. Melland Schill Studies in International Law, Juris Publishing, Manchester University Press.
Chimni, Bhupinder S (2017). Feminist approaches to international law: The work of Hilary Charlesworth and Christine Chinkin. In *International law and world order: A critique of contemporary approaches* (2nd ed., pp. 358–439). Cambridge University Press.
Chinkin, Christine, Heathcote, Gina, Jones, Emily, & Jones, Henry (2019). Bozkurt Case, aka the Lotus Case (France v Turkey): Ships that go bump in the night. In Hodson, Loveday & Lavers, Troy (Eds.), *Feminist judgements in international law* (pp. 27–54). Hart Publishing.
Choudhry, Shazia, & Herring, Jonathan (2019). Opuz v Turkey. In Hodson, Loveday & Lavers, Troy (Eds.), *Feminist judgements in international law* (pp. 253–278). Hart Publishing.
Collins, Patricia Hill (1990). *Black feminist thought: Knowledge, consciousness and the politics of the women's movement*. Unwin Hyman.
Combahee River Collective ([1977] 1997) A Black feminist statement. In L. J. Nicholson (Ed.), The second wave: A reader in feminist theory. Routledge, , pp 63–70.
Conaghan, Joanne (2009). Intersectionality and the feminist project in law. In Grabham, Emily (Ed.), *Intersectionality and beyond, law, power and the politics of location*. Routledge.
Conaghan, Joanne (2013). *Law and gender*. Oxford University Press.
Costa, Malena (2016). *Feminismos Jurídicos*. Ediciones Didot.
Crenshaw, Kimberlé (1989). Demarginalizing the intersection of race and sex: A black feminist critique of antidiscrimination doctorine, feminist theory and antiracist politics. *The University of Chicago Legal Forum, 139*, 139–167.
Crenshaw, Kimberlé (1991). Mapping the margins: Intersectionality, identity politics, and violence against women of color. *Stanford Law Review, 43*, 1241–1299.
Creutzfeldt, Naomi, Mason, Marc, & Mcconnachie, Kirsten (2020). *Routledge handbook of socio-legal theory and methods*. Routledge.
Davies, Margaret (2012). The law becomes us: Rediscovering judgment. *Feminist Legal Studies, 20*, 167–181.
Davis, Angela (1981). *Women, race and class*. Random House.
Delphy ([1980] 2006) Christine. "The main enemy". Feminist Issues 1, 23–40. https://doi.org/10.1007/BF02685557; "Antisexisme ou antiracisme ? Un faux dilemme". Nouvelles Questions Féministes 2006/1 Vol. 25. pp. 59–83.
Delphy, Christine (2009). *L'ennemi principal: Tome 2*. Penser le genre.
Derrida, Jacques (1976). *Of grammatology*. Johns Hopkins University Press.
Eisentein, Zillah R. (1979). Developing a theory of capitalist patriarchy and socialist feminism. In Z. R. Eisenstein (Ed.), *Capitalist patriarchy*. Monthly Review Press.

Engle, Karen (2005). Liberal internationalism, feminism, and the suppression of critique: Contemporary approaches to global order in the United States. *Harvard International Law Journal, 46*(2) https://ssrn.com/abstract=2157483

Engle, Karen, Nesiah, Vasuki, & Otto, Dianne (2022). Feminist approaches to international law. In Dunoff, Jeffrey L & Pollack, Mark A (Eds.), *International legal theory: Foundations and frontiers* (pp. 174–196). Cambridge University Press.

Feenan, Dermot (2013). *Exploring the 'Socio' of socio-legal studies*. Palgrave McMillan.

Foucault, Michel (1991). *Discipline and punish. The birth of the prison*. Random House.

Garbay Mancheno, Sussy (2018). El rol del Derecho en la construcción de identidades de género: replanteando el análisis de género desde los aportes de la teoría crítica. *Foro Revista de Derecho, 29*, 1–20.

Gilligan, Carol (1982). *In a different voice*. Harvard University Press.

González Hauck (2024) Sué et al. Public International Law. A Multi-Perspective Approach, Routledge

Greenman, Kathryn, & Lavers, Troy (2019). The Lockerbie Case (Libyan Arab Jamahiriya v United States of America). In Loveday Hodson & Troy Lavers (Eds.), *Feminist judgments in international law* (pp. 83–116). Hart Publishing.

Guillaumin, Colette (1992). *Sexe, Race et Pratique du pouvoir*. Côté-femmes.

Halley, Janet, Kotiswaran, Prabha, Rebouché, Rachel, & Hila, Shamir (2018). *Governance feminism: An introduction*. University of Minnesota Press. https://doi.org/10.5749/j.ctt2121736

Haraway, Donna (1988). Situated knowledges: The science question in feminism and the privilege of partial accounts of perspective. *Feminist Studies, 14*, 575–599.

Hartmann, Heidi I (1978). The unhappy marriage of marxism and feminism: Towards a more progressive union. *Capital & Class, 2*(1), 1–33. https://doi.org/10.1177/030981687900800102

Hodson, Loveday (2020). A feminist approach to Alyne da Silva Pimentel Teixeira (deceased) v Brazil'. In Gonzalez-Salzberg, Damian & Hodson, Loveday (Eds.), *Research methods for international human rights law* (pp. 42–68). Routledge.

Hodson, Loveday, & Lavers, Troy (2019). *Feminist judgements in international law*. Hart Publishing.

Holtmaat, Rikki (2001). *Gender: An analytical concept that tackles the hidden structural bias of law* (pp. 159–182). Recht Richting Frauen, Beiträge Zur Feministischen Rechtswissenschaft.

Hull, Akasha Gloria, Bell-Scott, Patricia, & Smith, Barbara (1982). *All the women are white, all the blacks are men, but some of us are brave*. The Feminist Press at CUNY.

Hunter, Rosemary (2013). The gendered 'socio' of socio-legal studies. In Dermot, Feenan (Ed.), *Exploring the 'Socio' of socio-legal studies* (pp. 205–227). Palgrave McMillan.

Hunter, Rosemary (2020). Feminist approaches to socio-legal studies. In Creutzfeldt, Naomi, Mason, Marc, & Mcconnachie, Kirsten (Eds.), *Routledge handbook of socio-legal theory and methods* (pp. 260–272). Routledge.

Hunter, Rosemary, McGlynn, Clare, & Rackley, Erika (2010). *Feminist judgments: From theory to practice*. Hart Publishing.

Indra, Doreen (1987). Gender: A key dimension of the refugee experience. *Refugee: Canada's Journal on Refugees, 3*(6), 3–4.

Jiménez Sánchez, Carolina (2015). La perspectiva de genero en las investigaciones y la docencia del Derecho Internacional Público. *Revista Jurídica de Investigación e Innovación Educativa, 12*, 2–12.

Jiménez Sánchez, Carolina (2017). La persecución de género en el Derecho Internacional de los Refugiados: nuevas perspectivas. *Revista Electrónica de Estudios Internacionales, 33*.

Jones, Emily (2023). *Feminist theory and international law. Posthuman perspectives*. Routledge.

Kapur, Ratna (2002). The tragedy of victimization rhetoric: Resurrecting the "Native" subject in international/post-colonial feminist legal politics. *Harvard Human Rights Journal, 15*, 1–37.

Keyes, Mary (2019). Women in private international law. In Harris Rimmer, Susan & Ogg, Kate (Eds.), *Research handbook on feminist engagement with international law*. Edward Elgar.

Kurki, Milja (2015). Stretching situated knowledge: From standpoint epistemology to cosmology and back again. *Millennium, 43*(3), 779–797. https://doi.org/10.1177/0305829815583322
Lacey, Nicola (1998). *Unspeakable subjects: Feminist essays in legal and social theory*. Hart Publishing.
Lamas, Marta (2000). *Diferencias de sexo, género y diferencia sexual*. Cuicuilco 18. ISSN 1405-7778: https://www.redalyc.org/pdf/351/35101807.pdf
Levit, Nancy, Verchick, Robert M, & Minow, Martha (2006). *A primer feminist legal theory*. New York University Press.
Lugones, María (2008). Colonialidad y género. *Tabula Rasa: revista de humanidades, 9*, 73–102.
Lutz, Helma, Vivar, Herrera, Teresa, María, & Supik, Linda (2011). *Framing intersectionality. Debates on a multi-faceted concept in gender studies*. Ashgate.
Macaya Andrés, Laura (2013). *Esposas nefastas y otras aberraciones, El dispositivo jurídico como red de construcción de feminidad*. Diletants.
Mackinnon Catharine, A. (1982). Feminism, marxism, method, and the state: An agenda for theory. *Signs: Journal of Women in Culture and Society, 7*(3), 515–544.
Mackinnon Catharine, A. (1991a). Reflections on sex equality under law. *Yale Law Journal, 100*(5), 1281–1328.
Mackinnon Catharine, A. (1991b). From practice to theory, or what is a white woman anyway? *Yale Journal of Law and Feminism, 4*(3), 13–22.
Martín Arribas, Juan José (2000). *Los Estados Europeos frente al desafío de los Refugiados y el Derecho de Asilo*. Dykinson.
McCall-Smith, Kasey, Smith, Rhona, & Yahyaoui Krivenko, Ekaterina (2019). Reservations to the convention on the prevention and punishment of the crime genocide. In Hodson, Loveday & Lavers, Troy (Eds.), *Feminist judgements in international law* (pp. 55–82). Hart Publishing.
McKenna, Miriam, & Arvidsson, Matilda (2024). Gendering public and private international law: Transversal legal histories of the state, market, and the family through women's private property rights. *AJIL Unbound, 118*, 12.
Mcneilly, Kathryn (2019). Sex/gender is fluid, what now for feminism and international human rights law? A call to queer the foundations. In Haris Rimmes, Susan & OGG, Kate (Eds.), *Research handbook on feminist engagement with international law* (pp. 430–440). Edward Elgar Publishing.
Meijer, Marika (1985). Oppression of women and refugee status. A discussion paper. In *Proceedings of the international seminar on refugees*. Dutch Refugee Association.
Miguel Juan, Carmen (2016). *Refugiadas*. Una mirada feminista al Derecho Internacional.
Mikkola, Mari (2006). Elizabeth Spelman, gender realism, and women. *Hypatia, 21*(4), 77–96. https://doi.org/10.1111/j.1527-2001.2006.tb01129.x
Millett, Kate (1969). *Sexual politics*. University of Illinois Press.
Minda, Gary (1995). *Postmodern legal movements. Law and jurisprudence at century's end*. New York University Press.
Minow, Martha (1988). Feminist reason: Getting it and losing it. *Journal of Legal Education, 38*, 47–60.
Minow, Martha (1989). Beyond universality. *University of Chicago Legal Forum, 1*, 115–138.
Minow, Martha (1990). *Making all the difference: Inclusion, exclusion, and American law*. Cornell University Press.
Mohanty, Chandra Talpade (2013). Transnational feminist crossings: On neoliberalism and radical critique. *Signs: Journal of Women in Culture and Society, 38*(4). https://doi.org/10.1086/669576
Moran, Leslie J (2012). In Rosemary Hunter, Claire McGlynn, & Erica Rackley (Eds.), *Feminist judgments: From theory to practice*. Hart Publishing., 2010, 504. Modern Law Review, 75(2): 287–290. https://doi.org/10.1111/j.1468-2230.2012.00901.x
Mossman, Mary Jane (1992). Feminism and legal method: The difference it makes. *Australian Journal of Law and Society, 3*, 30–52.

Mouffe, Chantal (1992). Feminism, citizenship and radical democratic politicism. In J. Butler & J. W. Scott (Eds.), *Feminist theorize the political* (pp. 369–384). Routledge.
Musalo, Karen (2005). La Convención de 1951 sobre el Estatuto de Persona Refugiada y la protección de las mujeres frente a las violaciones de sus derechos fundamentales. *Revista de Derecho Migratorio y Extranjería, 8*, 9–22.
Nadal, Kevin (2017). *The SAGE encyclopedia of psychology and gender*. Sage Publishing.
Nesiah, Vasuki, & Katsoni, Spyridoula (2023). Chatting with Vasuki Nesiah. *Völkerrechtsblog, 17*(03), 2023. https://doi.org/10.17176/20230317-185039-0
Nobus, Dany (2017). *The law sustains desire* (pp. 87–97). Springer.
Otto, Dianne (2006). Lost in translation: Re-scripting the sexed subjects of international human rights law. In A. Orford (Ed.), *International law and its others* (pp. 318–356). Cambridge University Press.
Peroni, Lourdes (2015). Selecting analytical frameworks across disciplinary boundaries. *Strasbourg Observers*. https://strasbourgobservers.com/2015/09/02/selecting-analytical-frameworks-across-disciplinary-boundaries/
Rackley, Erica (2010). The art and craft of writing judgments: Notes on the feminist judgments project. In Hunter, Rosemary, McGlynn, Clare, & Rackley, Erika (Eds.), *Feminist judgments: From theory to practice* (pp. 44–56). Hart Publishing.
Rubin, Gayle (1975). The traffic in women: Notes on the "Political Economy" of sex. In Reitner, Rayna R (Ed.), *Toward an anthropology of women* (pp. 157–210). Monthly Review Press.
Santolaya Machetti, Pablo (2000). Derecho de asilo y persecución relacionada con el sexo. In *Mujer y Constitución en España* (pp. 561–593). Centro de Estudios Políticos y Constitucionales.
Selim Alkan, Yavuz (2012). Feminist legal methods: Theoretical assumptions, advantages, and potential problems Ankara law review. *University of Leicester School of Law Research Paper: 13–12, 9*(2), 83–97.
Smart, Carol (2000). La teoría feminista y el discurso jurídico. In H. Birgin, (Comp.). *El Derecho en el género y el género en el Derecho* (pp. 31–60). Biblos.
Smart, Carol (1992). The woman of legal discourse. *Social and Legal Studies, 1*, 29–44.
Smet, Stijn (2015, September 4). *Some thoughts on case law selection and why it is ok to make mistakes (as long as you learn from them)*. Strasbourg Observers. https://strasbourgobservers.com/2015/09/04/some-thoughts-on-case-law-selection-and-why-it-is-ok-to-make-mistakes-as-long-as-you-learn-from-them/
Spelman, Elizabeth (1988). *Inessential women*. Beacon Press.
Spivak, Gayatri Chakravorty (1988). *Can the subaltern speak?* MacMillan.
Templeton Dunn, Jennifer, Lesyna, Katherine, & Anna, Zaret (2017). *The role of human rights litigation in improving access to reproductive health care and achieving reductions in maternal mortality* (Vol. 17, p. 367). BMC Pregnancy and Childbirth.
Van den Eynde, Laura (2015). *Selecting landmark cases*. Strasbourg Observers. https://strasbourgobservers.com/2015/08/28/selecting-landmark-cases/
Vogel, Lise (1983). *Marxism and the oppression of women: Toward a unitary theory*. Rutgers University Press.
Walby, Sylvia (1990). *Theorizing patriarchy*. Blackwell.
Walby, Sylvia (2007). Complexity theory, systems theory, and multiple intersecting social inequalities. *Philosophy of the Social Sciences, 37*(4), 449–470. https://doi.org/10.1177/0048393107307663
Young, Iris Marion (1990). *Justice and the politics of difference*. Princeton University Press.
Zoi, Aliozi, Schramm, Bérénice K., & Yahyoui Krivenko, Ekaterina (2019). Germany v Italy. In L. Hodson & T. Lavers (Eds.), *Feminist judgements in international law* (pp. 117–146). Hart Publishing.

Third World Approaches to International Law (TWAIL)

Davinia Gómez Sánchez and Eduardo S. Arenas Catalán

Contents

We are a network of scholars engaged in international legal studies, and particularly interested in the challenges and opportunities facing 'third world' peoples in the new world order. We understand the historical scope and agenda of the dominant voice of international law scholarship as having participated in, and legitimated global processes of marginalization and domination that impact on the lives and struggles of third world peoples.

Members of this network may not agree on the content, direction and strategies of third world approaches to international law. Our network, however, is grounded in the united recognition that we need democratization of international legal scholarship in at least two senses: (i) first, we need to context international law's privileging of European and North American voices by providing institutional and imaginative opportunities for participation from the third world; and (ii) second, we need to formulate a substantive critique of the

D. Gómez Sánchez (✉)
University of Deusto, Pedro Arrupe Institute of Human Rights, Bilbao, Spain
e-mail: davinia.gomsan@deusto.es

E. S. Arenas Catalán
Open University of the Netherlands, Faculty of Law, Heerlen, The Netherlands
e-mail: eduardo.arenascatalan@ou.nl

J. J. Garcia Blesa (ed.), *Contemporary Methods in International Legal Research*, Springer Textbooks in Law, https://doi.org/10.1007/978-3-031-69522-3_6

politics and scholarship of mainstream international law to the extent that it has helped reproduce structures that marginalize and dominate third world peoples.

Thus we are crucially interested in formulating and disseminating critical approaches to the relationships of power that constitute, and are constituted by, the current world order. In addition, we appreciate the need to understand and engage previous and prevailing trends in third world scholarship in international law.

To realize this vision, this network commits itself to the promotion of constructive dialogue among international scholars from diverse regions of the third world.[1]

1 Introduction

This chapter engages with Third World Approaches to International Law (TWAIL) as a diverse critical movement that aims at rethinking and democratising international legal scholarship. TWAIL, as a 'subaltern epistemic location',[2] contributes to rethinking the current model of International Law by challenging the Eurocentric paradigm and the coloniality of international law in order to redefine it within the context of modern colonialism and contemporary neo-colonialism.[3]

In line with the features outlined in the network's vision above, the following elements can be highlighted as the central features of TWAIL. Firstly, it is a scholarly network and a political project; a reactive and proactive intellectual and political movement. Reactive in that 'it responds to international law as an imperial project,'and proactive due to its transformative ambitions.[4] This 'scholarly enterprise and scholarship as political'[5] is connected to praxis, understood 'as reflection, agitation and transformative action'.[6] Secondly, TWAIL is guided by a historical approach to international law that rejects Eurocentric accounts and that seeks to formulate an alternative global history of international law placing imperialism at the centre. It connects and engages with earlier work in a critical way, including with TWAIL itself. This global historical perspective explores international law's patterns

[1] 'Vision Statement' of the Third World Association of International Law. Document circulated at the first TWAIL conference entitled 'New Approaches to Third World Legal Studies' which took place at Harvard Law School in March 1997.

[2] Kapur (2023), p. 775.

[3] Barreto (2018). For Martin Chanock '[t]he law was the cutting edge of colonialism, an instrument of the power of an alien state and part of the process of coercion. And it also came to be a new way of conceptualizing relationships and powers and a weapon within African communities which were undergoing basic economic changes, many of which were interpreted and fought over by those involved in moral terms', in Merry (2003), p. 572.

[4] Mutua and Anghie (2000), p. 31.

[5] Mickelson (2008).

[6] Sujith et al. (2016), p. VI. Praxis was the overarching theme of the TWAIL conference held Cairo in 2015.

of power and subordination seeking to overcome its Eurocentric bias.[7] Thirdly, its primary focus is on Third World peoples, their marginalisation and oppression.

Consequently, TWAIL puts the emphasis on a dialogue across cultures and on the incorporation of third world voices, in order to democratise international legal scholarship. Although many authors who can be identified as TWAIL scholars are based in the North (European and North American universities), there is undoubtedly a growing contribution from other sites of knowledge, including the geographical Third World. This ‘constructive dialogue’ therefore involves innovative work from scholars from different regions that incorporates voices from the excluded and dominated Third World, while restoring the thinking of pioneering intellectuals. However, as a type of international legal scholarship connected to the Third World, Professor Karin Mickelson claims that ‘TWAIL should be seen as a part of a Third World tradition of international law scholarship rather than the overarching framework into which all Third World scholarship can be fit’.[8] It is therefore not assumed that any scholarship coming from the Third World embodies a ‘Third World approach.’

Although it is not easy to demarcate TWAIL, following Kenyan critical scholar and professor Makau wa Mutua, Third World approaches can be traced back to the decolonisation period, to the confrontation between North and South and the anticolonial movement. He situates the Bandung Conference in 1955 as its symbolic birthplace, since it aspired at presenting a reformed world order, a new vision articulating an anti-colonial global system.[9]

However, TWAIL as an approach to the discipline of international law and a network of critical scholars emerged in the mid-late 1990s. It developed from a group of graduate students and visiting scholars at Harvard Law School[10] who were interested in law, development, critical race theory and postcolonialism. This subgenre of international legal scholarship aimed at questioning ‘colonial history, power, identity and difference, and what these mean for international law’.[11] Accounting for the consequences and impact of international law on the Third World, its peoples and aspects of global injustice and poverty: ‘TWAIL draws attention to how injustice is enabled and structured through law and its institutions, not only in local and domestic arenas but transnationally and globally’.[12]

---

[7] Mohammed Bedjaoui refers to the ‘poverty of international law’, that extends to its indifference towards human suffering, of which international law is complicit.

[8] Mickelson (2008), p. 362.

[9] For an exploration of the significance of Bandung for global history and international law see Eslava et al. (2017).

[10] Celestine Nyamu, Balakrishnan Rajagopal, Hani Sayed, Vasuki Nesiah, Elchi Nowrojee, Bhupinder Chimni, James Thuo Gathii with the support of Prof. David Kennedy, Jorge Esquirol, Antony Anghie and Makau wa Mutua among others involved who participated in the initial 1997 conference referred above.

[11] Gathii (2011), p. 27.

[12] Natarajan et al. (2020), p. 7.

In spite of the central features that guide TWAIL, there is neither a TWAIL canon nor a leading authority.[13] TWAIL is defined by a core of common interests, shared concerns and commitments. As such, it permits a diversity of voices, who align themselves with TWAIL precepts, to be part and to contribute to this project aimed at challenging power and knowledge hierarchies. Besides, and resulting from TWAIL not being a uniform approach or perspective, different scholars under this label can be identified as either reconstructionist or oppositional in their views on international law (conservative or reformist rather than revolutionary).[14] However, this lack of central authority or canon also prevents a more precise program or specific prescriptions for the reformative purposes that TWAIL claims to pursue. Furthermore, such vagueness or obscurity poses the risk of opening up to ideological positionings which may not be sufficiently substantiated.

TWAIL scholars (or TWAILers), share the ethical commitment to cross-examine the relationship between international law, global wealth and poverty.[15] As an anti-hegemonic approach to international law, TWAIL scholars' concerns and questions cover a broad range of topics, while seeking to explore the role of international law and policy in legitimising and maintaining unequal structures and a global unjust order stemming from the colonial and imperial legacies. TWAIL is therefore an expanding approach with evolving agendas enriched by a growing network and plural and dispersed scholarly production that draws from a wide range of areas within international law, namely: environmental law, carbon colonialism, international financial system and institutions, property law, foreign investment, corporations, labour law, human rights, migration and so forth. In doing so, TWAILers engage with international law in a dual way, as resistance and as transformation,[16] the reactive and proactive attitude introduced above. This duality is connected and dependent on authors' understanding of justice, the universal and the normativity governing the international realm. This ambivalent engagement enables to embrace deconstructive, constructive and reconstructive efforts and perspectives that reveal the contingency of international law. It also highlights both the potential as well as the limits of international law for those states which share a common history of colonialism. TWAILers are determined to use a reformed

[13] According to Mutua, TWAIL is antihierarchical, counterhegemonic, suspicious of universal creeds, a coalitionary movement.

[14] Following Ratna Kapur, its revolutionary strand 'draws inspiration from critical race theory, post-colonial feminism, decoloniality and the subaltern studies project,'dependency theory, Marxism, critical development studies.

[15] Quoting Canadian Professor Obiora Chinedu Okafor, they 'are solidly united by a shared ethical commitment to the intellectual and practical struggle to expose, reform, or even retrench those features of the international legal system that help create or maintain the generally unequal, unfair, or unjust global order' Okafor (2005), p. 177.

[16] Eslava and Pahuja (2011). These authors, in their taxonomy of attitudes towards international law, distinguish between conservative, reformists and revolutionary stances.

international law to further the interests of the Third World, and seek to de-silence marginalised voices 'within the *dominant discourses* of international law'.[17]

It is on the basis of these shared commitments, unifying objectives and core ideas, that TWAIL—despite its not being a 'monolithic epistemic community'—can be conceived as a theory, 'a chorus of voices'.[18] Thus, TWAIL offers a set of ideas for the study of international law whose internal diversity and richness does not imply incoherence or lack of articulation.

The term 'Third World' is used in TWAIL as an analytical category to evince the divide between the West and the rest as well as the lasting disparities between the North and the South. TWAIL adheres to this terminology of Third World 'as a counter-hegemonic discursive tool that allows us to interrogate and contest the various ways in which power is used'.[19] The Third World has been conceptualised as a political reality and a historical phenomenon.[20] The reference to the Third World is conceived to cluster a number of non-European states with similar historical experiences that, despite their diversity, resulted in a consciousness of resistance and liberation. It is therefore constructed in opposition to First World states involved in hegemonic and domination practices, pointing at a distinction that is still relevant today.[21]

Despite and against claims of fetishization,[22] essentialisation of identities and homogenisation of plurality, the strategic and intentional use of the label Third World is maintained cognisant of the shifting alliances, acknowledging the inequalities and imbalances within the South, as well as the existence of similar patterns that are currently present in the North. However, some scholars also use related terms such as South and Global South to mark this dichotomy.

In consequence, 'Third World' is not only used to designate a geographical-political space[23] but a reality defined by the experience of crisis derived from 'colonial, imperial and neo-colonial policies'.[24] It is mostly used to refer to non-European populations (the periphery) in contradistinction to European ones (the core), in that it carries with it the confrontation between Western hegemony (and other forms of empire) and the rest of the world. However, TWAIL scholars 'have increasingly redefined the content of the "periphery" beyond geographic or

[17] Gathii (2011), p. 35, emphasis added.

[18] Mickelson (1998), p. 360.

[19] Rajagopal (1999), p. 19.

[20] A political reality that 'describes a set of geographic, oppositional, and political realities that distinguish it from the West... it correctly captures the oppositional dialectic between the European and the non-European' Mutua and Anghie (2000), p. 35.

[21] Anghie (2023). 'Its very contingency, involving an insistence on history and continuity, may in fact be one of its strengths' Mickelson (1998), p. 360.

[22] 'fetishization of alterity' Dalglish (2018).

[23] Third world is used in a decentred manner from its geographic location, 'to focus on the various levels at which power operates to subjugate us and to engage in oppositional practices that challenge those power structures and flows' Rajagopal (1999), p. 3.

[24] Sujith et al. (2016), p. IX.

racial affiliations'.[25] Following Mickelson, the idea of the Third World would nowadays embrace groups such as women[26] and indigenous peoples.[27] Perhaps other collectives or entities (also political ones), who have undergone similar experiences of marginalisation and subjugation historically, could be further included as well.

1.1 Main Contributions and Shared Characteristics

The following develops the themes and views addressed by TWAIL.[28] Primarily, TWAIL distances itself from Eurocentric approaches to international law, also in relation to knowledge production. TWAIL challenges dominant narratives through the incorporation of a variety of approaches,[29] disciplines and features (class, economics, ethnicity, gender,[30] race,[31] sex…). Along with such standpoint, the colonial encounter, colonialism and neo-colonialism are key aspects for the study of international law. TWAIL explores the colonial origin and legacy of the international legal order, an allegedly neutral, non-political and objective regime. It focuses on the political economy of imperialism and the connection between old and modern forms of domination through a sophisticated look at the relationship between Third and First worlds. They do so by introducing 'under-represented and alternative knowledge about international law'[32] to confront the underlying structures of extant unequal relations.

Furthermore, TWAIL connects international law with dominant ideas and power relations (being them cultural, economic, military, or political power, which reproduce former settler-colonial relations of exploitation), together with the effects of displacing national legal systems. In doing so they reveal the lasting effects of patterns of dominance and underscore the imperialist traits of international law. TWAIL also explores the colonial origins and continuities of new legal technologies

---

25 Haskell (2014), p. 399.

26 See Fagbongbe (2008), on third world feminism Nesiah (2003), also in the collection of essays edited by Anghie et al. (2003), Nesiah (2022), Nesiah (2023), 'Borderline Jurisprudence' podcast.

27 In what has been termed as Fourth World Approaches to International Law (FWAIL), see Fukurai (2018).

28 For an extensive, even though not exhaustive account of the plurality of issues tackled by TWAIL scholars, see Anghie (2023).

29 'The approaches within TWAIL include critical, feminist, post-modern, Lat-Crit Theory (Latina and Latina Critical Theory Inc.), postcolonial theory, literary theory, modernist, Marxist, critical race theory and so on.' Gathii (2011), p. 37.

30 See Engle et al. (2021) feminist approaches international law.

31 'The ascendancy of Eurocentrism was and is contingent on anti-Blackness'(Adébísí 2023, p. 18). Ideas connected to civilisation, development and race gave rise to and supported the divide between us and the other/s, further sustaining the situation of domination and the expansion of a certain cultural universe.

32 Gathii (2011), p. 38.

(related to commerce and war, for example) that might deploy the same disempowering effects and hierarchisation.

TWAIL pursues the goal of achieving global justice. This aspiration stems from a dire rejection to the unjust global order and its effects in cultural, economic, legal, social and political spheres. A fair world that could not be achieved furthering capitalism. 'TWAIL scholars believe in the transformative potential of international law and in the ideal of law as a means of constraining power',[33] thus presenting counter-narratives to the history of international law. It is for these reasons, and on account of TWAIL's key themes and concerns, that TWAIL is also relevant for the First World, leading professor Anghie to consider it a cosmopolitan project.[34]

Although the emphasis within TWAIL is on the commonalities and interconnectedness of the ideas, priorities and concerns outlined above, different generations of TWAIL have marked the evolution of this intellectual movement. This classification refers to different periods distinguishing between phases and generations within TWAIL, thus, highlighting commonalities and connections, but also differences in answers and perspectives.

TWAIL I or first-generation scholars (1950s–1970s)[35] took a 'non-rejectionist' stance on international law. Under the conviction that international law was not an alien concept for non-European states, TWAIL scholars were confident about the opportunities that the international legal regime could provide for Southern states in their struggles towards emancipation invoking, for instance, the importance of principles such as non-intervention and equal sovereignty of states. They had trust in the United Nations system for transforming international law by means of the incorporation of recently independent countries, turning international law into a more democratic and participatory system. TWAIL I remained hopeful that international law could be amended in practice by getting rid of its colonial traits. In order to redeem this legal order, they looked at aspects such as the role of international law in legitimating oppression upon Third World peoples. Neo-colonialism and a critique of legal imperialism were at the centre of their critical analysis, and the need for a new international economic order to enable the complete liberation of former colonies were at the top of their agenda.

On the basis of the limitations encountered despite the efforts of previous scholars, a new generation continued their task and explored further theoretical

---

[33] Anghie and Chimni (2003), p. 101.

[34] Anghie (2023). 'TWAIL scholars argue that the realization of the (forever) incompleteness of international law's cosmopolitan project is itself the emancipatory core of the discipline that allows marginalized voices to assert their aspirations and needs on the global terrain and keeps international law attuned to the realities "on the ground"', Haskell (2014), p. 401.

[35] Including Third World jurists Georges Abi-Saab (Egypt), Ram Prakash Anand (India), M. Sornarajah (Sri Lanka), Justice Radhabinod Pal (India), Jacob Johannes Gustaaf Syatauw (Indonesia), F. Garcia-Amador (Cuba), Mohammed Bedjaoui (Algeria), Kéba Mbaye (Senegal), and Taslim O. Elias (Nigeria).

concerns that had emerged along this contestation. TWAIL II[36] questioned international law focusing on the need to reimagine and reform it in view of lasting power asymmetries. These scholars concentrated on the inadequacies of the international order of the time, driven by the specific context in the 90s, the liberal order and the centrality of ideas and values upon which different aspects of the international legal regime were founded.[37] Exploring major areas of international law, namely: economic integration, environmental governance, human rights, international criminal law, foreign investment law, trade regulations and regimes, and so forth.

Their analysis delved into the post-colonial states, with due consideration of development and nation-building projects. This critical examination resulted in powerful appraisals of third world states, the well-being of third world peoples and their lived experiences (including indigenous, minorities, women, workers and the most disadvantaged).[38] They focused on the production of knowledge on international law and the value of contributions from non-western cultures, systems and traditions in order to expand international law.

Theoretical work delved into the foundations of international law: colonialism and imperialism in their different forms and locations were addressed as central to international law, not as a peripheral question. Also the importance of international economic relations within international law was studied. TWAIL research further examined international law's defining characteristics. They focused on concepts, discourses, doctrines and institutions that were shaped and framed as a result of the colonial asymmetry. Aspects such as the central role of the state within international law was questioned. TWAIL studies highlighted how the idea of sovereignty acquired its meaning through the colonial encounter. In addition, other key categories were critically examined, in particular, how they emerged to respond to the situation created by imperialism, enabling its advancement.[39] Together with the idea of sovereignty and state centrism, other elements such as power, global governance and global institutions were critically scrutinised, leading to a solid theoretical apparatus that is central to TWAIL analysis.

The concept of the 'civilising mission'[40] guides the analytical framework used by these scholars in order to understand and explain the role of international law in

[36] Some of the scholars who are placed under this category (voluntarily or by reference) are involved in the online publication TWAIL Review (Anonymous), created in 2020 and dedicated to furthering, amplifying and consolidating TWAIL's aims and community.

[37] The Rule of Law, the individual, markets and their importance, deregulation, etc.

[38] On the possibilities for participation of these voices in the international law scenario, see Otto (1996).

[39] Ideas such as sovereign 'equality' of states, good governance, world peace, the use of force, the responsibility to protect, humanitarianism.

[40] One of the driving forces behind the imperial project: 'the civilising mission, the grand project that has justified colonialism as a means of redeeming the backward, aberrant, violent, oppressed, undeveloped people of the non-European world by incorporating them into the universal civilisation of Europe' Anghie (2007), p. 3). See Tzouvala (2020) on the 'standard of civilisation' in international law 'as a mode of international legal argumentation.'

suppressing third world peoples. The construction of 'the Other' and its rejection justified their exploitation as well as interventions aimed at transforming them. Through the decolonisation process, the gaining of independence of former colonies ascribed their self-determination in the form of nation states to obtain international legal personality. This formal equality of nation-states (a centralised administrative state as the subject of international law) was further connected to the liberal idea of separation between law and politics as well as politics and economics. International law and its institutions functioned as the framework that facilitated private property rights, free markets, trade and formal sovereign equality (rather than other models of economic, political and social organisation).

The categorisation just explained is disputed by some scholars who argue that this periodisation implies a linear conception of TWAIL's foundations and roots and further points at a gradual progression within TWAIL.[41] Despite these reservations, there are voices who claim an emerging TWAIL III consisting of younger scholars who are exploring other forms of imperialism 'semi-colonialism, settler colonialism, slavery, non-European versions of imperialism'.[42]

1.2 Locating TWAIL Within Critical Theories and Critical Legal Studies

As elaborated in the previous section, TWAIL implies an epistemological critical inquiry aimed at articulating reform proposals in the international legal order. In contrast to mainstream international legal scholarship (MILS),[43] TWAIL represents a critical approach aimed at deconstructing universal truths and transforming structures of domination and power. As such, TWAIL can be classified within anti-colonial theories, having in common with them several aspects.[44] They emerged in the twentieth century upon realisation that despite colonialism had ended as a political historical entity, it continued shaping relations and social imaginaries. Anti-colonial theories focused their attention on the consequences of European colonialism, considering the lingering effects of the colonial project and colonialism as an essential factor for understanding contemporary societies. At the margins of the

[41] Mickelson (2008).

[42] Anghie (2023), p. 107.

[43] 'At the heart of the MILS conception of international law is a sanitized universal framework of transnational legal regulation. MILS is infatuated with a legalist-cum-positivist mystique that strips international law of the global social imbalances that characterize the modern world, reducing it to a pedantic system of rules and norms. As a result, MILS adherents focus much on international treaties, judicial bodies, customary norms, and other embodiments of international legal formalism and little on the legitimacy of the corpus (which is presumed) or on the power that informs it (which is ignored)', al Attar and Tava (2010), p. 21.

[44] In broad term they differ in their respective intellectual and geopolitical traditions, as well as in relation to the authors they build on. Also, regarding the disciplines of study on which they focus, their geographic scope of analysis and in how they relate the social context and knowledge.

academic and political spectrum, and disillusioned with the processes of independence, they question the universality of Western-centred ideas and epistemic canons. Their deep knowledge of Eurocentric thinking was deployed as a tool of analysis as well as an instrument for political action to expose the provincialism of 'universal Eurocentric modernity' and its impact on the social, economic, political and cultural domains after independence.

Growing from those bases—the indeterminacy of international law and its bias favouring the global North, TWAIL's engagement with the colonial legacies of international law is informed by critical legal history and political economy. However, TWAIL overcomes the disconnection from reality of other critical approaches, apprehending the materiality of international law inserted in every day's practices (institutions, procedures, sites, shaping norms, subjects and so forth).[45] As a result, it stresses further the connections between the heterogenous array of phenomena that regulate life (cultural, economic, political) that are embedded in and influenced by international law.

Connected to the centrality given to the relationship between the construction of the Other and the assertion of the West (that defines itself by reference to it), TWAIL traces a 'genealogy of the modern subject that includes colonialism and slavery'.[46] TWAIL's critical historical approach going back five hundred years, re-reads the past through the gaze of the subaltern subject. In this way, it surpasses the theoretical narcissism that, according to Broeck,[47] characterises other critical theories. In addition, and stemming from the penetration of postcolonial approaches into critical studies of international law, the centrality of coloniality[48] is further expanded to engage with critical scholarship on class, caste, gender and race, as modes of domination.

Besides adopting this historical perspective, TWAIL scholars have undergone ethno-sociological analysis to dissect the dynamics of power within a given context,[49] as well as in relation to a plurality of actors (thus, not limited to the state). Although international law is still nowadays in hands of and driven by states, TWAIL challenges this traditional unit of analysis. It brings into the study Third World actors and communities, international institutions and new political units apart from the state form. In alignment with this and for an expansive take of international law,[50] it proposes the method of legal ethnography of international

[45] 'A specific kind of material practice, a practice which 'creates' and 'takes place' through the very materiality of the world' Eslava and Pahuja (2011), p. 109.

[46] Barreto (2013), p. 27.

[47] Preventing them from connecting the modern subject to colonialism and slavery, ibid.

[48] Understood as the lasting patterns of power that emerged as a result of colonialism and that survived that process of appropriation, control, subjugation and exploitation by force.

[49] Context: 'for us context means North-South relations and the civilizing mission that often structures these relations' Anghie and Chimni (2003), p. 89, together with the various complex economic, historical, political and social circumstances.

[50] Eslava and Pahuja (2011).

law's sites of practice, as well as covering what they refer to as 'new jurisdictions'.[51] They suggest embracing these fields of practice given the many jurisdictional forms where the international order unfolds nowadays (although these areas might appear unrelated to the international, more as bureaucratic, technical or commercial).

1.3 Methodology or Theory?

Although, above all, TWAIL is considered a 'political project',[52] it can be treated as a school of thought, a 'scholarly project', a field of study or a body of methods for international legal analysis. This section will reflect upon the question of whether TWAIL is a theory of international law or a methodology for the study of this discipline, as suggested by the title of this chapter.

As a theoretical framework, TWAIL can be seen as a discipline that provides the explanatory framework to support the study of international law. However, it can also be approached as a methodology, as an analytical tool including procedures, methods and research techniques that can help to interpret, understand and identify underlying principles and their impact in the discipline.

Obiora Okafor responds to this query concluding that TWAIL is a broad approach which offers both theory and method.[53] He tests TWAIL as a theory against the elements of his working definition of theory. Firstly, it is a description of a social phenomenon (international law, its institutions and related aspects and questions). Secondly, it is a predictive set of systematic expressions, offering logical and testable arguments, as well as a framework for analysis. He responds in the affirmative, arguing that the existence of internal differences within a school of thought is not at odds with its coherence. Its intelligibility comes with the core ideas shared by different scholars within this approach, making it self-consistent.

With regard to TWAIL as a methodology for the study of international law, as the title of this volume suggests, TWAIL could be seen as a methodology that is still developing, neither fixed nor established to be applied mechanically to solve the problems it confronts.[54] Despite charges pointing at its lack of methodological clarity, TWAIL implies a historically aware methodology for the understanding of the international system, an historical perspective that takes into account not just Western history, but also global history, and includes Third World shared

[51] Local municipalities, export processing zones, free trade areas, etc. to add to more traditional jurisdictions such as international courts and NGOs for example.

[52] Anghie (2008).

[53] Okafor (2008).

[54] TWAIL cumulative perspective is 'shaped by the experiences of the peoples and States of the Third World... In TWAIL, then, we offer instead an ongoing project that is continuously questioning not only the foundations and operations of international law, but also its own methodological premises' Anghie and Chimni (2003), p. 102.

experiences of subordination.[55] TWAIL emphasises the connection between old and modern forms of domination, the continuities and discontinuities of the techniques used by global powers in international development. TWAIL does present a collection of methods for the study of international law and legal analysis. This appears clear when considering the emphasis on analytical tools and categories such as: the centrality given to the idea of global justice, the historicization of the analysis of international law, the focus on the Third World, the questioning and distrust of universal narratives, and the rejection of Western-centrism.[56]

TWAIL is a distinctive way of thinking about international law guided by the following analytical tools and sensibilities. TWAIL is committed to revisiting 'all factors that create, foster, legitimize, and maintain harmful hierarchies and oppressions'.[57] In order to unveil and understand the asymmetries and contradictions at play, TWAIL problematises traditional international law concepts and dynamics, employing a specific body or 'set of methods used in a particular area of study or activity'.[58] These particular procedures for approaching a phenomenon, in this case international law, include attention to history and the dichotomy First World/Third World, which guides its resistance to the exercise of power and authority over oppressed peoples, and Third World as one key analytical category that points at the differentiation of geographies of injustice and misfortune.[59]

As already elaborated, central ideals to international law and policies receive special attention in order to unveil the underlying systemic structural and structuring legal arrangements that maintain and reinforce exclusion. The ideas of universality,[60] sovereignty and law itself, as well as other traditional notions, modes of

[55] On the limitations of the turn to history and TWAIL with regard to human rights, see Kapur (2023), who argues that these efforts to rethink human rights 'have not displaced rights as central to the emancipatory endeavour... they [these efforts] illustrate a reluctance to negate the value of human rights, worthy in and of themselves, as salvific, containing a beneficial essence and an effective tool of empowerment', Kapur (2023), p. 773.

[56] 'To embrace (as TWAIL does) the techniques of discourse analysis that was imported from French linguistics and philosophy to American legal studies through the Critical Legal Studies and New Approaches to International Law movements.'... 'The ideological preference for many scholars from this strand of analysis is oriented within the progressive liberal tradition: critical of any 'natural' foundations, attuned to ambivalence and the circularity of logic, interested in the contingencies and irrationalities of meaning. We should not lose this post-modern ambivalence towards truth and power.' Haskell (2014), p. 414.

[57] Mutua and Anghie (2000), p. 38.

[58] Definition of methodology according to the online Cambridge dictionary. Accessed 10 May 2024.

[59] Baxi (October 2002).

[60] Mutua asserts that the uncontested 'universality of international is geographic, not normative' Mutua and Anghie (2000), p. 31. It emerged from the colonial encounter, developing as a regime of global governance. After the independence of former colonial territories.

authority, jurisdiction[61] and legitimacy issues.[62] Concepts such as consent, resistance, rights, the significance of race, the silencing of the subaltern, development, state responsibility and excessive legalism[63] are further explored and analysed in how they operate nowadays.

Antony Anghie, who stresses the colonial origin of international law and its role in legitimizing imperialism, develops the idea of the 'dynamic of difference': 'a dynamic founded on the concept of "developed" versus "undeveloped", that remains with us'[64] conforming an international community with ranks of members and membership. The distinction of the savage and primitive evolved from the differentiation between the civilised and uncivilised (in racial and cultural terms) to the distinction between backward and advanced/developed people (based on economic development, a criterion 'that appears neutral and universal because it is based on economics... rather than on an assertion of cultural superiority by a European civilization'.[65] Derived from this hierarchisation, emerged the logic of inclusion/exclusion despite the equality of states. It is also constitutive of the act of 'othering', which implies a split-up between the West (the self) and the rest (the Other), a division that is intrinsic to such differentiation, which further secures its fixity and the civilising mission.[66]

A wide range of views and proposals are in place 'to understand the ways in which history shaped a particular approach to international law and how this approach precluded any inquiry into imperialism and its impact on the making of international law'.[67] They cover deconstructing judicial decisions, examining technologies of expropriation (of wealth and resources), considering incidents and cases relevant to the Third World (to extract the significance for international law), integrating voices and ideas on justice and governance other than Western ones to promote emancipation.[68] The problematization of analytical categories and theoretical developments advanced by TWAIL aim at 'taking the equality of Third-World peoples much more seriously',[69] and furthering equity all the more.[70] Finally,

[61] Chimni (2022).

[62] TWAIL disputes the legitimacy of law that is derived from its neutrality, objectivity and universality.

[63] A 'legalistic perception of international law that translates into an alienating narrative. Purported apoliticism produces an international legal corpus alienated from its origins and assimilative aims' al Attar and Tava (2010), p. 22.

[64] Anghie (2007), p. 267.

[65] Ibid. p. 189.

[66] Ibid.

[67] Anghie (2023), p. 52.

[68] Reflecting 'on ways of offering epistemic and ideational resistance to the global hegemonies' Okafor (2005), p. 179.

[69] Ibid.

[70] Bedjaoui (1979).

besides TWAIL's intellectual and political engagement, there is a pedagogical concern with intergenerational legacies and the teaching of international law.[71]

1.4 Problematising TWAIL

As has been explained above, TWAIL is in line with post-colonial thinking and theories. TWAIL seeks to contest the colonial world order established by European empires, continued hegemony and subjection, criticising the insularity of historical accounts. However, unlike other anti-colonial theories, it is argued that TWAIL's scholarly transformation and revindication of local and national contributions to knowledge (in what pertains to international law) lack a specific programmatic project with explicit objectives.[72] However, TWAIL scholars assert their political commitment in support of reversing inequality and injustice 'as TWAIL has sought to distinguish itself from other critical legal approaches through its political and transformative commitments'.[73]

In addition to this alleged absence of a concrete agenda for action and reform, critical voices argue that TWAIL conforms a less radical endeavour that combines both resistance and legitimation. As discussed in relation to the contested idea of universality, TWAIL's trust lies on common principles, a certain universality beyond the acknowledgement of extant plurality, aware that the idea of universality has long facilitated subjugation and exploitation. Universality is understood as an open universality, undefined, as quasi-trascendent, meaning that 'it recognises the impossibility of genuine universality, but also recognises that the impossibility of universality is precisely what makes a fruitful plurality possible'.[74] It is therefore connected with the contingency of law and, in the same logic, with the idea of justice—global justice understood in its openness. As such, TWAIL scholarship supports the existence of a global normative regime, considering international law redeemable, in different degrees.

In his mapping and appraisal of the movement, Haskell claims that TWAIL needs a profound radicalisation in order to challenge the inequality of the current international system on the basis that its argumentative logic 'operates according to the very

[71] See al Attar and Tava (2010) for a proposal of TWAIL as a pedagogical theory for legal education.

[72] As it is the case with the decolonial project that proposes among others: the idea of de-linking (Aníbal Quijano), critical border thinking as the method to connect the different colonial histories entangled with imperial modernity, transmodernity as a political world project of liberation (political, economic, ecological, pedagogic, etc.) (Enrique Dussel).

[73] Natarajan et al. (2016), p. 1947.

[74] Eslava and Pahuja (2011), p. 122. On the question of universality Pahuja asserts that the oscillation between 'the myth of universality and the nihilism of cultural relativism'is 'symptomatic of the post-colonial quality of law and the radical impossibility of closure it generates.' Pahuja (2005), p. 468.

conservative analytical framework it set out to transcend'.[75] He argues that as such, it ultimately betrays TWAIL's foundational critique on the imperialism of international law, further falling into certain transcendental traps it cannot resolve.[76] Therefore, Haskell considers that TWAIL is not radical or revolutionary enough, but remains conservative in orientation. However, some authors view this as a strategic decision, in order to remain able to interact and challenge the discipline without overturning it.[77] Employing 'the existing ideology and intellectual tools to try and "make good" on the system's promise',[78] rather than challenging the influence of 'a European capitalist orientation', in order to overcome the problems international law poses and TWAIL seeks to address. Thus, conservatives and reformists trust the emancipatory potential international law carries despite the criticism pertaining the 'impossibility of a post imperial international law'.[79]

However, although TWAIL's critical insights do contribute to this reformist goal of devising another international law, some of its proposed reforms do not entail much novelty or concretion, falling in what Haskell considers a long-standing fascination with non-Western beliefs and ways of life and perhaps an idealisation of fairer participation. The turn to 'local resistance movements should not be equated with emancipation'.[80]

Another criticism relates to the insufficient inclusion or neglect of certain questions and practices that result in discrimination. Some assessments compel TWAIL to engage in a more meaningful way with a more extensive range of issues to contest subjugation and hierarchies in order to reveal how exclusions operate.[81]

In conclusion, and related to TWAIL's needs for improvement, there is the question of expanding the disciplinary approaches in TWAIL-analysis to include insights from anthropology, sociology, in addition to the well-established historical

[75] Haskell (2014), p. 385.

[76] With regard to the cultural turn (the consideration of culture as pre-political) and the focus on imperialism (as exertion of power) in its connection with (international) law.

[77] 'There are real dangers in conceding the entire arena of international law to other methodologies and actors in the aspiration to find a more powerful discourse which would render injustice with such clarity and persuasion that it would compel the changes in international relations which TWAIL seeks. To the extent that CLS suggests this course of action, it runs the risk of merely supporting, if not furthering the status quo... TWAIL simply cannot afford this because international law has now become an extraordinarily powerful language in which to frame problems, suggest fault and responsibility, propose solutions and remedies. International law rules matter and must be taken seriously.'Anghie and Chimni (2003), p. 101.

[78] Haskell (2014), p. 386.

[79] Gathii (2022), pp. 153–173. TWAIL aims at transforming international law 'from being a language of oppression to a language of emancipation—a body of rules and practices that reflect and embody the struggles and aspirations of Third World peoples and which, thereby, promotes truly global justice', Anghie and Chimni (2003), p. 79.

[80] Haskell (2014), p. 406.

[81] This is the case of feminist accounts and practices in TWAIL scholarship and mainframe, besides TWAIL-feminist critique of international law and their analytical tools.

look. This would contribute to building alliances, synergies and solidarities between TWAIL and the agendas of similarly oriented projects and disciplines.

2 Examples of TWAIL Research in Practice

Following the structure of this book, this second section provides two examples where TWAIL methodologies have been used to tackle problems in international law. The first example connects the solidaristic conceptualization of social rights with a TWAIL perspective. The second example looks into the conceptualization of property of the San Indigenous People.

2.1 TWAIL Methodologies in Social Rights Research

In the first part of this section we comment on a work written by one of the authors of this chapter: *The Human Right to Health: Solidarity in the Era of Healthcare Commercialization*.[82] Though this work does not formally acknowledge reliance on TWAIL, its use of sources, its focus and critical angle of analysis draw upon that approach. Moreover, as we will see, the work aligns with the invitation made in the Introduction and Chapter 1 of this book, namely, that in carrying out legal research through TWAIL, we should avoid the stagnation produced by the apparent absence of a language common between doctrinal and alternative methodologies. This aims to show TWAIL's influence and applicability in social rights' legal research beyond the explicit use of analytical labels as a way to reaching out to the mainstream of the discipline. Our analysis in this section therefore attempts to provide room for methodological reflection, especially seeking to meet the needs of those conducting legal research in the field of social rights under international human rights law.

The analysis is divided into two parts. Firstly, we dissect the work's general methodological approach while emphasizing its connection to TWAIL. The second part assesses the way in which this work looks at social rights, seeking to provide opportunities for reflection to legal scholars relying on TWAIL.

2.1.1 Methodological Challenges

The work analysed studies the different ways in which the human right to health is interpreted. Presenting a dominant interpretation of this human right as judicially oriented, individualistic, and focused on minimum entitlements, the work shows how this focus fails the promise of guaranteeing equal access to healthcare for all. In opposition to this view, the work studies another possibility. Concentrating on the principle of solidarity, the human right to health unfolds a social and communitarian approach that contests the commercial delivery of healthcare, rendering access to healthcare a non-market entitlement.

---

[82] Arenas Catalán (2021).

In unfolding its methodological approach, the work carries out a plan in several (not linearly ordered) steps. In the first step, the book presents 'interpretations', i.e., a combination of various sources of international law coupled to philosophical, political, and historiographical materials (mainly historical facts, reference to philosophical ideas, and legal principles). Grounded on the idea of the law as an argumentative discipline, the process of building these interpretations is also argumentative: its merit does not depend on reliance to a formally valid source, but on its persuasiveness.[83] In a second step, following the same argumentative technique, the work links these interpretations with certain adjectives. The book speaks of: 'predominant', 'hegemonic' or 'solidaristic' interpretations. In a third step, the work associates the identified interpretations with processes of adjudication in the context of courts of law or with legislative expressions at the national level including countries from the North and the South, alike.[84] In doing so, the work describes the legal effect of these judgments and policies, suggesting a potential impact or interconnection with political and societal phenomena like economic inequality. However, the approach is modest in this regard. According to the work, nearly all remarks in this respect 'should be understood as formulating points for further research which may corroborate or dispute the normative claims that each of them makes'.[85] In a fourth step, the work provides a dialectic confrontation between these interpretations, addressing their limitations and potential to the goal of realizing the human right to health.

Despite its critical focus, the work makes no suggestion that doctrinal approaches to law should be set aside. Doctrinal methodologies would view law:

> uniquely from its interior within which the aim is to analyse and to explain in a coherent and logical manner a legal text or court decision and, continuing in this same methodological mode, to guide the reader towards future outcomes with respect to the positive law under consideration. One studies the law using analysis and synthesis in as strict a manner as the pharmaceutical chemist studies the body. A book on the sociology of law will thus not form part of *la doctrine*. Nor, indeed, would a work on legal history or, if too interdisciplinary, a text on comparative law.[86]

This is an opaque perspective on legal methodologies. Quite conveniently, as TWAIL denotes, such an approach sticks to a formal process that focuses on describing legal rules, limiting the possibility to pose questions regarding the origins or the (post) colonial uses and proclivities of international law. That most of the laws of war, for example, did not apply to colonial wars of conquest or counterinsurgency directed against liberation movements (up until Third World states forced law reform

[83] Escobar Roca and García Manrique (2019), pp. 18–19.

[84] The work considers examples from Europe and the Americas. See Arenas Catalán (2021) pp. 50–53, 149–154.

[85] Arenas Catalán (2021), p. 143.

[86] Samuel (2011), p. 180. See also Egan (2018), p. 24.

in the 1970s),[87] exemplifies the limitations of relying on a purely doctrinal framework in international law.

Yet, as mentioned, having contested formal reliance on traditional sources does not take the work to suggest that doctrinal methodologies should be set aside. As such, this method's ability to unpack the meaning, function and operation of law is acknowledged.[88] Neither does this work deny the authority of binding sources of international law, and the work significantly relies on treaty law as a binding rule in international law. By the same token, the work also relies on 'material' sources of international law, which would shed light on the existence of a legally binding rule. Furthermore, the work strongly relies on other sources that have been regarded as merely 'potential', namely, sources that would have not been yet universally recognized as such.[89]

Because it is helpful in letting us assess the specific way this work operationalizes TWAIL, we briefly describe the work's nuanced methodological approach. Two observations are in order here. Firstly, the theoretical meaning of using law as an argumentative discipline and secondly, some further methodological acommodations that the work makes in respect of the specific discipline of international human rights law.

Stemming from the idea of law as an argumentative discipline, law is neither true nor false, and it can only offer more or less persuasive answers to societal problems.[90] Does this mean that scientific research questions are political? Relevant scientific questions often engage with the political. And the reason for this is that law as an academic discipline should not be made exclusively dependent on law's internal normativity. Because law is accountable to society and not the other way around, legally sound research questions should engage both with internal and external dimensions of the law. For example, in the field of social rights, a pressing external question is whether law can bring social justice.[91] This interrogation demands both an external and an internal perspective. External questions may include the very question of what social justice is. And proposals to address this notion will remain partisan insofar only an excessively ambitious positivistic view of the law could expect answers so diverse to exclusively belong to the law's internal dimension. In the effort of integrating these external questions, classical internal issues might arise. The precise meaning of legal concepts, legal rules, legal

[87] Martineau (2016), p. 107, and Moyn (2022), p. 91.

[88] Egan (2018), p. 30.

[89] According to Hernández, formal sources would be legally binding and would include treaty law, custom and general principles of international law. Material sources of international law would not be legally binding, but would provide evidence on the existence of a legally binding rule. Potential sources would have not yet been universally recognized as such and would include resolutions of international organizations, codes of conduct, statements of bodies that monitor treaties and other forms of soft law. See Hernández (2022), p. 33.

[90] Escobar Roca and García Manrique (2019), pp. 18–19, and Van Hoecke (2011), pp. 4–5.

[91] Lettinga and van Troost (2015).

principles or legal constructions[92] might be of relevance in determining how these external questions will be processed.

In the intersection between external and internal dimensions, i.e., the way external concepts are embedded and operationalized by legal systems, the work adopts a critical stand towards the notion of legal rights.[93] This critical disposition has become a classical topic in critical studies, especially after the contributions of Marxist scholarship, in particular those of Yevgeny Pashukanis. Risking to over-reduce the problem, Pashukanis's basic thesis is that 'the legal subject of juridical theories is closely related to the commodity owner'.[94] Namely, a correlation would exist between 'commodity exchange with the time at which man becomes seen as a legal personality – the bearer of rights'.[95] There would be something typical in the nature of the commodity and of the commodity exchange that would be imprinted into fundamental legal subjects and relationships like legal personhood and rights. Pashukanis comes to this conclusion by observing how the commodity exchange necessitates both private property and formal equality. Insofar these two elements are pre-requirements to capitalism, their recognition by the law through the enforcement of private contracts would be a fundamental precondition to capitalism. Because legal rules can only derive from the fundamental relationship between persons as legal subjects and their relationship to commodities, legal rules themselves, even the State, would be secondary and contingent.[96]

The insights about the form of the law as theorized by Pashukanis challenges TWAILers to cautiously approach the wholesale promotion of rights. Since in its basic features rights tend to reproduce the elements of the legal form, their benefits might come at the expense of legitimizing property-oriented conceptualizations of these. However, this need not mean the enterprise of rights to be futile. Solidaristic and communitarian definitions of these rights, might help develop rights outside the framework of the legal form. Looking at social rights, Fernando Atria has opposed their conceptualization as rights to a minimum, explaining how social rights would fall within the idea of bourgeois rights. Contrarily, emphasizing the need 'of understanding human self-realization as reciprocal rather than individual', Atria conceptualizes these rights as 'anomalous grafts',[97] namely, 'rights that cannot be treated institutionally as individual rights.' The solidaristic interpretation of the human right to health (but also, the communitarian conceptualization of property as understood by the San Indigenous Peoples, which is presented in the next section), might be presented as instances of this ambition.

In the second place, the work takes distance from two methodological dispositions of common currency in international law. On the one hand, the work

[92] Van Hoecke (2011), p. 14.

[93] Arenas Catalán (2021), p. 6, n 20.

[94] Miéville (2008), p. 106.

[95] Ibid, p. 106.

[96] Ibid, p. 107.

[97] Atria (2015), p. 610.

distances itself from a position that appears to ascribe *automatic* binding value to interpretative documents or opinions emerged from the monitoring bodies of international human rights conventions.[98] Strategically adopting a more positivistic methodological position, the work argues that these views are better accounted as prospective or *lege ferenda*.[99] This understanding allows for a clearer distinction between these sources and the canonical legal texts that they seek to interpret (*lege lata*), to which the work gives more authority to support its argument. One key example in this regard is the way the work treats the International Covenant on Economic, Social and Cultural Rights (ICESCR) and the value assigned to the interpretative work of its monitoring body—the United Nations Committee on Economic, Social and Cultural Rights (UNCESCR). While the work devotes significant attention to the views issued by this organ (especially in the form of general comments or concluding observations in processes of international periodic review), they are not treated differently than the work of other UN bodies, such as that of Special Rapporteurs or Independent Experts.[100]

On the other hand, the work takes equal distance from another traditional positivistic position according to which valid rules of international human rights law—'the rules that now exist'—would be those that had attained the status of customary international law.[101] As it can be appreciated from a work written by William Schabas on the topic, restricting the corpus of international human rights law norms in that way would limit the human rights enterprise in general and TWAIL in particular. For a start, it might limit the content of international human rights law exclusively to the areas where the greater powers acquiesce, something that those working with TWAIL should at least problematize.[102]

Moreover, it would fail to account for processes of dialogue in the field of international human rights law which have been key in providing meaning to formal sources. This would be the case with international fora where new interpretations crystallize, for example, in the context of decisions issued by international judicial and quasi-judicial bodies, international UN declarations, reports issued by UN Special Rapporteurs, interpreting principles issued by academic experts or decisions adopted by national courts in the field of international law.[103]

---

[98] This approach could be grounded on the 'great weight' the ICJ ascribed in the *Ahmadou Sadio Diallo (Republic of Guinea v DRC)* case, to the interpretation of human rights treaties adopted by the relevant court or committee. See Crawford (2019), p. 633.

[99] For an overview of the traditional positivistic elements of Mainstream Approaches to International Law (MAIL), see Chapter "Legal Method in the Context of Social Thought".

[100] Some of whom work with TWAIL, for example: Prof. Obiora Okafor, Prof. Michael Fakhri, Prof. Tendayi Achiume or Prof. Balakrishnan Rajagopal.

[101] Schabas (2021), p. 8.

[102] Consider how the concept of 'specially affected States' allows nuclear states to bloc the emergence of new customary rules in the face of opposition from non-nuclear States, See Hernández (2022), p. 39; Chimni (2018), p. 11.

[103] Consider, for example, the topic of reservations in respect of multilateral human rigths treaties and the acknowledgment of the International Law Commission regarding the need of developing a

Yet, it is important to emphasize that the need to account for these processes and dialogues should not be exaggerated. The opposite extreme—to automatically validate any views discussed in these fora as 'emerging' expressions of what the law is—would probably be as problematic in legal rhetorical terms and might weaken the overall persuasiveness of the strategic use of traditional human rights law methodologies undertaken.[104] It is only in view of arguments considered persuasive by the target audience (e.g., 'intersubjective consensus' for institutional or academic conservative audiences), that an interpretation might be regarded as persuasive.[105] Conceiving 'the rest of the world' as 'most of the world',[106] TWAILers should move to demand the recognition of perspectives less salient among the Western community of scholars.

Faced with a mixed audience that considers questions of legal validity from a traditional positivistic viewpoint, the work takes a stand that brings together formal, material, and potential sources of international law, juxtaposing sources that traditional law doctrine regards as binding and those it regards as non-binding. From a TWAIL perspective, this approach is advantageous because it allows to direct the attention towards the blind spots and inequalities produced by traditional formal sources.[107]

Be that as it may, the main added value of this approach might be indirect: while the construction of alternatives to dominant interpretations remains challenging, the methodological fragility of dominant interpretations does come to light. As the analysis shows, both dominant and counterhegemonic interpretations may strategically rely on a combination of international law sources (formal, material and potential). Namely, the approach allows to highlight the role potential sources play in dominant interpretations.[108] To give an example, the ICESCR's obligation to 'the creation of conditions which would assure to all medical service and medical attention in the event of sickness'[109] has been interpreted by the UNCESCR in association with equal opportunity,[110] an ideological position linked to political liberalism which does not forcefully stem from the ICESCR. Contrarily, the rather maximalist text of the convention: *the right of everyone to the highest attainable standard of health*, could well be associated to ideas of substantive equality, namely, to regard the pursuit for equality of condition both within and between nations as a human rights objective. The combined effect of this analysis leads to relativize the

'reservations dialogue' between reserving states and human rights bodies. See Hernández (2022), p. 193.

[104] Coomans (2010), p. 185.

[105] See Chapter "Mainstream Approaches to International Law" on critical legal rhetoric.

[106] Natarajan (2016), p. 1953.

[107] A discussion that invites reflection on the approaches of the ICJ towards 'literary works' from 'time immemorial', as argued by China in the South China Sea dispute. See Singh (2022), p. ix.

[108] Alter (2020), p. 847.

[109] International Covenant on Economic, Social and Cultural Rights (1966), Art. 12(2)(d).

[110] 'the right to a system of health protection which provides equality of opportunity for people to enjoy the highest attainable level of health'. See UNCESCR (2000), para. 8.

legal force of official perspectives in the field of international human rights law, while at the same time opening space for alternative interpretations.

Obviously, the methodological choices of this work suggest distance from the formalistic and positivistic ambitions of doctrinal methodologies.[111] While the work does not deny rhetorical force to traditional sources in international law, the work's nuanced approach allows to problematize the *formal* validity of this system. This is of interest to those relying on TWAIL as a lens to look critically at international human rights law. The South lacks the financial resources to object, let alone monitor the emergence of customary rules. At the same time, these countries do not benefit from the dominant dynamics in academic publishing, which contribute to perpetuate North-South relations with its taxonomies of academic performance.[112] By exposing the dependency of dominant interpretations on potential sources, the work shows the need for a more critical approach towards legal sources, in opposition to a purely formalistic one. While relying on potential sources might be a stretch too far for legal scholars working within doctrinal methodologies, the suggestion of the book is not to break up with this method, but to mobilize it for critical purposes. While readers will find a great deal of referencing towards formal sources, acknowledging thus its legal authority, readers will also become more aware about the strategic need to push for the diversification of the sources of international law that traditional or mainstream approaches to international law allow for.[113] In so doing, readers will recognize the ideological, historical, and geopolitical imbalances in international law, a concern central to TWAIL.[114]

2.1.2 A TWAIL Focus on Advancing the Human Right to Health

The work devotes quite some attention to addressing and contrasting conceptualizations of social rights. In what comes next, we address the cleavage the work proposes between two interpretations, focusing on its legal effect. The work looks first at a more traditional theoretical approach that it calls: 'the predominant interpretation of the human right to health'.[115] Further, the work looks at an alternative interpretation to this human right grounded on the principle of solidarity.[116] In identifying the main features of these interpretations, the work conceptualizes the predominant interpretation both procedurally and in terms of

[111] Which would be best expressed in the 'ultra-positivist' direction that Kelsen and his followers gave to international law by means of their 'technical, rational, scientific and antipolitical approach to law'. *See* Eslava and Pahuja (2012), p. 216.

[112] Scott and Zahava (2017), pp. 14–15.

[113] About the eclectical foundations and flexible features of MAIL, see Chapter "Legal Method in the Context of Social Thought".

[114] A case in point being the failed attempt of the Non-Aligned Movement to push for the implementation of the New International Economic Order Declaration by relying fundamentally on declarations issued by the United Nations General Assembly. See Knox (2022), p. 58, and Scott and Zahava (2017), p. 15.

[115] Arenas Catalán (2021), ch 2.

[116] Ibid, pp. 9–13.

content. Procedurally, reliance on judicial measures is highlighted. Contentwise, the predominant interpretation leads to a healthcare minimum for vulnerable individuals in ways that do not conflict with the commercial delivery of healthcare.[117]

In contrast to this perspective, the work proposes a defense of social rights from the point of view of solidarity. This perspective would be non-hegemonic or even counter hegemonic. Associating solidarity to critical traditions both in the North and in the South, including the Latin-American Theology of Liberation, the development agenda promoted internationally by the South in the 1970s and the contributions from the European *New Liberals* and social democrats, the work links solidarity in the right to health to collaboration and interdependence, redistribution, citizenship and medical need. Following Chilean legal philosopher Fernando Atria, the question of access to the human right to health, is understood as a proposition to de-commodify healthcare, i.e., to remove healthcare services from the market.[118]

A key focus of this work lies in its assessment of the different way in which social rights have been conceptualized. This is a TWAIL-related problem, because the interpretation the work identifies as dominant would have worked towards the exclusion of Southern perspectives on social rights, which would be of a more social and communitarian content.[119] While for the predominant interpretation social rights would be protections to attain a minimum level of dignity however understood, solidarity would take issue with privileged forms of access in the current political economy, in particular, those grounded on unequal ability to pay in the context of healthcare commercialization. Healthcare commercialization made its entry in systems of health protection from the 1980s onwards through the introduction of neoliberal style market reforms.

Ultimately, the predominant and the solidaristic interpretations fail meeting each other because of the different underlying values that serve as their starting points. Following a distinction similar to the one proposed by Amartya Sen, the work draws on the opposition between struggle against poverty and struggle against inequality.[120] The predominant interpretation would seek to build a minimum dignity floor. It would make the struggle against poverty its principal focus of attention.[121] Solidarity, on the other hand, would be motivated by the struggle against inequality,

[117] Ibid, pp. 5–7.

[118] Ibid, pp. 86.

[119] In his account of Third World histories of human rights, especially in the field of economic and social rights, Barreto, for example, accounts for the contributions of Chilean international law scholars Hernán Santa Cruz and Alejandro Álvarez, who would have been among the main sources of John Humphrey's final draft to the Universal Declaration of Human Rights. See Barreto (2019), p. 174; reflecting critically on post-apartheid South Africa, the rights' based approach to reform in particular, Mutua stated: 'majoritarian democratic rule constrained by particular notions of property rights does not necessarily lead to the economic empowerment of the majority'. See Mutua (2002), p. 140.

[120] As documented by Samuel Moyn in justifying his attention to the the dychtomy between sufficiency and inequality, Moyn (2018), p. 137.

[121] See OHCHR (2012).

namely, it would tackle poverty, but it would go beyond it, taking issue with too large economic distances between and within countries.[122]

Stemming from these different stands around the nature and function of human rights law, the predominant interpretation developed a set of legal frameworks. The work concentrates on an issue TWAIL scholars have also addressed: the utilization of the law and politics distinction in order to position questions of distributive justice away from the sphere of what human rights law is or does.[123] To take an example from those addressed in the work, General Comment Number 3 on the Nature of State Parties' Obligations, of 1990, allowed the predominant interpretation to understand and apply human rights law as an issue entirely distinguishable from the institutional setting (public or private) in charge of implementing social rights obligations.[124] Thanks to a focus on minimum obligations and the stark separation between law and politics, the predominant interpretation could push institutional and distributive questions away from human rights law, regarding them as non-legal or political issues.

On the other hand, the work recounts how a more recent legal framework—General Comment 14 on the Right to the Highest Attainable Standard of Health, from 2000—did advance distributive justice. It did so by incorporating the challenge of economic accessibility (affordability) in a legal framework known as the AAAQ. The AAAQ is an all-encompassing legal framework, that includes questions of availability, accessibility, acceptability and quality. Only in the field of accessibility, which is the area the work focuses on, there would be four dimensions: non-discrimination (for example, of vulnerable or marginalized sections of the population), physical accessibility (for example, ensuring that medical facilities would be within physical reach), information accessibility (for example, by treating personal health data with confidentiality) and the abovementioned economic or financial accessibility.[125] While the work recognizes these issues, it criticizes that economic accessibility was not prioritized as a human rights response to a political economy revolving around commodification and individual responsibility. Both in this general comment, but also further in the context of international processes of periodic review, affordability is not understood as a mandate to challenge the private provision of healthcare. This is in spite of the fact that the private search for profits under commercial healthcare schemes entails the greatest challenge to keep healthcare services affordable.

Looking at the solidaristic interpretation of the right to health, the work addresses several perspectives developed at the instance of the South. These included: the 1978

[122] American historian Samuel Moyn, documents several equality approaches emerged from the South, including the contributions of African leaders such as: Nkrumah, Nasser, Nyerere, Kaunda or Dia. See Moyn (2018), pp. 98–104, Eslava (2017), pp. 18–22, and Arenas Catalán (2021), p. 3, *n* 8; a similar account is provided by Jessica Whyte, see Whyte (2019), pp. 213–214.

[123] eg, Kennedy (1999), pp. 34–35, Baars (2015), p. 277, and Hodson (2020), p. 60.

[124] UNCESCR (1990), para. 8.

[125] UNCESCR (2000), para. 12.

Alma-Ata Declaration, the 1969 Declaration on Social Progress and Development, the 1974 Declaration on the Establishment of a New International Economic Order or the 1975 Charter of Economic Rights and Duties of States. These international declarations were attempts to develop more equitable exchanging conditions between the North and the South. Moreover, States in the South sought the improvement of social conditions in ways that would be beneficial to their national development. The policies developed in these documents were of a marked redistributive orientation and were far from limited to questions of health. Yet, when it came to health, there was a recognition about the importance of addressing health inequalities and an acknowledgement about the communitarian nature of health challenges.[126]

Unlike what was the case in the West and the Soviet orbit, the solidaristic agenda on the protection of health, had a long way to go in the developing world. The work points out the case of Chile, referring to the incipient development of equity-oriented policies in the field of health promotion and local medical attention, very much in line with what was later suggested in the Alma-Ata Declaration or the Ottawa Charter of Health Promotion.[127] With the 1973 coup that ousted the socialist Salvador Allende, Chile became a laboratory of the neoliberal policies that decades later would become common place in the rest of the world. The work also pays attention to the Cuban healthcare system highlighting how a socialist approach to healthcare around health promotion and primary care, manages to obtain results comparable to those of the developed world, but with a fraction of the necessary financial resources.[128]

Critical to the work's argument is how the neoliberal policies that commodified the provision of healthcare from the 1980s onwards did not conflict with the conceptualization of social rights under the predominant interpretation.[129] Hence, the relevance of the work's method for scholars using TWAIL. The work's approach shows the importance of challenging the idea that social rights have an exclusive or uniform conceptualization. The uncovering of different meanings through documents and historiographies, especially those relating to the South, shows that there was more than one view. Secondly, the work contests the idea that in the 1990s the West would have succeeded to include social rights to the family of human rights. Claiming that from the perspective of solidarity social rights cannot be regarded as fulfilled, the work proposes healthcare commercialization as antithetical to the right to health. In so doing, the function of human rights law expands beyond the hegemonic understanding of protection against state abuse, expanding into challenges derived from the commercialization of health.

---

[126] E.g., WHO (1978), and Arenas Catalán (2021), pp. 33, 41, 62.

[127] WHO (1986).

[128] Arenas Catalán (2021), pp. 150–153.

[129] Ibid, pp. 80, *n* 88.

2.2 Human Rights and Property from an Indigenous Peoples' Perspective

In this section, another example of work that distances itself from the orthodoxy of rights as per their articulation in the International Human Rights Corpus is presented. It refers to three articles which are part of a broader research on the reformulation of human rights from an indigenous perspective.[130] In an attempt to revert epistemic injustice and the insularity of historical narratives, the aim of such extensive study falls under the ambition of decolonising the Western epistemic canon that underlies the language of rights, challenging the hegemonic design by the West of human rights constructs. It further explores ways in which the plurality of non-dominant knowledges and epistemic communities could be brought into an inter-epistemic dialogue in order to redefine law beyond eurocentrism, focusing on marginalised perspectives, peripheral knowledge(s) and subaltern legalities; those of the San, indigenous peoples from Southern Africa.

This research starts by examining the hegemonic human rights grammar[131] from a decolonial perspective and TWAIL. Its point of departure is a critique of the dominant human rights discourse; its epistemological grounds and conceptual underpinnings, which are conceived as Western-centric, the embodiment of a secular, rational and anthropocentric worldview.[132] From this standpoint, the research interrogates human rights as power categories that emanated from a particular context, epistemic location and legal culture.[133] In line with decolonial and TWAIL critical approaches, this study aims to contribute to the transformation of international human rights law and to redefine it in pluralistic terms.[134] By acknowledging alterity, it seeks to remedy epistemic asymmetries and the ideological coloniality of such a prevailing narrative.[135] To this end, property paradigms and land conceptualisations are examined under two different perspectives: Western legal regimes and the San's world-views. An alternative to the conceptualisation of the liberal right to property is therefore advanced on the basis of aspects such as communality, egalitarianism, mutual dependence and obligations, sharing, redistribution, reciprocity and earth's boundaries. It is based on those premises that property, ownership and uses of land could be reframed beyond their economic

---

[130] Gómez Sánchez (2020, 2022, 2023, 2024).

[131] In reference to the language around the mainstream idea of human rights. This is in line with TWAIL's stance that, following Ratna Kapur, 'involves provincializing the dominant scholarship, unmasking its Eurocentric, imperial, racial and civilizational underpinnings and exploding the myth of universality' Kapur (2023), p. 772.

[132] Gómez Sánchez (2020).

[133] 'The justification of Christian evangelization was no longer available to legitimate imperial control, nor was that of the religiously more neutral concept of the civilizing mission of colonial powers. The rhetorical language now shifted to a concept that came to have new meaning and strength in this postcolonial era: human rights.' Wallerstein (2006), p. 12.

[134] Rajagopal (2004).

[135] Gómez Sánchez (2022).

significance and materiality, laying down the foundations for a different understanding of property that could transform and enrich the hegemonic human rights' discourse, transcending its limitations.[136]

These objectives are in line with the TWAIL defining features discussed in the introduction of this chapter, namely: placing the Third World at the centre, resisting global hegemony, calling for global equality and unmasking power in relation to knowledge construction. Following those ideas, this research work defends the validity of alternative approaches to the mainstream human rights grammar and challenges traditional connections between the normative order and the political and structural power dynamics. It is from this perspective that the hegemonic articulation of the human rights discourse is examined, tracing the relationship between the context of modernity, the emergence of international law and the human rights conceptual framework. This analysis reveals the protection of certain values over others and the subsequent dominance of one narrative to the detriment of other epistemic cultures, values and traditions.[137]

It is argued that the sanctioning of such superiority implies a representational violence, the emptying of alternative discourses, on the basis of what dominant voices believe is the correct and morally superior perspective. However, problematising what is being referred here as the dominant human rights grammar or hegemonic discourse, does not entail a rejection of the human rights paradigm. Rather, it strives for an ameliorated version built on premises that are inclusive of neglected epistemological views and 'universes of meaning'.

2.2.1 Human Rights: 'The Moralized Expression of a Political Ideology'[138]

The relevance of human rights is undeniable. They are enshrined in numerous binding and non-binding legal documents. They have inspired innumerable protection instruments at global, regional, national and local levels and influenced countless governmental policies and strategies. Their normative and institutional expansion as well as the proliferation of rights is remarkable and manifests itself in our everyday lives. This centrality is reinforced by the actuality of challenges around culture, health, poverty and other areas being framed as legal concerns to be addressed through human rights claims. However, this legalistic approach prevents focusing on the root causes of such issues. Consequently, the prominence of the human rights grammar compels us to critically approach what has become hegemonic in view of the implications law can have in defining socio-economic structures. Sometimes as a liberating and transformative tool or instrument for

---

[136] Gómez Sánchez (2024).

[137] According to Dianne Otto: 'law has the constitutive power to universalize certain knowledges and to disqualify others' Otto (1996), p. 359.

[138] Mutua (1996), p. 592.

resistance, but also as a limiting and oppressive force, insufficient for achieving social change, dignified lives and global equality.[139]

The research commented explains how this dominant human rights framework was conceived as a set of shared and common values across cultures, which were elevated to universal. However, it has been argued that their conceptual foundations rest on Western ideological components, embodying a particular worldview.[140] A genealogy of the dominant rights discourse traces their ideological underpinnings back to Western traditions and ideals: a liberal rights paradigm with universal ambitions, built on a particular understanding of justice, of the person, of a good life and a good society. The frame of reference being the epistemological frame of modernity, that of Eurocentrism; a conceptual apparatus and set of beliefs that places the European worldview at the centre. This geopolitical perspective is integral to the European colonial project, the asymmetrical world system that resulted from the dichotomy centre-periphery (the metropolis and the colony), which will be further reproduced in contemporary relations of power as well as in other spheres such as knowledge. This modern conceptualization of the world is characterised by individualism, a capitalist economy, a techno-scientific epistemology, as well as a longing for universality that led to the expansion of Eurocentrism, and the West becoming the holder of truth, the source of legitimate signification and knowledge validity.[141] It is within this context that the international law order emerged, as a result of the colonial encounter and as part of an economic, normative and political framework of domination.[142]

The imposition of this Western imaginary and its ensuing hierarchisation extended to knowledge production systems. It resulted in the subordination of other views, numerous erasures and non-dominant socio-cultural contributions being depicted as unimportant, including those of Indigenous Peoples as holders of valid knowledges and subjectivities. The circulation and transfer of legal ideas has so far taken place in an unbalanced way from the dominant knowledge frameworks to the less powerful ones towards homogenisation and legal transplantation. Thus, the ability of indigenous peoples to pursue their self-determined pathways to fulfilment still encounters numerous structural barriers, including ideological ones.

[139] The 'neo-liberalist human rights discourse functions as part of an empire of law used to structure the implementation of neoliberal changes to social, political, and legal organizations' Goodale (2013), p. 103.

[140] Gómez Sánchez (2020).

[141] 'The metaphysical epistemology of the West has had world-political consequences: it has advanced and sustained imperialism by selecting the holders of truth, dictating the colonization of culture and propelling the West to world hegemony', Barreto (2012), p. 6.

[142] As exposed by TWAIL and explained in the introductory section of this chapter, critical legal perspectives condemn international law for its colonial roots and its constitutive elements that played a role in legitimating imperialism, namely: sovereignty and ostensible equality of states, the construction of the other as well as the understanding of nature as an exploitable resource, and land appropriation as a constitutive process.

The perspective of this work responds to the need to uphold the views of those who have been historically left at the margins, whose narratives have been ignored, and whose struggles and suffering derived from historical and structural forms of discrimination.[143] It is from the premises of these undermined knowledges that counter-hegemonic alternatives can be advanced, opening up to alterity.[144] However, the significance of subaltern worldviews is still peripheral. Not only at a global level but also in the African continent, where the focus on indigenous peoples usually responds to a different interpretation of indigeneity (understood as nativeness),[145] and land tenure laws 'are for the most part based on colonial legislation and norms".[146]

Already during the drafting of the Universal Declaration of Human Rights (UDHR), the question around the philosophical foundations and status of human rights appeared as a controversial topic. It was understood that human rights could not be circumscribed by the standards or aspirations of any single people, nor the values inspiring a declaration aimed at having global applicability and validity emerge from a single culture.[147] However, the lack of consensus around opposing conceptions of rights, ideas of justice and the question of universality resulted in a strong polarisation around their content, nature and value.[148] Despite the discrepancies, a pragmatic approach was adopted in order to reach an agreement, leaving the unsolved controversies aside, an agreement rooted on the longing for a world-wide normativity (what Jack Donnelly has referred to as functional universality). Nevertheless, concerns about the document becoming a product of western ethnocentrism have continued to be at the centre of many debates, and the human rights grammar the object of ideological and cultural contestation ever since. Furthermore, it is within the international law framework that the human rights grammar was legitimised by legal means conferring a sense of a neutral, non-political, non-ideological normativity to this anthropocentric, secular and universal framework, while concealing the imbalanced power relations the system sustained.[149]

This particular conceptualisation is based on the individual as the unit of society, on rights as the basis for securing human existence, and legalism and juridification as the method for securing rights with the state as the ultimate guarantor. This

[143] Gómez Sánchez (2022).

[144] See Rajagopal (2006) where he suggests delving into the 'radical democratic potential' of human rights to feed a counter-hegemonic international law.

[145] For an overview of the criteria characterising indigenous peoples in the African context, see (ACHPR 2005).

[146] Crawhall (2011), p. 18.

[147] See the statement on human rights by the American Anthropological Association (1947), p. 542.

[148] See Goodale (2018) for a detailed account of the theoretical debates around the elaboration of the UDHR. For a commentary on the discussions around the United Nations Declaration on the Rights of Indigenous Peoples (UNDRIP), see Hohmann and Weller (2018).

[149] On the language of legality: 'Its charm also lies in the fact that it obscures the most brutal of truths: that power produces rights, not rights power; that law is itself a product of the political, not a prime mover in constructing social worlds' Comaroff and Comaroff (2012), p. 79.

perspective clashes with other understandings that emphasise aspects such as: a connection between the person and the community, ideas of togetherness and harmony, a duty-rights conception, a holistic unity with nature, a broader temporal scope that encompasses the past and the future, the idea of membership, a linkage between religion, law and morality, and a non-state centric logic. Nevertheless, it is the former western ethnocentric perspective that has become hegemonic as stated above, privileging a particular cognitive, normative and value framework as the guiding standards in the absence of a global ethics.

The focus on an indigenous conceptualisation aims at redressing epistemic coloniality and the 'enduring indifference towards peripheral knowledges that have been disregarded specially in the construction of the global rights discourse".[150] The following lines describe how the work analysed engages with a counter-hegemonic perspective from which to articulate an alternative formulation of property and uses of land.[151]

2.2.2 Property and Land

The following explains the main ideas around property in two different legal orders: that of the San and their collective *ethos*, on one hand; and the dominant legal paradigm and liberal conceptions of property, on the other. In order to contrast both understandings of property, the following analyses a range of aspects related to the relationships between people and resources, including the diverse actions and entitlements attached to each view, related rights, the modes of governance on which the regulation of property depends, the distinct tenure systems and degrees of enforceability, as well as related dimensions, interests and values served by property.

The content reviewed here relies on the solid corpus of literature on the San which includes socio-cultural and legal anthropological studies. In addition to these sources and ethnographic records, the arguments and conclusions described build on data drawn from reports and policy papers on African indigenous peoples that deal with different dimensions of the legal domain as grounded in their social practices and lived experiences. The impossibility of carrying out empirical work in this case limits the ability to contrast part of that input. However, the exploration of secondary sources and narratives around entitlements, land and nature enabled to determine the main aspects related to the San understanding and relationship to resources and the territory they inhabit, as well as their conceptions of land uses, property tenure and ownership schemes. Notwithstanding, the author is aware of the fact that the attempt of reconstructing the position of the subaltern does not equal to the subaltern speaking by itself. In addition, the author acknowledges the limitations attached to exogenous interpretations, blurred conceptual boundaries of key notions as well as

[150] Gómez Sánchez (2024), p. 346.

[151] 'Africa must not just be taken as a problem to be solved but must also be seen as a contributor to positive global development. It has values that could give meaning to the fullness of human society.' Ndlovu-Gatsheni (2007), p. 7.

the complexity of achieving conceptual clarity when putting in dialogue two different conceptualisations of rights. Different categories are bound to their respective universes of meaning and are often not readily translatable or even identifiable as parallel or directly related dimensions.

On account of these challenges, questions of legitimacy, ethnocentric approaches to knowledge as well as relations of power in knowledge production (extractivism of ideas and appropriation of knowledge) must be carefully pondered throughout the entire research process. All those aspects must be dealt with respect, responsibility and, above all, openness and clarity, trying to remain informed by indigenous methodologies, sensibilities and approaches to inquiry that conceive knowledge as relational and culturally centred.

Bearing this in mind, the work begins by looking into the approach to property in Western liberal orders. This is a legal construct based on the expectation of attaining the exclusive right to 'own', where the value of the individual and their connection to the thing is privileged over the group's connection with it. The right to property is considered a civil liberty, a marker of individual autonomy that entails a collection of prerogatives, generally vested on an individual upon what is owned (material or immaterial), from which others are excluded unless the owner allows it.

This conception of property has its roots in the agglomerative propensity of Roman Law that reinforced ownership in parallel to a process of increase in population pressure, market integration, rising individualization, and rights' holders calling for the creation of formalized rights, where evidence of ownership was required to solve disputes. The state's sanctioning of private property was seen as pre-condition for economic growth and poverty alleviation, based on the assumption that formal title provides guarantee of tenure, more productive uses of resources, efficient markets and wealth. Although empirical evidence in this regard is controversial, this overlooks the fact that the consolidation of land tenure registration often results in dispossession in the absence of a formal title. Besides, the commodification of what is owned, together with the monetary and individualistic rationales behind this logic disregard fairer distribution and inequalities, putting those with low buying and social power at a disadvantage. In sum, individual property ownership is understood as a 'bundle of rights', which enables the holder of that right to dispose, divide, sell, use and principally, to exclude others, privileging land tenure and property registration through individual titling and ownership.

Among the San, on the other hand, property is understood in terms of its social function, an approach that closely connects the autonomy of the individual with the communal and personal freedom with the collective. Their egalitarian *ethos* together with social relationships based on mutual dependence and sharing, result in communal tenure, users' rights and obligations, and access rights to subsistence resources being taken for granted. 'Even though different categories of ownership can be identified depending on the objects at stake, this does not immediately imply excluding others. With regards to personal items, for example, consumable goods, clothes, cooking tools, the San developed forms of tenure and possession marked by re-distribution and the delayed exchange rule that enable establishing a social security network'.[152]

The institutionalised modest approach to life, entails a moral obligation to share and the moral inadmissibility to accumulate. This is exemplified by gift-giving reciprocation practices that contribute to minimise internal social differentiations. This generalised reciprocity allows them to grow lasting symmetrical relationships and to increase the social security network of people with mutual rights and obligations, while providing them with a sense of belonging and comfort. It further contributes to avoid jealousy and mitigate tensions (due to distress or hunger), and to secure living conditions against potential risks. Sharing and demand sharing operate as a redistribution practice of the produce of activities such as hunting and gathering firewood, food, honey, plants and water. And 'this sharing can be read as generosity, in the sense of responding positively to demands'.[153] Besides, communal property agreements take into consideration a non-dualistic understanding of human/nature, as well as an intergenerational dimension of human solidarity which is inclusive of future generations and limits the ability to alienate resources, imposing an obligation to protect and preserve them.

All these aspects influence the San's consideration and relationship to land, which is one of custodians. Therefore, their understanding of land goes beyond its materiality, it is not considered an economic asset. Their uses of land are non-exclusive and security of tenure is ensured by communal ownership. The individual has a claim to such land by virtue of belonging to the community. Additionally, this communal ownership is seen as a right 'vested in the descendants of the original ancestors',[154] and as a consequence, it does not encompass an alienation right. Besides, rights are not formally bestowed and the state is not regarded as the guarantor but as the usurper.

Land is the source of their culture and identity, being essential for their collective survival in a material and spiritual sense, and the territory is conceived as the unit of management and stewardship, further connected to other rights.

The main features of the San understanding of land, property and relationships to other beings have the potential to inspire a decolonised human rights alternative, providing human rights with new content on the basis of the following elements: complementary interests, egalitarianism, mutual dependence, redistribution, sharing and the right to make claims on others—with the obligation to respond in return.

In sum, the social function of property, redistribution patterns and the obligation to share, together with an equalised access to resources, are features that could constitute the foundations of a different conception of property. In this way, to the self-interest of the owner, the consequences for what is owned would be added, as well as a human/social dimension that acknowledges the implications for others. Thus, together with a reorientation towards solidarity and a broader understanding of

[152] Gómez Sánchez (2024), p. 349.

[153] Ibid.

[154] Barnard (2002), p. 15.

harm, an ecological perspective would be attached, connected to the idea of custodianship.

Accordingly, by accommodating the existing diversity of lived-worlds, the basis for articulating a reformulation of human rights would include a more nuanced interpretation of rights and obligations, a more holistic relationship with nature, an understanding of community not as aggregated individuals, but with an emphasis on the sense of belonging, mutual dependency and solidarity towards other human beings (present and future ones), as well as a stronger environmental awareness. These are elements that could effectively permeate development initiatives, government policies, land reforms and legislation, in a global scenario where ideological coloniality and liberal logics are still prevalent.

The answer to current collective challenges will arrive from the ascertainment of a common and shared future. It demands contributions beyond the usual hegemonic sites of reflection and knowledge production, also with regard to law, thus, acknowledging human plurality and the inherent incompleteness of every culture.[155] It is in times of uncertainty that people long for universal valid principles, in need for guidance. However, it is also in times of crisis that alternative approaches might provide the ideas needed for change and direction. Some features drawn from alternative epistemic locations have already permeated the international law corpus, where influence and cross-pollination have occurred and consolidated, representing a path for the future.[156] A future in which, maybe, in the absence of universals, there can at least be widespread recognition of what is not acceptable when we encounter it.

3 Optional Exercises

We started our analysis in Sect. 2 asking: what should researchers consider when working with TWAIL? And in what way should they relate to doctrinal and other dominant legal methodologies? In our reviewing of *The Human Right to Health: Solidarity in the Era of Healthcare Commercialization* and on works that challenge the dominant conceptualization of human rights and property, in particular, the conceptualization of property of the San Indigenous People, Sect. 2 delved into the methodological choices adopted by these works. We conclude this contribution by suggesting two exercises that aim to help readers apply TWAIL to practical research issues and anticipate challenges that those using TWAIL are likely to face

[155]Wisdom is like a baobab tree; no one individual can embrace it alone (Ewe proverb).

[156]Examples of these are the recognition of collective rights (in the African Charter of Human and Peoples' rights and the United Nations Declaration on the Rights of Indigenous Peoples to name a few), as well as ideas around the rights of nature and nature as a legal person, aspects that have achieved different degrees of protection, from constitutional guarantees (in the cases of Ecuador and Bolivia) to domestic legislation (Uganda and New Zeland) to courts decisions (Colombia and India) and advocacy initiatives.

when conducting international legal research, especially in international human rights law.

The exercises seek to subordinate academic reflection to the need of incrementing the political power of subjects in a subaltern position. This entails that TWAIL will remain truncated if legal work is limited to explaining why or how the law is hegemonic.[157] Legal researchers should not limit themselves to discussing where the law should be taken; they should also seek to gain greater influence. In the view of Okafor this requires, among other things, to take the pedagogies of the oppressed towards the institutions exerting power.[158] To ensure that the content of this more activist role remains transformative, TWAILers should avoid assuming the positive contribution of certain frameworks.[159] This caution is especially required when evaluating whether these frameworks may increase the developed-developing world gap.

On the other hand, in strategizing emancipatory trajectories, TWAILers should be mindful to avoid an excess of theoretical purity in the sense of limiting themselves to hypothesize the ideal law. This includes suggestions of fundamental break-ups with dominant epistemologies of legal meaning.[160] As much as in military history frontal and open confrontation has rarely served the weaker parties, the same is true in strategizing legal change. Asserting that only political revolutions can correct 'wrong' legal dynamics might inhibit socially committed legal scholars.[161] Contrarily, as Costas Douzinas put it,

> in law and politics . . . the task is not so much to discard 'wrong'ideological concepts, like human rights, but to re-define them against whatever conservative connotations they may have acquired, adjust them to the project of popular politics and build around them a 'hegemonic'bloc'.[162]

Exercise 1

Read the United Nations Guiding Principles on Business and Human Rights: Implemeting the United Nations "Protect, Respect and Remedy" Framework, (UN Doc HR/PUB/11/04), 2011, available at: <https://digitallibrary.un.org/record/720245?v=pdf>

[157] As argued by Jodoin and Lofts, 'critical theorists cannot satisfy themselves by criticizing the world for the sake of criticism; they must do so with an unwavering commitment to ethics and justice'. Jodoin and Lofts (2014), p. 334.

[158] Okafor (2016), pp. 24–25.

[159] Coomans (2010), p. 182.

[160] Although in his stimulating contribution Robert Knox appears to conclude somewhere along those lines, his perspective is mainly about contextualizing and re-politicizing rights by pushing courts into addressing more political questions such as: asking for the 'interests' at play within legal conflicts, Knox (2020), pp. 36, 38.

[161] Gearty (2020), p. 252.

[162] Douzinas (2000), p. 169.

- According to Principle 1, States have the obligation to protect against human rights abuse within their territory by third parties, including business enterprises. States are especially advised to integrate preventive and remedial measures. Equality before the law must also be ensured. According to Sect. 2.1.2, dominant interpretations within human rights law 'push institutional and distributive questions away from human rights law'. Might this way of implementing human rights law be doing that, and why?
- According to Principle 26, when addressing business-related human rights abuses, 'States should take appropriate steps to ensure the effectiveness of domestic judicial mechanisms'. The commentary attached to this principle navigates between a requirement that the State should accord 'due process', and the need to pay 'particular attention' to the rights and specific needs of certain groups. Does this view reproduce the Western 'particular understanding of justice' as per Sect. 2.2.1? What are the strengths and limitations regarding the goal of establishing thos sort of remedies to protect the rights of indigenous peoples?

Exercise 2

Read the United Nations Committee on Economic, Social and Cultural Rights, General Comment Number 24 on State obligations in the context of business activities (UN Doc E/C.12/GC/24), 10 August 2017, available at: <https://www.ohchr.org/en/documents/general-comments-and-recommendations/general-comment-no-24-2017-state-obligations-context>

Consider the following questions.

- According to the General Comment, privatization is not 'prohibited by the Covenant' and States are instead required to impose 'public service obligations' on private providers (para 21). If human rights are not supposed to break up with the market as a principle of distribution domestically and internationally, how can human rights law bring social justice and what are the prospects of legitimizing human rights as a viable political vocabulary in the South and in the North?
- The General Comment mentions indigenous peoples several times. On the one hand the general comment stresses the duty of states to ensure access to effective remedies (para 46), something that may require the recognition of these people's customary laws and customary ownership over their lands (para 52). On the other hand, the obligation to protect translates in 'human rights impact assessments', where the issue at stake is whether mechanisms are in place to identify negative impacts, allow for compensation and make possible for these groups to get a share in extractive benefits (para 17). Would you say that this focus addresses the structural imbalance of power experienced by indigenous people's? Do you find the Free, Prior and Informed Consent (FPIC) to be the right approach to address power imbalances? Can these instruments be regarded as effective whenever they express indigenous people's concerns over their lands where land is understood as a commodity? Does this focus create an incentive to prevent violations and if they still occur, effectively account for the created damage? And finally, what role

may cross-cultural differences play in the definition and application of FPIC and how could TWAIL researchers help make these differences have an impact on mainstream legal debate?

Exercise 3

Read the United Nations Committee on Economic, Social and Cultural Rights, General Comment Number 25 on science and economic social and cultural rights (UN Doc E/C.12/GC/25), 30 April 2020, available at: <https://documents.un.org/doc/undoc/gen/g20/108/12/pdf/g2010812.pdf?token=dOUdBoXSCkpntqiBwy&fe=true>

Consider the following questions.

- Does paragraph 69 of the General Comment strike a fair balance when considering the right to the enjoyment of the benefits of scientific progress a right that mediates between the right to health and private patents as an expression of the right to property? Is the patent-based intellectual property regime the expression of a human right? If it is a human right, does this perspective contribute to facilitate access to health and scientific progress for 'the rest of the world'?
- Considering paragraphs 39 and 40, how do you imagine 'special intellectual property regimes' and a 'global intercultural dialogue' in order for them to become effective tools to protect the identity, lands and knowledge of indigenous peoples?

References[163]

ACHPR (2005) Report of the African Commission's Working Group of Experts on Indigenous Populations/Communities

Adébísí, F. (2023). *Decolonisation and legal knowledge: Reflections on power and possibility*. Bristol University Press.

al Attar, M., & Tava, V. I. (2010). TWAIL pedagogy - legal education for emancipation. *Palestine Yearbook of International Law, 15*(7).

Alter, K. (2020). LJIL Lecture 2019. Visions of international law. An interdisciplinary retrospective. *Leiden Journal of International Law, 33*, 837–869.

American Anthropological Association, Executive Board. (1947). Statement on human rights. *American Anthropologist, 49*(4), 539–543. https://doi.org/10.1525/aa.1947.49.4.02a00020

Anghie, A. (2007). *Imperialism, sovereignty and the making of international law* (1st pbk ed.). Cambridge University Press.

Anghie, A. (2008). TWAIL: Past and future. *International Community Law Review, 10*, 479–481.

Anghie, A. (2023). Rethinking international law: A TWAIL retrospective. *European Journal of International Law, 34*(1), 7–112. https://doi.org/10.1093/ejil/chad005

Anghie, A., Bhupinder, C., Mickelson, K., & Okafor, O. (Eds.). (2003). *The third world and international order: Law, politics and globalization*. Brill Academic Publishers.

[163] For an extensive bibliography on TWAIL see Gathii (2011), pp. 49–64.

Anghie, A., & Chimni, B. S. (2003). Third world approaches to international law and individual responsibility in internal conflicts. *Chinese Journal of International Law (Boulder, Colo.), 2*(1), 77–103. https://doi.org/10.1093/oxfordjournals.cjilaw.a000480

Arenas Catalán, E. (2021). *The human right to health. Solidarity in the era of healthcare commercialization*. Edward Elgar.

Atria, F. (2015). Social rights, social contract, socialism. *Social and Legal Studies, 24*, 598–613.

Baars, G. (2015). From the Dutch East India Company to the corporate Bill of Rights. Corporations and international law. In U. Mattei & J. Haskell (Eds.), *Research handbook on political economy and law*. Edward Elgar.

Barnard, A. (2002). The foraging mode of thought. *Senri Ethnological Studies, 60.*

Barreto, J. (2019). Eurocentric and third-world histories of human rights. Critique, recognition and dialogue. In B. Schippers (Ed.), *Critical perspectives on human rights*. Rowman & Littlefield International.

Barreto, J. M. (2012). Decolonial strategies and dialogue in the human rights field: A manifesto. *Transnational Legal Theory, 3*(1), 1–29.

Barreto, J. M. (2013). *Human rights from a third world perspective: Critique, history and international law*. Cambridge Scholars Publishing.

Barreto, J. M. (2018). ¿Qué Es TWAIL? Un Estudio De Las Aproximaciones Tercermundistas Al Derecho Internacional.

Baxi, U. (2002, October). Operation 'enduring Freedom'.

Bedjaoui, M. (1979). Towards a New International Economic Order UNESCO.

Chimni, B. S. (2018). Customary international law. A third world perspective. *The American Journal of International Law, 112*, 1–46.

Chimni, B. S. (2022). The international law of jurisdiction: A TWAIL perspective. *Leiden Journal of International Law, 35*(1), 29–54. https://doi.org/10.1017/S0922156521000534

Comaroff, J., & Comaroff, J. (2012). *Theory from the South: Or, how Euro-America is evolving toward*. Africa Paradigm Publishers.

Coomans, F., Grünfeld, F., & Kaminga, M. (2010). Methods of human rights research. A primer. *Human Rights Quarterly, 32*, 179–186.

Crawford, J. (2019). *Brownlie's principles of public international law*. OUP.

Crawhall, N. (2011). Africa and the UN declaration on the rights of indigenous peoples. *The International Journal of Human Rights, 15*(1), 11–36.

Dalglish, C. (2018). *What is the ontological turn, and to what extent are 'ontological' approaches relevant for the anthropological study of development? — an anthropological essay*. Medium.Com.

Douzinas, C. (2000). *The end of human rights. Critical legal thought at the turn of the century*. Oxford.

Egan, E. (2018). The doctrinal approach in international human rights law scholarship. In L. McConnell & R. Smith (Eds.), *Research methods in human rights*. Routledge.

Engle, K., Nesiah, V., & Otto, D. (2021). *Feminist approaches to international law*. University of Texas Law, Public Law Research Paper (716).

Escobar Roca, G., & García Manrique, R. (2019). *Argumentación e investigación en derechos humanos*. Tirant Lo Blanch.

Eslava, L., Fakhri, M., & Nesiah, V. (2017). The spirit of Bandung. In L. Eslava, M. Fakhri, & V. Nesiah (Eds.), *Bandung, global history, and international law. Critical pasts and pending futures*. CUP.

Eslava, L., & Pahuja, S. (2011). Between resistance and reform: TWAIL and the universality of international law. *Trade, Law and Development, III*(1).

Eslava, L., & Pahuja, S. (2012). Beyond the (Post)Colonial. TWAIL and the everyday life of international law. *Verfassung und Recht, 45*, 195–221.

Fagbongbe, M. (2008). The future of women's rights from a TWAIL perspective. *ICLR, 10*(4), 401–409. https://doi.org/10.1163/157181208X361449

Fukurai, H. (2018). Fourth world approaches to international law (FWAIL) and Asia's Indigenous struggles and quests for recognition under international law. *Asian Journal of Law and Society, 5*(1).

Gathii, J. T. (2011). TWAIL: A brief history of its origins, its decentralized network, and a tentative bibliography. *Trade, Law and Development, 3*(26).

Gathii, J. T. (2022). The Agenda of third world approaches to international law (TWAIL). In J. Dunoff & M. Pollack (Eds.), *Critical approaches to international law. Foundations and frontiers* (p. 153). Cambridge University Press.

Gearty, C. (2020). Afterword: Human rights research beyond the traditional paradigm. In D. Gonzalez-Salzberg & L. Hodson (Eds.), *Research methods for international human rights law*. Routledge.

Gómez Sánchez, D. (2020). Transforming human rights through decolonial lens. *The Age of Human Rights Journal, 15*. https://doi.org/10.17561/tahrj.v15.5818

Gómez Sánchez, D. (2022). Deconstructing the dominant human rights grammar: An alter-native narrative based on indigenous peoples' world-views. *African Journal of International and Comparative Law, 30*(4). https://doi.org/10.3366/ajicl.2022.0421

Gómez Sánchez, D. (2023). *Reformulating human rights from an indigenous perspective: Embedding the san views on property rights*. Deusto University.

Gómez Sánchez, D. (2024). Our human rights are our land. An alter-native conceptualisation of the right to property from an indigenous perspective. In A. Diala & C. Rautenbach (Eds.), *Reimagining legal pluralism in Africa: Balancing indigenous, state, and religious laws*. Brill.

Goodale, M. (2013). *Human rights at the crossroads Oxford*. Oxford University Press.

Goodale, M. (2018). *Letters to the contrary: A curated history of the UNESCO human rights survey*. Stanford University Press.

Haskell, J. (2014). TRAIL-Ing TWAIL: Arguments and blind spots in third world approaches to international law. (Towards a radical approach to international law). *Canadian Journal of Law and Jurisprudence, 27*(2), 383–414. https://doi.org/10.1017/S0841820900006408

Hernández, G. (2022). *International law*. OUP.

Hodson, L. (2020). A feminist approach to Alyne da Silva Pimentel Teixeira (deceased) v Brazil. In D. Gonzalez-Salzberg & L. Hodson (Eds.), *Research methods for international human rights law*. Routledge.

Hohmann, J., & Weller, M. (2018). *The UN declaration on the rights of indigenous peoples: A commentary*. Oxford University Press.

International Covenant on Economic, Social and Cultural Rights (1966) 993 UNTS 3

Jodoin, S., & Lofts, K. (2014). What's critical abour critical international law? Reflections on the emancipatory potential of international legal scholarship. In P. Sing & B. Mayer (Eds.), *Critical international law. Postrealism, postcolonialism, and transnationalism*. OUP.

Kapur, R. (2023). TWAIL and alternative visions: 'Talking about a Revolution': Afterword to the Foreword by Antony Anghie. *European Journal of International Law*. https://doi.org/10.1093/ejil/chad054

Kennedy, D. (1999). The disciplines of international law and policy. *Leiden Journal of International Law, 12*, 9–133.

Knox, R. (2020). A Marxist approach to R.M.T. v the United Kingdom. In D. Gonzalez-Salzberg & L. Hodson (Eds.), *Research methods for international human rights law*. Routledge.

Knox, R. (2022). Imperialism, hypocrisy and the politics of international law. *TWAIL Review, 3*, 25–67.

Lettinga, D., & van Troost, L. (Eds.). (2015). *Can human rights bring social justice? Twelve essays*. Amnesty International Netherlands.

Martineau, A. (2016). Concerning violence. A post-colonial reading of the debate on the use of force. *Leiden Journal of International Law, 29*, 95–112.

Merry, S. E. (2003). From law and colonialism to law and globalization. *Law Social Inquiry, 28*(2), 569–590. https://doi.org/10.1111/j.1747-4469.2003.tb00206.x

Mickelson, K. (1998). Rhetoric and rage: Third world voices in international legal discourse. *Wisconsin International Law Journal, 16*(2), 353–419.
Mickelson, K. (2008). Taking stock of TWAIL histories. *ICLR, 10*(4), 355–362. https://doi.org/10.1163/187197308X366605
Miéville, C. (2008). The commodity form theory of international law. In S. Marks (Ed.), *International law on the left: Re-examining Marxist legacies*. CUP.
Moyn, S. (2018). *Not enough. Human rights in an unequal world*. HUP.
Moyn, S. (2022). *Humane: How the United States abandoned peace and reinvented war*. Verso.
Mutua, M. (1996). The ideology of human rights. *Virginia J Int Law, 36*(589), 589–657.
Mutua, M. (2002). *Human rights. A political and cultural critique*. University of Pennsylvania Press.
Mutua, M., & Anghie, A. (2000). What is TWAIL? *Proceedings of the annual meeting (American Society of International Law), 94*, 31–40. http://www.jstor.org/stable/25659346.
Natarajan, U., Betancur-Restrepo, L., Bhatia, A., Reynolds, J., Tzouvala, N., & Sujith, X. (2020). Third world approaches to international law review: A Journal for a Community. *TWAIL Review, 1*, 7–13.
Natarajan, U., Reynolds, J., Bhatia, A., & Sujith, X. (2016). Introduction: TWAIL - on Praxis and the intellectual. *Third World Quarterly, 37*(11), 1946–1956. https://doi.org/10.1080/01436597.2016.1209971
Ndlovu-Gatsheni, S. J. (2007). Giving Africa Voice within Global Governance: Oral History, Human Rights and the United Nations (UN) Human Rights Council. ASC Working Paper Series 73.
Nesiah, V. (2003). The ground beneath her feet: Third world' feminisms. *Journal of International Women's Studies, 4*(3).
Nesiah, V. (2022). *TWAIL feminist perspectives on conflict*. Völkerrechtsblog.
Nesiah, V. (2023). Lawfare, CVE, and international conflict feminism. In L. Abu-Lughod, R. Hammami, & N. Shalhoub-Kevorkian (Eds.), *The cunning of gender violence: Geopolitics and feminism*. Duke University Press.
OHCHR. (2012). Guiding Principles on Extreme Poverty and Human Rights UN Doc A/HRC/21/11.
Okafor, O. (2005). Newness, imperialism, and international legal reform in our time: A twail perspective. *Osgoode Hall Law Journal, 43*.
Okafor, O. (2008). Critical third world approaches to international law (TWAIL): Theory, methodology, or both? *International Community Law Review, 10*, 371–378.
Okafor, O. (2016). Praxis and the international (human rights) law scholar. Toward the intensification of Twailian dramaturgy. *Windsor Yearbook of Access to Justice, 33*, 1–35.
Otto, D. (1996). Subalternity and international law: The problems of global community and the incommensurability of difference. *Social & Legal Studies, 5*(3), 337–364. https://doi.org/10.1177/096466399600500304
Pahuja, S. (2005). *The postcoloniality of international law, Journal of International Law, 46*.
Rajagopal, B. (1999). Locating the third world in cultural geography. *Third World Legal Studies, 15*(2).
Rajagopal, B. (2004). *International law from below: Development, social movements, and third world resistance* (Repr 2004 ed.). Cambridge University Press.
Rajagopal, B. (2006). Counter-hegemonic international law: Rethinking human rights and development as a third world strategy. *Third World Quarterly, 27*(5), 767–783. https://doi.org/10.1080/01436590600780078
Samuel, G. (2011). Does one need an understanding of methodology in law before one can understand methodology in comparative law? In M. Van Hoecke (Ed.), *Methodologies of legal research. Which kind of method for what kind of discipline?* Hart.
Schabas, W. (2021). *The customary international law of human rights*. OUP.
Scott, S., & Zahava, O. (2017). *Developing countries and international law*. Oxford Research Encyclopedia, International Studies.

Singh, P. (2022). Editorial. Tales of multiple decolonisations. *Indonesian Journal of International Law, 19*, iii–xii.
Sujith, X., Bhatia, A., Natarajan, U., & Reynolds, J. (2016). Placing Twail Scholarship and Praxis: Introduction to the Special Issue of the Windsor Yearbook of Access to Justice, *33*(3).
Tzouvala, N. (2020). The Standard of civilisation in international law: Politics, theory, method. In *Capitalism as civilisation: A history of international law* (pp. 1–43). Cambridge University Press.
UNCESCR. (1990). General Comment 3. The nature of states parties obligations (Art 2, Para. 1, of the Covenant). UN Doc E/1991/23.
UNCESCR. (2000). General Comment 14: The right to the highest attainable standard of health. UN Doc E/C.12/2004/4.
van Hoecke, M. (2011). Legal doctrine. Which method(s) for what kind of discipline. In M. Van Hoecke (Ed.), *Methodologies of legal research. Which kind of method for what kind of discipline?* Hart.
Wallerstein, I. (2006). *European universalism. The rhetoric of power*. The New Press.
WHO. (1978). *Primary health care*. Report of the international conference on primary health care. Alma-Ata, USSR.
WHO. (1986). Ottawa charter for health promotion. WHO/HPR/HEP/95.1.
Whyte, J. (2019). *The morals of the market. Human rights and the rise of neoliberalism*. Verso.

Empirical Legal Research

Marijke Malsch

Contents

1 Introduction

This chapter deals with the introduction of empirical research methods and findings of empirical research into legal scholarship and the practice of law. The first part of the chapter describes Empirical Legal Research (ELR)[1] as a field that is concerned with empirical research into the law. After having sketched ELR and its history, the chapter presents several basic empirical methods that can be used by lawyers who are not highly familiar with social science research and its outcomes. These methods

[1] Some scholars in the field use the term 'Empirical Legal Studies'. I will use the term 'Empirical Legal Research' most of the time. In my opinion, both terms are interchangeable.

M. Malsch (✉)
Open University of the Netherlands, Faculty of Law, Heerlen, The Netherlands
e-mail: marijke.malsch@ou.nl

J. J. Garcia Blesa (ed.), *Contemporary Methods in International Legal Research*, Springer Textbooks in Law, https://doi.org/10.1007/978-3-031-69522-3_7

can be helpful to gain some knowledge of what the law 'does' in society and how its operation might be changed. In doing so, the chapter makes use of the existing literature that focuses on Empirical Legal Research and ELR methods.

The second part of the chapter discusses a number of ELR studies that combine a doctrinal perspective with empirical research. These examples feature studies about the right to lay participation in the administration of justice; stalking legislation; suspects with an intellectual disability in the criminal justice system; and the fundamental wishes of victims of crime. The outcomes of the studies discussed can help researchers learn how to deal with particular types of empirical information. Studies mentioned here generally aim at both enriching our knowledge on the law's operation and pointing at possibilities to change the law's functioning.

The third part of the chapter presents a number of exercises that aim to help the reader to transfer the information presented in the previous sections into their research practice. These exercises ask the reader to use basic empirical methods themselves and test their understanding of the outcomes of empirical research in practice.

2 Empirical Legal Research: History, Trends and Relevance

Empirical legal research is not a discipline in the traditional sense, but a combination of research methods that study how the law is practiced and its impact on social life. It also explores the assumptions on which that practice is based.[2] The insights of ELR can be of the utmost relevance to legal work. ELR therefore strongly advocates that the study of law be enriched with knowledge of empirical methods and that lawyers become better acquainted with social sciences.[3] There is a slight overlap between ELR and disciplines such as Sociology of Law, Psychology of Law, and Criminology. However, ELR distinguishes itself from these disciplines by its strong focus on the search for knowledge about the practice of law.

Empirical legal research is not a new field; its origins date back to the late 19th century. Oliver Wendell Holmes in his famous *The Path of the Law* concluded that judges make decisions first and then come up with reasons to explain them.[4] And Jerome Frank was of the opinion that judicial decisions would be more influenced by psychological factors than by legal premises.[5] Frank said that judges and legal

[2] Bijleveld (2023). See also Galligan (2010), p. 983. For a different take, see Posner (2016).

[3] Malsch (2021).

[4] Holmes (1987).

[5] Frank (1931).

[6] Kritzer (2010), p. 876.

[7] Cane and Kritzer (2010a), and Kritzer (2010), p. 876.

[8] Kritzer (2010), p. 879. See also Schlegel (1995). For a more recent example of legal realism, see Spamann et al. (2021).

[9] For an overview, see Cane and Kritzer (2010a).

scholars should acknowledge the gaps and uncertainties in the law, and think of law pragmatically as a tool for human betterment.

In the 1920s and 1930s, interest in ELR increased in some parts of the world, especially in the United States.[6] Legal Realists in America were interested in establishing 'the facts' of the practice of law, the 'law in action.'[7] According to Kritzer, much of the research conducted by legal realists aimed to document problems in how courts handle various types of cases ranging from criminal cases through divorce to tort.[8]

Today, however, there are many journals, research institutes and university departments specialized in empirical research into the law[9]—not only in the United States, but also in other countries.[10] Governments and law enforcement agencies make regular use of quantitative methods for policy making, focusing on the law in practice. For example, Public Prosecution Offices and law enforcement agencies frequently make statistical overviews of the (types of cases) they deal with as well as their outcomes, and so do many courts. Such statistical reports are also an important source of knowledge that can be used by empirical legal researchers.[11]

Notwithstanding, the customary workwise of lawyers, both in academia and in legal practice, has tended to focus on the study of legal materials, while the use of more quantitative methods generating larger data bases has traditionally been limited to the social sciences. Empirical legal research, however, may resort to the full range of sources from individual case investigations and decision-making (more typical for traditional legal work) to large scale databases.

Empirical legal research often takes a longitudinal and comparative perspective, which is being helped by the increasing collection of large databases by empirical legal researchers. This enables trends and patterns to be identified, as well as comparisons to be made between groups.[12] For instance, jury decision-making can be compared to judicial decision-making showing that the differences are only superficial.[13]

The array of empirical legal methods, themes and areas of interest has been substantially refined and diversified since the origins of empirical legal research. New lines of empirical research into the practice of law developed during the

[10] Marseille et al. (2020), van den Bos (2021).

[11] Kritzer (2010), p. 877.

[12] Eisenberg (2004).

[13] Kalven and Zeisel (1966).

[14] Lind and Tyler (1988), and Webley (2010), p. 972.

[15] Genn et al. (2006), Cane and Kritzer (2010a), Hensler and Gasperetti (2017), Grootelaar et al. (2019), and Bijleveld et al. (2020).

[16] See e.g. in the Netherlands, Leeuw and Schmeets (2016), van Boom et al. (2018), Bijleveld et al. (2020), van den Bos (2023), Bijleveld (2023), Bijleveld et al. (2020), Marseille et al. (2020), and Malsch (2023).

[17] Cane and Kritzer (2010a).

twentieth century, like studies on Alternative Dispute Resolution (ADR) and Procedural Justice.[14] These major areas of empirical legal research have turned out to be extremely fruitful in terms of their substantial influence on legal practice.[15] Empirical legal research has also intensely influenced legal education where there has been a dramatic increase in the offer of academic courses and textbooks in recent years.[16]

One of the central debates about empirical methods of legal research is whether qualitative methods are more suitable or practicable for legal researchers than quantitative methods. In their famous Oxford Handbook of Empirical Legal Research, Cane and Kritzer advocate for a plurality of empirical approaches to the study of law and legal phenomena.[17] According to these authors, both types of methods can and should be applied in legal research. Other authors suggest the use of various types of methods as well.[18]

In terms of this book's more modest goal of getting legal researchers acquainted with the basic practice of empirical legal research and its outcomes, however, a focus on qualitative methods seems justified. There are several reasons for this. In general, researchers trained in law can be expected to understand qualitative methods more easily than quantitative tools. In other words, lawyers are more likely to do qualitative empirical work themselves and much more reluctant to use quantitative tools. In addition, qualitative methods might be easier to apply. Although the choice of the method is also dependent on the research question addressed, qualitative methods have a more direct and explicit focus on the 'qualities' of how the law functions in practice than quantitative methods and outcomes.

Cane and Kritzer are hesitant about the actual reach of empirical legal research among legal scholars. They conclude that '. . . many [legal scholars] remain more or less ignorant of the importance and value of empirical research and may find empirical legal scholarship difficult and somewhat mysterious'.[19] Also other authors conclude that ELR has no strong impact on the legal world at present.[20] The connection between legal work and empirical legal research, thus, still seems erratic.[21]

There might be different reasons for that. Above all, lawyers may lack insight into the complicated nature of empirical research and how long it takes to carefully and systematically conduct such investigations in legal practice.[22] On the other hand, certain legal issues and procedures may not always be clear for people participating

[18] Bijleveld (2023), and van den Bos (2023).

[19] Cane and Kritzer (2010b), p. 3.

[20] Galligan (2010), Nielsen (2010), Malsch et al. (2016), and Malsch (2023).

[21] Cane and Kritzer (2010a), and Malsch (2021).

[22] Malsch (2021).

[23] I leave out the traditional collection and analysis of case law, because most lawyers use this method already in their daily work (see Cane and Kritzer (2010b), p. 5, who also leave out this method for similar reasons). For similar reasons, I do not consider the method of document research. I do not discuss the method of experiment either for that method is more quantitative in nature and might be slightly too complicated for the scope of this chapter, meant as a basic introduction into empirical methods. Furthermore, the methods I discuss here are not primarily focused on

in empirical research without a legal background. Therefore, it is important for ELR-scholars to explain empirical methods and findings to lawyers, to other disciplines and the general public, and vice versa.

3 Methods of Qualitative Empirical Legal Research

This section briefly introduces some basic methods of qualitative legal research that can be applied by legal scholars who lack a background in empirical research.[23] More specifically, it considers the use of interviews, observation, case study and multi-method research. However, it will concentrate on interviews and observation due to their being even more intuitively accessible for legal researchers than the others. It will also discuss a number of guidelines for doing interviews and observations in the section devoted to the exercises below.

Typically, when lawyers do empirical research, they investigate how a certain legal issue plays out both in traditional doctrine and in legal practice by conducting *expert interviews*. To a large degree, this empirical method is familiar to anyone because it resembles a regular conversation between two individuals. Therefore, legal researchers may feel less hesitation about the use of this empirical method than, for example, about the collection and analysis of a large databases which require sophisticated statistical analysis. Also approachable for lawyers with no experience with empirical research is *observation*. Observations can be done anywhere outside (and even inside) the office. It is relatively easy to learn and to do, and it may satisfy the basic curiosity that any researcher has. The third method discussed here is *case study*. This method also largely aligns with how lawyers work in daily practice. In an *empirical* case study, however, one example or situation is studied from various perspectives including empirical methods of investigation.

The most immediately apparent difference between these three *qualitative* methods vis-à-vis quantitative methods is the amount of the data collected and the use of statistical analysis. Qualitative methods have a different scope and more depth as they focus on the specific qualities and characteristics of the issues at hand, facilitated by the smaller number of units studied. For example, a qualitative study may focus on ten recorded interrogations of suspects of a particular crime, and scrutinize how the interrogations were conducted, the kind of questions that were asked, the kind of answers that were given, non-verbal behaviour of both the interrogators and the individual who is questioned, etc. None of this is normally possible in quantitative studies.

Qualitative methods in general do not depend on statistical quantification; instead, they aim to capture and categorize social phenomena and their meanings.[24]

---

establishing causal relations between variables; they are more appropriate for investigating how the law works in daily practice and for increasing insights into the operation of some legal institutions.

[24] Webley (2010), pp. 927–928.

[25] Webley (2010).

The information obtained can then be compared with the outcomes of other empirical research and add to our understanding of individuals' experiences, behaviours and opinions, improving our knowledge about how institutions function in practice or providing insights about other social issues.[25]

In contrast, *quantitative* methods generally focus on a relatively small number of characteristics or features, but of a large number of subjects/units, in which relations and trends can be uncovered. For example, a question of quantitative research may be whether certain minor offences, like shoplifting, are committed on a larger scale in big cities as compared to small villages, and if there is a relation with the number of police cars driving up and down the streets.

3.1 Interviews

Interviews largely resemble everyday talks between people. As an empirical method, however, interviews are more structured. It is the interviewer who asks the questions and the respondent who gives the answers, although some deviation is possible on this rule. The interviewer is in charge and the interview's aim is the collection of information. The interview, thus, is not a two-sided friendly exchange of words without any obligation, as between family or friends. During the interview, the interviewer does not give opinions or react in an emotional way to what the respondent says. Lawyers or law students conducting an ELR interview for the first time, should keep in mind these essential differences between everyday talks and interviews.

Several types of interviews can be distinguished, such as the ethnographic interview, the respondent interview and the informant interview (or: focus group).[26] Of these types, the *ethnographic interview* resembles most an everyday conversation. It feels most like a casual talk during which the researcher and the respondent are in their natural roles. A *respondent interview* is far more formal, and the interviewer assumes a more official role. Questioning is more in-depth. An *informant interview* or *focus group* is an interview with a group of people that has special knowledge and/or experiences.

Interviews, thus, may range from more unstructured (ethnographic interviews) to highly structured (informant interviews, focus groups, or surveys).[27] Unstructured interviews are more often in-depth in nature and they may be lengthy. The role of the interviewer is important in unstructured interviews; how the interviewer asks the questions, may influence the outcomes. That is less so in more structured interviews. The more structured the interview is and the more standardized the questions asked are, the easier it becomes to conduct the interview in a form other than face-to-face, like in writing or online (e.g. via online survey). In this case, the questions are not asked by an interviewer, but the respondent reads them and answers them, for

[26] Tracy (2013), and Bijleveld (2023).

[27] Tracy (2013), and Bijleveld (2023), p. 64.

example via the computer. The interviewer as a person then plays no more a role during the interview. This heightens the comparability—and, thus, the reliability—of the outcomes of the interviews (in the situation where more than one interview is conducted), since incidental factors related to the individual characteristics of the interviewer have been removed. The interviews, then, can more easily be done with a large sample of respondents, and they become more quantitative in nature.

During the more unstructured types of interviews, use can be made of a *topic list*. Topic lists contain a number of topics or issues about which the interviewer wishes to ask questions to the respondent. How questions are phrased is to the discretion of the individual researcher. *Questionnaires* are more elaborated and standardized than topic lists, and the questions have been written down in full. They are used more regularly in more quantitative studies, or surveys, that aim at standardization in order to minimize distortion. Standardization also helps statistical analysis of the outcomes. Standardization is deemed less necessary for more qualitative types of research where the individual perceptions, experiences and opinions of respondents are of importance and where in-depth questioning takes place.

A further distinction can be made between *expert* interviews and interviews with members of the *general public*. Both are possible in case of lawyers doing empirical work, but most lawyers taking the first step in the field of empirical research will interview experts. Lawyers should be aware that they must adjust the language they use to the type of respondent they interview. Some lawyers may have difficulty in using everyday language when approaching and talking to members of the general public. Supervisors should be aware of that, and urge the lawyer to use colloquial language in that situation.

If the respondent consents, interviews are generally *taped*, to allow the researcher to analyse a full transcript or summary later on. Taping instead of taking notes makes listening to the respondent easier.[28] The processing of the interview or interviews that has been taped or noted can take place afterwards in a written report. Such a report can either be a literal transcription of the interview(s), or a summary of the most important respondent statements. Such a report may be the basis for an analysis which will be included in the thesis, article or other research document.

Interviews generally provide none or very limited information about the respondent's behaviour—that aspect is missing in this method. During the interview, the researcher generally has no time or opportunity to make extensive observations on how the respondent acts. However, studying behaviours can be done with help of the empirical method of 'observation' explained below.

3.2 Observation

The method of observation can be *participatory* or *non-participatory* in nature. As a participatory observer, the researcher takes part in a group as a member of this group.

[28] For more information about practical guidelines, see below.

In case of non-participatory observation, the researcher remains on the outside and observes what is going on.

When the researcher participates in the observed group, they may do so *covertly* or *openly*. In the case of covert participation, that is, when the researcher makes not clear that their aim is to do research, ethical dilemmas may arise; in principle, lying or deceit is not allowed during scientific research. In addition, when the group observed, for instance a street gang or a criminal group that smuggles cocaine, discovers that one of their members is a researcher and, thus, has other aims than just the smuggling, different types of issues and risks may emerge for the researcher. In principle, the assessment of the research project by an *ethical committee* is necessary in situations like this. Today, most universities have such an ethical committee.

When people know they are being observed, they may alter their behaviour. To avoid such effects, participatory researchers sometimes immerse themselves in a situation for an extended period. This is called: ethnographic observation. After some time, the observed persons may get used to the researcher's presence and forget this, thereby taking away some of the awareness-effects.[29]

Empirical legal researchers regularly make observations in courts or at other legal, state or private institutions and organizations, with the aim to gain knowledge on how professionals and citizens (inter)act and make decisions, or how the institution functions in general. These are types of *non-participatory observation*. In such situations, the professionals and other individuals involved may be less aware that they are being observed—for example, in the event that the researcher is a member of a general audience witnessing the hearing of a legal case at the public gallery of a court. Sometimes empirical legal researchers succeed in getting access to a judge's chambers in order to more intimately observe the work of judges. Some researchers even have been allowed to sit in (confidential) meetings of judges where decisions are made, for instance, regarding a defendant's guilt and sentencing in criminal cases. In that situation, they are still conducting non-participatory observations, but have managed to get very close to where the important decisions actually are being made. Yet, getting this type of access is not easy; most courts are not very willing to get monitored by a researcher during their decision-making processes, or are not allowed to do so by their organizations.

The observing researcher may take notes (on a laptop or on paper) of the event they observe, and they may do so with help of a (digital) *topic list* or a more structured *questionnaire*.[30] When it is permitted through express consent or when it is considered ethically acceptable, auditive or audio-visual recordings can be made, which can be analysed afterwards.[31]

The growth in numbers of CCTV footage in the street, in public or private buildings, bodycams, and the recording of, for example, police interrogations of

---

[29] Webley (2010).

[30] On topic lists and questionnaires, see the rubric on Interviews.

[31] For more information about practical guidelines, see below.

[32] Malsch et al. (2018).

suspects and witnesses, has significantly expanded the existing possibilities to do observations. Systematic research with help of those recordings and images can now take place more easily thanks to their wider availability. That can be done, for example, in case of a study of police interrogation methods, of the interaction between citizens and officials, or of conflicts occurring in the street, etc.[32]

3.3 Case Study

A case study can be considered an 'umbrella strategy' that combines a range of data from different methods. It investigates an event within its real-life context. Qualitative or quantitative empirical sub-methods may be used, or both, on top of more traditional doctrinal or critical methods. An event, a court case, an individual's course of life, an organization, or a specific situation may be subject of a case study.[33] Case study research is meant to focus in detail on a given situation rather than to provide findings that are generalizable to other situations.

In its basic design, case study as a qualitative empirical legal method is akin to what lawyers working in legal practice often do: studying a legal case while paying attention to many of its other constituting elements. However, as an empirical legal method, it includes more non-doctrinal elements and methods than a purely black-letter case study. In the field of *Law and Psychology*, for example, studies of criminal cases presenting unsafe convictions are regularly made in which due attention is paid to interrogation techniques, expert reporting, reliability of eyewitness testimonies and the accuracy of judicial and other law enforcement decision-making.[34] So-called 'triangulation', the use of multiple data sources and/or methods, also is of great relevance in these case studies.[35] The doctrinal element in most empirical legal case studies decreases; it is more about the legal system or institution as a whole, its various constituting phases and how it operates that is under scrutiny in these studies in *Law and Psychology*.

3.4 Multi-Method Research

Multi-method research ('triangulation') is any research that uses more than one technique or method, thereby generating more reliable outcomes than the use a single one.[36] Obviously, the use of multiple methods is only possible when sufficient time and budget is available.

---

[33] Webley (2010).

[34] van Koppen et al. (2017).

[35] Another term for this is 'mixed methods approach'. See Nielsen (2010) p. 970, and below.

[36] Nielsen (2010), p. 953.

[37] See for illustrations of these interactions, the examples of ELR presented below.

[38] Nielsen (2010), p. 955, and Bijleveld (2023).

The use of more than one method may be of special relevance to empirical legal research, because law and its operation are characterized by many different aspects: legal, social, psychological, emotional, procedural and professional. Moreover, these aspects are in continuous interaction with each other.[37] When acquiring knowledge on only a few of these aspects while neglecting others, some aspects may exert an unforeseen, disruptive influence. Therefore, when time and facilities are available, the use of more than one method is highly advisable.[38]

The following may serve as an example of this requirement. Comparisons between written reports of police interrogations and (audio)visual recordings of the same interrogations have shown that the recordings are far more exhaustive and accurate. On the basis of this information, it would be advisable to use the recordings on a larger scale, instead of the written reports, which most of the time are summaries of the interrogations, that even sometimes may be biased.

On the other hand, expert interviews demonstrated that watching or listening to these recordings is generally considered too time-consuming and, thus, does not happen on a large scale. The preference of law enforcement officials is to employ the written, summarized reports instead, because these are more manageable, even if there are risks of bias.[39] The information obtained via expert interviews thus adds highly relevant insights in how the law works in practice.

4 Examples of Empirical Legal Research

This part of the chapter presents four examples of empirical legal research that combine a traditional doctrinal perspective with empirical-legal research. The examples feature empirical research work dealing with different issues that have ramifications both in national and international law, particularly, in relation to human rights law. In such cases, empirical studies must necessarily take place at the local level. This does not preclude the importance of the direct study of international institutions and procedures and the empirical insights that can be gained from them.[40] The examples below, however, aim to connect more explicitly with the experience of most international legal researchers around the world who might not have the opportunity or resources to get direct access to relevant international institutions.

4.1 Lay Adjudication

Two decades ago, Jackson and Kovalev noticed a growing interest in the use of lay adjudication in a number of Member States of the Council of Europe.[41] Thus, they

[39] Malsch et al. (2018).

[40] E.g. van den Meerssche (2022).

[41] Jackson and Kovalev (2006).

investigated the role of lay adjudication in criminal justice systems in relation to the human rights and democratic standards required by the Council of Europe. The authors noted that, on one hand, lay adjudication can help to give citizens a meaningful role in the administration of justice, which may have been previously denied to them, and can help boost confidence in the administration of justice. On the other hand, the use of lay adjudication may raise questions about the extent to which systems can deliver a fair trial according to Article 6 of the European Convention for the Protection of Human Rights and Fundamental Freedoms (ECHR), and, in particular, about the safeguards that are required to assure that the system of adjudication is independent and impartial vis-à-vis defendants in criminal procedures.

Although, as Jackson and Kovalev observed, none of the international human rights instruments require lay adjudication to be part of the judicial system of a state, there are a number of arguments that can be advanced in favour of the view that lay adjudication can help promote civil and political rights.[42] The right of every citizen to take part in the 'government of the country' or in the 'conduct of public affairs', directly or through freely chosen representatives, is acknowledged in a number of international documents.

The subject of lay adjudication has also been investigated with help of empirical legal methods.[43] In this case, the central issues researched were: what kinds of systems of lay participation do exist in Europe, how do they function in practice, and what are the experiences and views of both lay and professional participants in these systems? It was found that systems of lay adjudication vary greatly between the countries, as does the satisfaction of participants and the society at large. Some countries generally are very satisfied with their systems of lay participation (e.g., England and Denmark), while other countries are much more sceptical and important amendment have been debated over the past decades (e.g., Belgium and, to a lesser extent, Germany). Drawn on the basis of the comparison of various features of lay participation across a selection of countries, the general conclusion is that lay adjudication my provide a certain degree of 'democracy in the courts'. On the other hand, lay participants may be confused about their role, e.g., as Jackson and Kovalev have warned, in decisions about guilt. Thus, it seems lay people need to be better prepared for their participation in the administration of justice, even if the 'lay perspective' is partially lost. Indeed, the research suggested that citizens should be encouraged to become acquainted with and participate in the criminal justice system of their own country and courts should be as open and welcoming as possible to lay participants and the general public.[44]

---

[42] Ibid.

[43] Malsch (2009, 2016).

[44] Malsch (2009), pp. 213–214.

[45] 'Snowballing' describes the practice of asking respondents to suggest other potential respondents for the study and so on.

The empirical legal methods applied in this line of research were: interviews with lay and professional judges, as well as criminal lawyers (a total of 66 interviews), observations of court sittings, and extensive document research. Respondents in the interviews, which were conducted in five different European countries, were partly selected via the 'snowball method':[45] asking respondents to suggest other potential respondents, and so on. For example, in both Denmark and Germany, the professional judges contacted lay judges they worked with. Almost no potential interviewee declined participation in the research. The Councils of the Judiciary in some of the countries included in the research were also helpful in suggesting and contacting potential respondents, as were several organizations of lay judges (e.g., in England) or professional judges.

Interviews were mostly conducted face-to-face, with help of topic lists. A few interviews were conducted by telephone. The interviews most of the time took place in the courthouses where the judges worked. The interviews were combined with observations of hearings with lay adjudicators in the same courts. In the case of Denmark, professional judges joined the observations and helped the researchers by translating what was said during the hearing of the cases. Observations of the local and cultural situation in each country helped to get a comprehensive impression of the differences between national legal systems of lay participation and how they operated.

Document research on the systems of lay adjudication was mostly conducted through online sources; official websites provided most valuable information. When queries arose, for example, regarding the actual operation of systems of lay participation, the researchers approached academics, practicing lawyers and other professionals via email, and obtained clarification about confusing points. Indeed, the research project was an example of a mixed methods approach.[46]

4.2 Stalking Legislation

This second example describes the introduction and implementation of anti-stalking laws in several countries. It examines the ideas and assumptions underlying these laws, their implementation and effects in legal practice, as well as the degree of recidivism after a conviction by a court. Since this is about research into how the law works in practice, the study is a classic example of ELR.[47]

A few decades ago, anti-stalking laws came into force in several countries. These laws generally forbid the intentional, repeated harassing of another person against his or her will. In some countries, like the US, a requirement for a conviction is that violence was committed or a credible threat was uttered. In other countries, like the Netherlands, repeated, unlawful harassment, even without violence or a threat, is

[46] Malsch (2009, 2016).

[47] The examples in this part of the chapter come from Malsch (2021).

[48] Malsch (2007, 2021).

legally sufficient for establishing the crime of stalking. At that time, negligible or no empirical research had been conducted into the phenomenon of stalking.[48] The assumption was generally held that the primary victims of stalking would be public figures, such as pop-stars, politicians, etc. This was not an unlikely assumption because it was stalking on public figures that had attracted the most media attention. Stalking in the private sphere went largely unnoticed at that time.

When stalking was empirically investigated in more detail after these laws had come into force, it was found that the primary victims were non-celebrity women. In most stalking cases, these women had recently separated from their husbands or male partners, who could not accept the separation and would start repeatedly seeking contact with the woman with the aim of restoring the relationship. After this harassing behaviour had persisted for some time, it amounted to stalking under the new laws.[49]

The legislatures of various countries had, therefore, started from a wrong assumption. Empirical legal research could then help to examine whether this erroneous assumption required a legislative or doctrinal change to achieve the general policy goals or whether it had other negative effects. Yet, this appeared not to be the case: stalking laws can be applied in situations where a relationship has ended as well as in situations where a public figure has been harassed.

Moreover, before the new laws had come into force, law professors as well as legislators had expected that victims would not be prepared to notify the police and, even if they did so, it would be problematic to prove stalking for reason of the difficulty to collect evidence. But, also that turned out otherwise: women appeared willing to go to the police and many cases were brought before a criminal court. And courts convicted most defendants brought before them.[50] Evidence-collection of stalking appeared easier than expected. Stalking leaves many traces, such as a plethora of digital contacts, but also neighbours and family members who witness the stalker repeatedly visiting the victim's home and who can make a statement in court, and so on. In terms of the number of convictions, the new laws were effective.[51] But then, a new question came up: did the convictions affect the prevalence of stalking? Did the stalkers stop their harassing behaviour after having completed their sentence?

After the laws had been in force for a number of years, recidivism of convicted stalkers could be investigated. Predominantly first-time offenders appeared to stop their harassing behaviour after having served their sentence. However, there is a (small) group of stalkers with a large number of previous convictions that continues stalking their victims, avoids obstacles of any kind, or switches to other victims such as relatives or children if the primary victim makes herself unapproachable.[52] In the

[49] Malsch (2007, 2021).

[50] Malsch (2007).

[51] Rosenfeld (2004), Spitzberg and Cupach (2007), and Malsch et al. (2009).

[52] Rosenfeld (2004), Spitzberg and Cupach (2007), and Malsch et al. (2011).

[53] The total recidivism rate for all convicted stalkers is over 50 per cent, Malsch et al. (2011).

Netherlands, for instance, about 80 per cent of this persistent group commits a new crime after having been convicted for stalking.[53] Criminalization and the trial of stalking behaviour, thus, has different effects on different kinds of perpetrators. The limits of a criminal justice approach have become clear in respect of this group of offenders. It is helpful for legislators, legal practitioners, social workers, psychologists and psychiatrists to be aware of the law's impact, or lack of impact, on different types of offenders, as demonstrated by this research.

In this research into the impact of stalking legislation, several different empirical methods were applied (mixed methods approach). Apart from the analysis of legal materials, case file analysis and interviews with victims of stalking were conducted. This was combined with quantitative methods of analysis, such as analysis of databases of the Public Prosecution Office, court decisions, survival data analysis, etc.

Case files were obtained from a number of district courts in the Netherlands. The researcher first asked permission from both the Council of the Judiciary and the courts where the investigations were to be conducted. When the permissions were obtained, the courts selected a number of stalking cases where the offender was convicted for stalking (acquittals were omitted). The researcher then visited the courts and was offered a working place there. She analysed the case files *in situ* with help of a topic list.

Face-to-face interviews were conducted with both celebrities and public officials that were stalked (among others: writers, musicians, politicians, members of Parliament and a minister). Snowballing was used to find and to approach these respondents. Interviews took place at locations chosen by the interviewees.

The case files analysed probably do not accurately represent all case files and all victims of stalking. However, in combination with each other and with further research into stalking, the samples provide useful insights into stalking actions, how the law is being used in practice in those cases, and to what extent other measures may be effective in combating this type of harassment.

Quantitative methods were also applied to the study of stalking, for example, in the analysis of large data bases for establishing the types of stalking behaviour, what kinds of penalties have been imposed and with what type of crime, and the question of convicted stalkers' recidivation. This combination of the qualitative and quantitative methods is helpful to obtain more comprehensive insights into the stalking behaviour. The use of several methods was also dependent on time. As the research covered several decades, sufficient information had become available, for instance, regarding a considerable body of court decisions, or recidivism rates. On the other hand, additional research became necessary when changes in the field occurred (e.g., legislative amendments of the original statutes).

---

[54] Garrett (2009), Kassin et al. (2010), and van Koppen et al. (2017).

[55] Kassin et al. (2010), Teeuwen et al. (2020).

4.3 Suspects with an Intellectual Disability

Over the past decades, increasing attention is being paid to the involvement of suspects with an intellectual disability in the criminal cases. One reason is that, in a number of cases of miscarriage of justice in the United States and other countries, the wrongfully convicted suspects suffered from an intellectual disability. Undue police pressure may have led them to wrongfully confess to having committed the crime.[54] Another reason is that the cases of young people having a minor intellectual disability who cause nuisance in the streets of big cities have increased and encouraged empirical legal research into this group.[55]

Empirical findings suggest that a criminal justice approach without accompanying psychological support is not very effective for this group and may even lead to negative side effects, such as an increased recidivism rate.[56] There is a risk of false confessions due to suggestibility and acquiescence tendencies within this group, when put under pressure during police interrogations. Such risks are increased by the invisibility of their disability, which implies that police officers may remain unaware of it and thus do not adjust the interrogation methods to the defendant's restricted intellectual abilities.[57]

In the US, empirical findings about the risks of false confessions in criminal investigations concerning this group of population have led to an increased awareness and attention to interrogation techniques used by the police.[58] Also in the Netherlands, empirical legal research has influenced legal practice and education: special courses for the police dealing with such suspects have been created, law enforcement has become more aware of problems related to suspects with an intellectual disability; tools for a better detection of intellectual disabilities have been developed; and research groups have been instituted.[59]

However, problems with this special group of suspects are still insufficiently addressed. Law enforcement professionals need *continuing* education on this issue, because such knowledge can be 'forgotten' in the heat of the daily practice of policing and criminal investigation. The expertise such professionals should acquire is generally coming from disciplines other than legal training. Law enforcement and law practitioners need to be made aware of these problems both during their training and later on the job as well.[60] But that is not always the case.

Like the example discussed above (stalking legislation) this research is usually conducted with the help of several empirical methods, among which analysis of various kinds of databases, observation of court hearings and decision making by other professionals, and interviewing of both professionals and suspects. In particular, researchers sat in as observers at specific professional meetings where the way a

[56] Teeuwen et al. (2020), and Malsch (2021).

[57] Kassin et al. (2010), and Teeuwen and Malsch (2017).

[58] Kassin et al. (2010), Garrett and Neufeld (2009), Garrett and Mitchell (2017), and Garrett (2020).

[59] Teeuwen et al. (2020).

[60] Malsch et al. (2016).

criminal case was to be investigated and dealt with by different professionals and institutions had to be decided. The aim of this special procedure is to provide for a meaningful solution of a case early on for both the suspect, the victim and society at large. The participants at these meetings came from the Public Prosecutions Office, the Police, Victim Support, the Probation Office and Youth Care. The researchers were admitted to these meeting on condition of confidentiality. They took notes and were, afterwards, allowed to briefly interview the participants. The topics raised by the interviewers were: whether the professionals had identified a certain intellectual disability with the suspects, and how they dealt with it.

The researchers also sat in as observers in open court hearings of a number of cases where the defendant had an intellectual disability. These observations were supplemented with interviews with judges who had experience with this type of case. Also, a small number of the suspects were interviewed. Some of the problems related to police interrogations of such suspects consisted of their lack of basic understanding of legal and other complicated language, their lack of insight into their own interests in the case, and their wish to go home as soon as possible when arrested. A further issue was the so-called 'streetwise behaviour' of this group which caused problems for the police to detect their special vulnerability and made it more likely that they be punished for crimes they did not commit, or that they did not receive the social help they needed.

The combination of various empirical methods in this research example enabled the researchers to detect problems inherent to investigations against suspects with an intellectual disability and to make recommendations for legal professionals.

4.4 The Wishes of Crime Victims

Today, victims play a far more important role during criminal proceedings than was the case several decades ago. This increasing role affects both the criminal procedure, defendants' rights, and the experiences, wellbeing and perspectives of victims themselves. Legal doctrinal as well as empirical research into the role and position of the victim within the criminal justice system is abundant. However, how victims' increased participation in the criminal process affects their private life and what their wishes are in this respect has only recently received more detailed attention.[61]

A general assumption that seemingly underlies legislation, policy making and research of the past decades, is that victims would continually strive for a more dominant and visible position within the legal system. It can, however, be questioned whether this is actually the case for each and every victim. Empirical legal studies have shed light on this assumption: research has shown that there are victims who are

---

[61] Malsch (2022).

[62] Malsch et al. (2015).

[63] Tolsma (2011).

[64] de Mesmaecker (2012).

not eager to take a visible role in the criminal case, generally out of fear to come face-to-face with the suspect or to have their identity revealed.[62] Such victims would prefer to shield at least some of their personal information when getting involved in the criminal justice system, and to refrain from speaking in open court or appearing in public.[63]

Safety concerns appear to play an important role when victims decide whether to make a victim impact statement or not.[64] The hearing of a criminal case in open court may be experienced by victims as 'confrontational' or even 'intimidating'. Some victims are happy to take a seat in the back of the public gallery, in order to avoid visibility and confrontations, or to stay away from the hearing altogether.[65] In the Netherlands, most victims prefer to submit a *written* impact statement and to do so *before* the actual hearing of the case, thereby remaining in the background.[66] These statements are then read out by the judge in open court, a procedure preferred by many victims.[67] Some victims even deliberately avoid attending court sessions due to fear of being confronted with the defendant.[68]

In sum, thanks to empirical studies about victims' safety and privacy wishes in criminal proceedings, pertinent legal measures can be taken to protect them. The victim's identity may be concealed, for instance by omitting their name and/or address from the case file; face-concealing facilities and voice distortion may be applied; victims may be questioned outside the presence of the defendant; written testimonies, blurring intimate photo/video footage may take place, as well as making it possible for victims to follow the court hearings from a different room via live video streaming.[69]

Furthermore, other situations with which some victims do not feel comfortable can be prevented,[70] such as physically coming face-to-face with the defendant before the actual hearing of a case. For example, victims and defendants may access the courthouse through the same entrance and may find themselves next to each other in line for the security check. When waiting for the case to begin, victims often sit opposite to defendants in the waiting area.[71]

The hearing of a criminal case in open court may be experienced by victims as 'confrontational' or even 'intimidating'. Some victims are happy to take a seat in the

[65] Malsch et al. (2015).

[66] That option has been made available in the Netherlands, see Lens et al. (2010), and Malsch et al. (2015).

[67] Lens et al. (2010).

[68] Malsch et al. (2015).

[69] Malsch (2022).

[70] That may also be the case in other countries, Malsch (2022).

[71] Malsch (2022).

[72] Malsch et al. (2015).

[73] de Mesmaecker (2012).

[74] Kunst (2015) and ELbers et al. (2023).

[75] Staub (2004) and ten Boom (2021).

back of the public gallery, in order to avoid visibility and confrontations, or to stay away from the hearing altogether.[72] Making an oral statement at the hearing of the case may frighten victims; they may feel insecure or uncomfortable and therefore refrain from doing so.[73] A literature review found no clear evidence for the therapeutic effects of speaking in open court.[74]

Empirical findings show that about one third of victims entertain wishes related to their needs for safety and privacy. In view of the fundamental character of these needs, these wishes should be fulfilled first; other needs could be pursued afterwards.[75] However, the legislations, policy making and legal practice in various countries tend to go in a different direction: speaking in court is encouraged; while safety and privacy measures for victims' risk to be neglected. Rights that give the victim an important and visible role during (the hearing of) criminal cases are generally considered as more important than other types of rights, like the suspect's rights and victims' privacy rights.

The presumption of innocence, a suspect's right that seems at odds with ever extending victim rights, tends to be ignored in favour of increasing victims' rights such as the right to speak in open court.[76] Some political motives (for instance, advocacy for victim rights and visibility of victims is more popular) seem to prevail over others, discarding the use of empirical findings that reveal victim wishes such as that of remaining in the background. A more balanced implementation of empirical findings would thus be desirable to meet fundamental victim wishes and protect the presumption of innocence.

Like in the previous examples presented above, the line of research into victim wishes was conducted with help of a mixed methods approach.[77] Semi-structured interviews were conducted with police officers, public prosecutors and judges with help of topic lists drawn up on the basis of literature and desk research. Lawyers and employees of Victim Support Netherlands (SHN) were also interviewed. Most interviews were conducted face-to-face, although a small number of them were conducted by telephone. The topics on which the professionals were interviewed concerned their organization's policy on protecting the privacy of victims and their relatives; the way in which that policy was implemented in criminal justice practice; discrepancies between policy and practice; the reasons for this and the respondents' perceptions in this regard.

Victims and their relatives were also interviewed with a view to assessing their experiences and perceptions of privacy protection. An electronic and a written version of the questionnaire was composed. The questions focused on possible violations of the victims' privacy during criminal proceedings; actual protection measures taken by the police; the Public Prosecution Office and the court;

---

[76] In many countries, Victim Impact Statements are presented at some point during the hearing, when the guilt of the defendant has not yet been established by the court. Victims generally are allowed to say everything they want to the defendant, such as calling them a 'monster', and reproaching them for what they allegedly did. This situation may present a substantial risk of impinging upon the presumption of innocence.

[77] Malsch et al. (2015) and Malsch (2022).

effectiveness of these protective measures; contacts with the media, how these were experienced; and, finally, needs and wishes regarding the protection of their privacy.

A link to the questionnaire was distributed by several organizations, and a paper version was sent by post to a sample of 200 victims from a database. Electronically completed questionnaires were automatically entered into an anonymized online database. The written questionnaires could be returned by regular mail using a reply envelope. In addition, eleven telephone interviews were conducted with victims who had indicated at the bottom of the questionnaire that they wanted to participate. During these interviews, the respondents' experiences with (possible) privacy violations, the protective measures during the criminal proceedings and how they experienced them were discussed in more detail.

5 Optional Exercises

This part of the chapter aims to acquaint the reader with the application of some of the methods described above. It presents a few exercises that can be completed both individually or in groups. In these exercises, the reader is invited to conduct a small empirical research themselves. This starts with the formulation of a concise research question on the basis of existing literature, it continues with the application of some basic empirical methods, and it ends with the presentation of the empirical findings and the development of relevant conclusions. In order to support the conduct of these research exercises, the basic empirical methods of *interviews* and *observation* are explained in more detail at the end of this section in relation to the exercises.

General Guidelines

The empirical methods applied in these exercises are interviews, observations or a combination thereof. The choice of the subject-matter and research question(s) is left to the reader. The reader is encouraged to select a topic related to their own research.

Time frame: the exercises proposed can last several months and imply a workload of about 200 hours in total.

First steps:

- Conduct a literature review on your topic of interest;
- Develop a concise research question based on the previous literature review;
- Select the empirical method(s) you intend to use
- Make a topic list or brief questionnaire;
- Define respondents and locations for interviews and/or observations (or case study). 'Snowballing' is a regularly used way of getting respondents: asking respondents to suggest other potential respondents and so on. This method is easier and more manageable for unexperienced empirical researchers than trying to draw a representative sample from a population group;

- Get acquainted with the rules on data protection and data saving applicable at your university or by your employer.

For interviews (for more detailed guidelines, see below):

- Try to conduct at least 3 interviews. Interviews may be conducted by one or more interviewers;
- Confidentiality/anonymity of respondents must be guaranteed. Topic lists/ questionnaires should not be too long and complicated, and must be adjusted to the type of respondent (expert or general public);
- The names of respondents must not be mentioned on reports/records of interviews or in the papers, only professional background and, if relevant to the interview, some personal details. Exceptions are possible to this rule; you should discuss this with respondents in advance;
- In case interviews are recorded, secure respondents' permission first and destroy the records after making written copies of the interview. Take notes in case no permission for recording is obtained.

For observations (for more detailed guidelines, see below):

- Find adequate locations for observation (e.g., a courtroom; the streets). Observations may be conducted by one or more researchers. Take care that you plan to do sufficient observations to be able to answer your research questions.

Processing results: When processing and presenting the results of your exercise, you are encouraged to use the *Standard Table of Contents for Empirical Legal Research* suggested below. Each part of this table has its own function and deserves due attention. Make sure that the information you insert under each heading belongs there. The method(s) section should contain only information about methods, the results section should contain only information about the results and so on. The results section explains the outcomes of the empirical research, as well as what the interviews, observations, etc. have added to previous knowledge on the topic. Try to indicate what you have learned by conducting this empirical research. The criteria for choosing location(s) and, in case of interviews, for choosing and approaching respondents must be indicated in the report. The discussion of interviews' and observations' results should be as concrete as possible without mixing them with your own conclusions. Due to the brief duration and limited character of these research exercises, the representativity of the group of respondents needs not be explicitly considered.

Self-evaluation criteria:

1. Is the approach sufficiently empirical-legal in character?
2. Was the *Standard Table of Contents* for *Empirical Legal Research* applied and each of its elements sufficiently addressed?

3. Does the work pay sufficient attention to the relevant literature on the topic chosen?
4. Are the methods used appropriate for answering the research question?
5. Has the use of these methods been clearly explained in relation to the research question(s)?
6. Is more empirical (or theoretical) work necessary to address the question(s)? And is that properly explained?
7. Have accurate conclusions be drawn from the research in view of the research question(s)?
8. Have limitations to the research and its findings sufficiently been reported?

Standard Table of Contents for Empirical–Legal Papers

When putting your exercise in writing try to use the following table of contents:

- Introduction/problem definition/literature review
- Research question(s)
- Method(s)
- Results
- Conclusions
- Limitations of the research and the findings
- References
- Appendices

Exercise 1 Interviews

Choose a topic (e.g., something related to your own research), develop a topic list or questionnaire, approach possible respondents (both expert interviews and interviews with members of the general public are possible), conduct interviews.

Possible respondents

- Interviewing refugees, victims, perpetrators or relatives of victims of human rights violations on consequences experienced;
- Interviewing legal officers of a Ministry of Foreign Affairs, International Organizations, NGOs, etc.;
- Interviewing diplomats;
- Interviewing international judges or arbitrators;
- Interviewing domestic judges on their experience with international legal issues;
- Interviewing domestic administration or police officers on how they deal with international legal issues (human rights, refugees, transnational crime, etc.);
- Interviewing members of legislatures on topics related to international legal relations;
- Interviewing the general public on topics related to international legal relations.

Exercise 2 Observations

Choose a topic (e.g., something related to your own research), develop a topic list, select locations for observation, and conduct observations.

Possible locations for observation:

- Observations of court sittings in domestic or international courts, monitoring bodies or dispute resolution panels; comparisons between courts, behavior of professionals and (lay) participants, or members of the public; how procedures take place in practice;
- Observations in open sessions of international organizations' councils, committees or other bodies;
- Observations in areas or offices where refugees are treated or human rights issues are processed by public authorities (police, administration) or NGOs. For instance, areas where policing is intense or demonstrations are being held.

Detailed Guidelines for Interviews

1. Make a list of topics or a questionnaire. Adjust the language you use, as well as the phrasing of the questions you ask, to the respondent—lay people and experts need a different language. Ask clear, simple questions. Avoid asking 2 questions in 1;
2. Decide whether the interviews will be conducted face-to-face, online or by phone. Discuss this with the respondent(s) in advance. Respondents' preferences will be respected as much as possible;
3. Inform the respondents in advance about the planned length of the interview (45 to 60 mins. max.);
4. In case you want to record the interview, ask for respondents' permission in advance. Indicate that recording will be destroyed after processing of the interview (and actually do so!). In case no permission is granted, take notes yourself. Forward the written report of the interview (anonymously) to the respondents and give them the opportunity to amend and/or supplement it;
5. Interviews must be processed anonymously in the report/essay, unless the respondents themselves wish to be mentioned by name (or have no objection to this). In consultation with the respondents, note their (professional) position and/or other background information, so that the reader can see from which expertise/experience the respondents speak;
6. Note/mention the date, time and location of the interview on the report you write, or say it aloud on the record, so that you can yourself identify the interview/respondent later;
7. During the interview, define the concepts you use (this is called 'operationalization'), so that you and the respondent both know what you are talking about. For example: the concept of 'open justice' can be interpreted differently, so make clear how you wish to use it;
8. The order of the topics or questions on your list can be altered, but keep track of the changes and make sure that all topics are covered during the interview;
9. Ask respondents follow-up questions;
10. Don't display your own knowledge or take a stand. Don't react (emotionally) to the respondent's answers;

11. Limit yourself to listen and look at the respondent;
12. You may sometimes keep quiet, for example to give the respondent a chance to think about the answer;
13. Try not to suggest anything, do not to give your own opinions, do not steer answers, and do not jump to conclusions;
14. During the interview, you may occasionally summarize or paraphrase the respondent's answers, for example to clarify whether you have understood the respondent correctly, but stay close to what the respondent says;
15. When the interview is finished, transcribe the interviews or summarize them as good and completely as you can. Delete recordings afterwards;
16. In your report/essay/thesis, properly explain how you conducted the interviews (face-to-face, online, other), how many respondents and what backgrounds they have, how you found them, how long the interviews lasted, how you analysed/processed them;
17. Analysis of interviews: create codes to summarize the statements of the respondents. Those codes will roughly match the items of your topic list, but sometimes interviews bring up new interesting topics that deserve their own code or item. You may include these in your analysis. You can further refine these codes as you go (e.g., make several rounds). Write down illustrative quotes from your respondents in your report/essay at the place where you deal with the code or topic they relate to;
18. Present the interviews in your report/essay under different headings (which usually relate to the topics/codes you defined). Do not include the full interviews one after the other, not even as an appendix (unless necessary for your research goals). It is important that you actually analyse the interviews, that the aggregated results are discussed in your report/essay, and that you draw relevant conclusions from them;
19. Before you decide to make use of the method of interview in your masters or PhD thesis, please consult with your supervisor first.

Detailed Guidelines for Observation

1. Observations are often combined with other research methods, such as interviews and document research;
2. Make a list of topics you want to make observations about. The initial topic list may be slightly later when strictly necessary;
3. Use a clean topic list for each observation and note on each topic list the date, time, and the place of the event you are observing, who filled in the topic list (in case you work together with other researchers), and what the event or case was about. In your paper, you should also summarize this information on the events or cases in an aggregated manner when justifying your research methods;
4. In your report/essay, properly explain how you conducted the observations: at which areas or event(s), how many, how long the events/observations took, etc.;
5. Analysis of observations: create codes to summarize the observed events. Those codes will roughly match the items from the topic list, but sometimes

observations bring up new interesting topics that deserve their own new code or item. You can further refine these codes as you go (e.g. make several rounds);

6. Discuss the observations in your essay/thesis under different headings (trying to match the topics/codes you defined). Do not include the full written observations one after another in your report/essay/thesis, not even as an appendix (unless necessary for your research goals). It is important that you actually analyse the observations, that the aggregated results are discussed, and that you draw relevant conclusions from them;
7. Striking observations can be picked out and described in detail. This can liven up the report/essay. For example, if a defendant in a court hearing suddenly says something strange or funny, or if a conflict arises at a police control or demonstration, this can be noted. You may also add descriptions of the courthouse, the courtroom where a case is heard, or the area/location where observations take place, if this adds something relevant in light of your research question(s);
8. Before you decide to make use of the method of observation in your masters or PhD thesis, please talk to your supervisor first.

References

Bijleveld, C. (2023). *Research methods for empirical legal research: An introduction*. Boom Juridische uitgevers.

Bijleveld, C., Akkermans, A., Malsch, M., Marseille, B., & Smit, M. (Eds.). (2020). *Nederlandse encyclopedie empirical legal research*. Boom juridisch.

Cane, P., & Kritzer, H. (Eds.). (2010a). *The Oxford handbook of empirical legal research*. Oxford University Press.

Cane, P., & Kritzer, H. (2010b). Introduction. In P. Cane & H. Kritzer (Eds.), *The Oxford handbook of empirical legal research* (pp. 1–10). Oxford University Press.

de Mesmaecker, V. (2012). Antidotes to injustice? Victim statements' impact on victims' sense of security. *International Review of Victimology, 18*(2), 133–153.

Eisenberg, T. (2004). *Why do empirical legal scholarship?* Cornell Law Faculty Publications. Paper 346. https://scholarship.law.cornell.edu/cgi/viewcontent.cgi?article=1359&context=facpub

Elbers, N., van den Berg, C., & Kragting, M. (Eds.). (2023). *What works: Effectieve ondersteuning voor slachtoffers*. Boom criminologie.

Frank, J. (1931, 2009). *Law and the modern mind*. Transaction Publishers,

Galligan, D. (2010). Legal theory and empirical research. In P. Cane & H. Kritzer (Eds.), *The Oxford handbook of empirical legal research* (pp. 976–1001). Oxford University Press.

Garrett, B. (2009). *The substance of false confessions*. University of Virginia Law School. Public Law and Legal Theory Working Paper Series, Paper 136, Virginia.

Garrett, B. (2020). Wrongful convictions. *Annual Review of Criminology, 3*, 245–259.

Garrett, B., & Mitchell, G. (2017). *The proficiency of experts*. University of Virginia School of Law: Public Law and Legal Theory Research Paper Series 2017–55, Virginia.

Garrett, B., & Neufeld, P. (2009). Invalid forensic science testimony and wrongful convictions. *Virginia Law Review, 95*, 1–97.

Genn, H., Partington, M., & Wheeler, S. (2006). *Law in the real world: Improving our understanding of how law works*. Final Report and Recommendations. The Nuffield Foundation.

Grootelaar, H., Hulst, K., & van den Bos, K. (2019). Ervaren procedurele rechtvaardigheid. In D. de Groot & H. Steenberghe (Eds.), *De mondelinge behandeling in civiele zaken* (pp. 85–137). Boom Juridische uitgevers.

Hensler, D., & Gasperetti, M. (2017). *The role of empirical legal research in legal scholarship, legal education and policy–making: A U.S. perspective*. Cambridge University Press.
Holmes, O. (1987). The path of the law. *Harvard Law Review, 8*, 457–478.
Jackson, J., & Kovalev, N. (2006). Lay adjudication and human rights in Europe. *Columbia Journal of European Law, 13*, 83–123.
Kalven, H., & Zeisel, H. (1966). *The American jury*. Little Brown.
Kassin, S., Drizin, S., Grisso, T., Gudjonsson, G., Leo, R., & Redlich, A. (2010). Police–induced confessions: Risk factors and recommendations. *Law & Human Behavior, 34*, 3–38.
Kritzer, H. (2010). The (nearly) forgotten early empirical legal research. In P. Cane & H. Kritzer (Eds.), *The Oxford handbook of empirical legal research* (pp. 975–900). Oxford University Press.
Kunst, M. (2015). De therapeutische werking van slachtofferdeelname aan het strafproces, Eenspiepr146 kritische beschouwing vanuit een psychotraumaperspectief. *Beleid en Maatschappij, 42*spiepr132(1), 32–45.
Leeuw, F., & Schmeets, H. (2016). *Empirical legal research – A guidance book for lawyers, legislators and regulators*. Elgar.
Lens, K., Pemberton, A., & Groenhijsen, M. (2010). *Het spreekrecht in Nederland: een bijdrage aan het emotioneel herstel van slachtoffers?* Intervict.
Lind, E., & Tyler, T. (1988). *The social psychology of procedural justice*. Plenum.
Malsch, M. (2007). Stalking. Do criminalization and punishment help? *Punishment and Society, 2*, 201–209.
Malsch, M. (2009, 2016). *Democracy in the courts. Lay participation in European criminal justice systems*. Ashgate
Malsch, M. (2021). *Law is too important to leave to lawyers. Eleven International Publishing*. Den Haag
Malsch, M. (2022). Victims' fundamental needs for safety and privacy and the role of legislation and empirical evidence. *Erasmus Law Review, 3*. http://www.erasmuslawreview.nl/tijdschrift/ELR/2021/3/ELR–D–21–00018.pdf
Malsch, M. (2023). Empirical Legal Studies in Nederland: overzicht en relevantie voor rechtspraktijk en -wetenschap. *Boom Strafblad, 5*, 1–8.
Malsch, M., de Keijser, J., & Debets, S. (2011). Are stalkers recidivists? Repeated offending by convicted stalkers. *Violence & Victims, 1*, 3–15.
Malsch, M., Dijkman, N., & Akkermans, A. (2015). *Het zichtbare slachtoffer: Privacy van slachtoffers binnen het strafproces*. Boom criminologie.
Malsch, M., Groenen, A., de Keijser, J., & Vervaeke, G. (2009). Dealing with stalking: Police intervention or court decision? *International Review of Victimology, 16*, 51–65.
Malsch, M., Kranendonk, P., de Keijser, J., Komter, M., de Boer, M., & Elffers, H. (2018). Reporting on police interrogations: Selection effects and bias related to the use of text, video and audiotape. *Investigative Interviewing: Research and Practice, 1*, 61–76.
Malsch, M., ten Hove, L., & Elffers, H. (2016). Het belang van empirisch onderzoek voor de rechtspraktijk: een analyse van toepassing van rechtssociologische en rechtspsychologische bevindingen. *Justitiële Verkenningen, 6*, 60–78.
Marseille, B., Smit, M., Akkermans, A., Bijleveld, C., & Malsch, M. (2020). Empirical Legal Research in Nederland. Tussenstand en toekomst. *Nederlands Juristenblad, 36*, 2767–2773.
Nielsen, L. (2010). The need for multi–method approaches in empirical legal research. In P. Cane & H. Kritzer (Eds.), *The Oxford handbook of empirical legal research* (pp. 951–977). Oxford University Press.
Posner, R. (2016). *Divergent paths. The academy and the Judiciary*. Harvard University Press.
Rosenfeld, B. (2004). Violence risk factors in stalking and obsessional harassment. A review and preliminary met–analysis. *Criminal Justice and Behavior, 9*, 9–36.
Schlegel, J. (1995). *American legal realism & empirical social science*. University of North Carolina Press.

Spamann, H., Klöhn, L., Jamin, C., Khanna, V., Zhuang Liu, J., Mamidi, P., Morell, A., & Reidel, I. (2021). Judges in the lab: no precedent effects, no common/civil law differences. *Journal of Legal Analysis, 13*(1), 110–126. https://doi.org/10.1093/jla/laaa008
Spitzberg, B., & Cupach, W. (2007). The state of the art of stalking: Taking stock of the emerging literature. *Aggression and Violent Behavior, 12*, 64–86.
Staub, E. (2004). Basic human needs, altruism, and aggression. In A. Miller (Ed.), *The social psychology of good and evil* (pp. 51–84). The Guilford Press.
Teeuwen, M., Bruggeman, M., Dirkse, M., & Malsch, M. (2020). *Levenslange obstakels. Een levensloopstudie naar licht verstandelijk beperkten in het strafrecht en in de zorg*. NSCR.
Teeuwen, M., & Malsch, M. (2017). *Licht Verstandelijk Beperkte jongeren in de strafprocedure: knelpunten en risico's*. NSCR.
ten Boom, A. (2021). How do victims with the need for protection judge their experiences with the police in the Netherlands? *Erasmus Law Review, 14*(3), 2021. Available at SSRN: https://ssrn.com/abstract=4089694
Tolsma, J. (2011). Aangiftebereidheid: Welke overwegingen spelen een rol bij de beslissing om wel of niet aangifte te doen? In L. Smets, J. de Kinder, & L. Moor (Eds.), *Proces–verbaal, aangifte en forensisch onderzoek, 4* (Vol. 21, pp. 11–32). Cahiers Politie Research.
Tracy, S. (2013). *Qualitative research methods*. Wiley.
van Boom, W., Desmet, P., & Mascini, P. (Eds.). (2018). *Empirical legal research in action: Reflection on methods and their applications*. Elgar.
van den Bos, K. (2021). *Inleiding empirische rechtswetenschap*. Boom juridisch.
van den Bos, K. (2023). *The fair process*. Cambridge University Press.
van den Meerssche, D. (2022). *The World Bank's lawyers: The life of international law as institutional practice*. Oxford University Press.
van Koppen, P., de Keijser, J., Horselenberg, R., & Jelicic, M. (2017). *Routes van het recht. Over rechtspsychologie*. Boom juridisch.
Webley, L. (2010). Qualitative approaches to empirical legal research. In P. Cane & H. Kritzer (Eds.), *The Oxford Handbook of empirical legal research* (pp. 926–950). Oxford University Press.

MIX
Papier aus verantwortungsvollen Quellen
Paper from responsible sources
FSC® C105338

If you have any concerns about our products,
you can contact us on
ProductSafety@springernature.com

In case Publisher is established outside the EU,
the EU authorized representative is:
Springer Nature Customer Service Center GmbH
Europaplatz 3, 69115 Heidelberg, Germany

Printed by Libri Plureos GmbH
in Hamburg, Germany